STANFORD
CENTER ON ADOLESCENCE

INVESTOR POLITICS

INVESTOR POLITICS

The New Force That Will Transform
American Business, Government, and Politics in
the Twenty-First Century

JOHN HOOD

TEMPLETON FOUNDATION PRESS

Philadelphia & London

Templeton Foundation Press
Five Radnor Corporate Center, Suite 120
100 Matsonford Road
Radnor, Pennsylvania 19087

Designed and typeset by Kachergis Book Design, Pittsboro, North Carolina

LIBRARY OF CONGRESS CATALOGING-IN-PUBLICATION DATA

Hood, John.
    Investor politics : the new force that will transform American business,
government, and politics in the twenty-first century / John Hood.
        p.   cm.
    Includes bibliographical references and index.
    ISBN 1-890151-51-3 (alk. paper)
        1. Saving and investment—United States.   2. Stockholder—United States.
3. Social security—United States.   4. Welfare state.   I. Title.
HC110.S3 H66 2001
306'.0973—dc21

                                                            2001034738

Printed in the United States of America

01 02 03 04 05 06   10 9 8 7 6 5 4 3 2 1

CONTENTS

INVESTOR POLITICS

INTRODUCTION
THE GRASSHOPPER SYNDROME

ONE OF AESOP'S MOST BELOVED FABLES, THE STORY of the ant and the grasshopper has delighted and instructed many generations. It has also been translated several times to television, most recently providing the opening plot of *A Bug's Life,* an immensely entertaining Disney motion picture using computer-generated animation. The traditional version of the fable is short and to the point:

> In a field one summer's day a grasshopper was hopping about, chirping and singing to its heart's content. An ant passed by, bearing along with great toil an ear of corn he was taking to the nest.
>
> "Why not come and chat with me," said the grasshopper, "instead of toiling and moiling in that way?"
>
> "I am helping to lay up food for the winter," said the ant, "and I recommend you do the same."
>
> "Why bother about winter?" said the grasshopper, "we have got plenty of food at present."
>
> But the ant went on its way and continued its toil. When the winter came, the grasshopper had no food and found itself dying of hunger, while it saw the ants distributing corn and grain from the stores they had collected in the summer. Then the grasshopper knew: It is best to prepare for the days of necessity.

While watching *A Bug's Life* recently with my young son, it suddenly hit me that the fable of the ant and the grasshopper encapsulated perfectly the state of American politics as we enter the twenty-first century. The polls show that Americans are an increasingly contented lot. The Cold War is over. We won. The painful recessions of the 1970s and 1980s seem distant memories. More recent downturns have been comparatively mild and brief. The federal budget is in surplus. But there are very real problems facing us. It is no exaggeration to say that despite its short-run fiscal health, the federal government is facing the equivalent of long-term bankruptcy and the collapse of Medicare, Social Security, and the rest of the welfare state on which most Americans have become dependent. Even before the appearance of a budget surplus in the late 1990s, and especially afterward, Americans have not seemed particularly concerned. Nor have we rewarded leaders who, like the workaholic and humorless ants, wagged their fingers at us, warned of the fiscal crisis to come, and suggested policy changes that would address it. As the "Mediscare" campaign in 1996 demonstrated, we are more likely to vote these sourpusses out of office in favor of those politicians more like the easygoing, carefree grasshopper (known, by the way, for its constant mating calls and proclivity to overeat).

There is another parallel between the ancient fable and today's politics. It involves the centrality of saving and investment. The modern, costly federal welfare state about which most serious political discussions occur was assembled piece by piece, program by program, in an attempt to provide for Americans at times of great need—from the blizzards of disability or unemployment to the bitter winds of retirement. For the better part of the twentieth century, our national government added promise after promise, one government program on top of the other, without ever spelling out how these promises can truly be kept when winter finally arrives. From the creation of Social Security and unemployment insurance in 1935 to Medicare and Medicaid in 1965, Washington has created an artifice of income-transfer programs that promise to relieve us of the need to prepare for life's most costly and stressful events—losing a job, becoming disabled, educating children, buying a home, caring for elderly parents, and retiring from work. The fact that all of these programs combined cost us a third or more of our incomes every year—with higher rates of taxation to come as the Baby Boom generation begins to retire early in the next century—is hidden by devices such as "employer contributions" to the payroll tax, indirect charges through corporate income taxes, withholding of income taxes, and, when necessary, inflation of the nation's money supply. Furthermore, the extent to which federal "trust funds" have not been invested in real, income-generating assets but simply paid out to past beneficiaries remains unrecognized by millions of trusting Americans who believe there is a stockroom full of food for the winter. Instead, the stockroom is full of paper IOUs. In essence, Americans believe that the federal government is their ant, when it is really an amazingly loquacious and irresponsible grasshopper.

Not just our pocketbook is imperiled by this Grasshopper Syndrome—our personal freedom is at stake. Indeed, the federal government has become more than just a massive flood of benefit checks, loan guarantees, and special tax subsidies. All these promises have brought federal bureaucrats into every nook and cranny of our lives. What was once private is now public, primarily because the public is paying for much of it. The recent, shameless national campaign against the tobacco industry is a perfect example. Politicians sued cigarette companies not for being "nasty" and "peddling addictive drugs," but on the specific grounds that the companies had increased the cost to taxpayers of treating smokers through Medicare, Medicaid, and other health care entitlements. Government funding of health care turned into the conduit through which personal behavior became subject to regulatory control.

Unfortunately, Americans have yet to recognize the Grasshopper Syndrome for what it is. While the growth of government expenditures and power since the 1930s has been massive, most Americans do not yet realize its full implications. The end of the 1990s may have brought a federal budget surplus on paper, but viewed by standard accounting principles, the federal budget is way out of balance. By the middle of the next century, it is highly unlikely that federal expenditures currently promised can be financed with the current rate of federal taxation. The combined effect of political irresponsibility since the 1930s has created a staggering long-term gap—in the tens of trillions of dollars—between expected revenues and expenditures. Our national grasshoppers in Washington have made no provisions for it and even now deny that the winter will ever come. In this, as in so many other things, they lack the wisdom of Solomon, who exhorted "sluggards" in the Book of Proverbs to "look to the ant . . . observe her ways and be wise, which, having no chief, officer or ruler, prepares her food in the summer, and gathers her provision in the harvest. How long will you lie down, O sluggard? When you will arise from your sleep?"[1]

SHOCK THERAPY OR GRADUAL REFORM?

Of course, there is a reason why so few politicians spend their days warning about the coming winter and the bankruptcy of the welfare state. It is not conducive to continued election. Nor is it feasible to announce one day to an American population that has ceded much of its own responsibilities to government the following news: "Sorry, but we screwed up. There is no money to pay for the program we promised you. We hereby withdraw that promise. You are on your own." To the extent that advocates of smaller government and lower taxes come across as scolds or as living in a libertarian dream world of their own, they have no chance at all of overcoming the Grasshopper Syndrome. Because government has, through high taxes and false entitlement promises, taken away our desire and ability to finance the big-ticket items in our lives, there is no immediate solution to the problem of an overextended welfare state. No sixty-year-old has time enough to save for retirement or nursing home care. No forty-year-old parent of a high school junior has the time to save enough to finance a four-year university education. An immediate end to the federal Unemployment Insurance program would leave many a twenty-something worker with no savings in the event of a layoff.

Nor are conservative dreams of a sudden rewriting of the nation's tax system along the lines of a flat tax or national sales tax either feasible or necessarily desirable, even though both of these ideas represent serious attempts to shrink the size and power of the federal government and encourage personal responsibility. Several decades of biased tax policies have firmly established, for example, the tax-free status of employer-provided health insurance. Health insurers, doctors, nurses, hospitals, and employers will fight any tax reform—such as the flat tax—that would take such tax benefits away. A national sales tax, which would certainly do wonders for America's savings rate, is not going to happen, either. No state sales taxes apply to the retail sale of services such as legal aid, health care, investment advice, or accounting. They apply only to goods. If you buy a lawn mower, you pay a sales tax. If you hire someone to mow your lawn, you do not. A national sales tax must apply evenly to goods and services to be fair and efficient, but doing so will pick a fight with virtually every powerful lobby in Washington.

If the end is to shrink the size and scope of the welfare state, reformers must select means that are really up to the task. They must be willing to think strategically about the long term and tactically about the short term. Both perspectives are needed for success. The welfare state was not built overnight; it will not be dismantled overnight. Nor was it built against the wishes of the American people. We *are* worried about our retirement, our health care, our education, and our job security. Politicians knew that and built government programs around these worries. Replacing those government programs with personal responsibility means proposing realistic, credible alternatives for supplying the security we want without disguising the costs or shifting responsibility to someone else. It also means, frankly, recognizing the breadth and depth of the Grasshopper Syndrome. Most Americans living today have never been Ants. They will have to relearn the skills and strategies necessary to save and invest for their own futures. Let us face it: The path of the grasshopper is enticing precisely because it is easier and more enjoyable. Being an ant means hard work and responsibility. In the past, people have believed government leaders who said they could spare Americans such responsibility.

THE SAVINGS STRATEGY

Fortunately, at the same time that government was growing beyond all bounds of reason and affordability, the private sector was undergoing its own dramatic changes. Innovative new ways of organizing, operating, and funding businesses have created a personal financial revolution, particularly during the last two decades of the twentieth century. An unprecedented number of Americans now own stock in American corporations directly through discount brokerages and Internet trading accounts or indirectly through individual retirement accounts (IRAs), 401(k) accounts, and traditional pension systems. Indeed, about half of all Americans were stockholders in one form or another in 1999. Many members of this new "investor class" are, in effect, reclaiming personal responsibility for their own retirement and other needs. The good news is that it has never been more rewarding or fun to be an ant. Technology and other innovations have made personal investments relatively easy to understand. Personal computers and money-management software are taking some of the complexity out of managing a household budget, computing alternative rates of return, planning for the future—even paying taxes. And new forms of money such as Internet bank accounts and debit cards will make it easier in the future to track a variety of savings vehicles and expenditure categories, allowing consumers to debit particular accounts when they visit the doctor, buy educational software, or withdraw retirement funds.

These private financial innovations come at an opportune time. Over the next few decades, Americans must stop looking to Washington as a source of the money they need to take care of themselves—there is no alternative. They will need instead to look to investment and wealth creation on Wall Street and Main Street as the guarantors of their retirement security, their health security, their job security, and their children's futures. The debate now raging in Congress and elsewhere about converting all or part of the Social Security program into private savings accounts reflects this realization, but the stakes go far beyond that one program. In fact, Medicare and Medicaid are probably more financially imperiled in the short term than Social Security and need more immediate attention. What is needed is not just one reform, but a broad strategy of reform across a range of issues: taxes, health care, education, anti-poverty programs, and housing, to name a few. Simply put, the goal should be to replace government entitlement programs with a system that exempts savings and investment from taxation. This will allow individuals and families to invest their own money, rather than expecting the government to "invest" it for them in failed programs and pyramid schemes. The accumulation of personally owned assets will allow Americans to make their own plans for sudden job loss, disability, education, and retirement. Over time, some existing federal entitlements can be ended. Others can be scaled back or "means tested" to serve only as true safety net programs for the poor. Once the middle class is invested in the private sector instead of government, federal expenditures can better be controlled and federal entitlement obligations kept relatively modest.

Such a strategy will require a paradigm shift no less for traditional opponents of the welfare state than for its traditional defenders. The Republican revolution of 1994 brought to Washington a motley band of would-be budget cutters and reformers who, in a few short months the following year, found themselves stymied by the Grasshopper Syndrome. Their attempts at modest reforms in Medicare and other programs were successfully portrayed as mean-spirited and unnecessary. They failed to eliminate even one federal department or major federal spending program. For most Americans, it was easy to support a smaller, less costly federal government as long as it was just rhetoric. The reality of eliminating departments or programs turned out to be less appealing.

The welfare reform bill of 1996 appears to be a counterexample, but not really. On that issue, Republicans had the American people on their side. After all, the average middle-income taxpayer saw cash assistance for poor women and children as benefiting those who were not working, who were not pulling their own weight. They were willing to see work requirements, time limits, and other restrictions imposed on a program far removed from their own lives. But Medicare—well, that was a different story. Attempts by the Republican Congress to make even modest headway in Medicare reform were met with political opportunism by Democrats, demagoguery from the Clinton White House, and either purposeful or reckless misrepresentation by the news media.

Fiscal conservatives need to stop looking for some "grand deal" to reform entitlements or rewrite the tax code. Washington does not work that way. Seemingly small things such as the creation of IRAs and 401(k)s can grow to be far more important than "big" pieces of legislation consuming months of hard work and frustrating negotiations. Those who search for the grand deal need a refresher course on the biannual political cycle. What is done today may well be undone two years from now. Alternatively, the gradual introduction of new ways for Americans to shield their savings from excessive taxation and to substitute their own judgment for bureaucratic decisions will have revolutionary impacts in the long run, even if it fails to provide the immediate gratification of "solving" a major national problem. We already know this to be true with respect to IRAs, 401(k)s, and recent additions to the tax code such as Education IRAs and Roth IRAs. The future offers greater possibilities. The potential of the "savings strategy" to build a constituency for free markets and limited government remains mostly untapped.

This book represents an attempt to sketch out, across a host of public policy topics, a realistic strategy for shrinking the welfare state. Albert Einstein once wrote that the most powerful force he knew of in the world was compound interest. That is not far from the truth. Most politicians have yet to comprehend fully how the personal financial revolution can be made to change the relationship between the governing class and the governed. One politician that understood this well was America's third president, Thomas Jefferson. For those like me who have viewed Jefferson as an intellectual hero and a peerless advocate for freedom and limited government, his economic views have often seemed curious, even embarrassing. After all, Jefferson championed an agrarian republic as contrasted with the more urban, commercial republic envisioned by Alexander Hamilton and, it would seem, more congenial to those who believe in trade, free markets, and capitalistic innovation.

Hamilton was, of course, right about the economics. Show me a land where a majority of citizens are still engaged in farming, and I will show you a basket case. Consolidation of agriculture and the movement of people from farms to cities is certainly a sign of progress and affluence. However, a closer reading of Jefferson shows that he was not making an economic case for an agrarian republic. Indeed, he granted that the growth of manufacturing would increase American prosperity. Throughout his career, Jefferson was far more concerned about the survival of political, religious, and intellectual freedom than he was about economic progress. And he saw a trend of farmers leaving the land and seeking employment in cities to be inconsistent with a limited, self-governing republic. In this, Jefferson and his sympathizers were influenced by their intimate familiarity with ancient political history. They admired the self-governing Greeks and the yeoman farmers of the Roman Republic. They viewed the later Rome, swollen by conquest, immigration, and rural strife, as the source of corruption of the entire empire, with the city's huge urban population dependent on government-provided "bread and circuses," rather than their own labor and thrift. As Jefferson wrote in a 1787 letter to James Madison:

> I think we will be virtuous . . . as long as agriculture is our principal object, which will be the case while there remains vacant lands in any part of America. When we get piled upon one another in large cities, as in Europe, we shall become corrupt as in Europe, and go to eating one another as they do there.[2]

Jefferson argued that farming led to virtue and to support for limited government "by the most lasting bonds." Working the soil and waiting, with patience and thrift, for a subsequent return created a sense of ownership in the community and a long-run, rather than a short-run, perspective. Those who labor in manufacturing or other trades in which the capital is owned by someone else come to feel dependent—and "dependence begets subservience and venality, suffocates the germ of virtue, and prepares fit tools for the designs of ambition."[3]

Certainly Jefferson's proposed solution—to sacrifice the economic advantages of commercialism to protect the liberty of an agrarian society—seemed extreme at the time and was bowled over by the evolution of modern capitalism, as well it should have been. However, the political consequences of this transformation have proven to be markedly similar to Jefferson's warnings. As Americans left the farm during the late 1800s and early 1900s to seek their fortunes in the cities, new constituencies for government growth were created as homeowners became renters and as owners of agricultural capital (land, livestock, and farm implements) became mere users of industrial capital (including plants, machinery, and new inventions).

The relationship between ownership and political behavior is clear. Social scientists have long observed the tendency of homeowners to perceive issues and express themselves in local politics differently from renters, even when earning similar incomes or coming from similar backgrounds. One of the most tantalizing aspects of the new Investor Politics is the early evidence that a similar transformation begins to occur to those who become owners, rather than just users, of capital assets through stock and bond investing. They come to think about issues such as taxes and regulations quite a bit differently than they did when they were only "renting" assets as workers. To understand why savings and investment are so important, and how they can be harnessed to entice Americans back into the ranks of ants, is to understand the deeper meaning of Jefferson's political economy—and the likely contours of politics in the first few decades of the twenty-first century.

CHAPTER 1

A SHORT HISTORY OF SAVING
AND INVESTMENT

L ET US BEGIN WITH SOME DEFINITIONS. SAVING AND investing are ways to delay consumption so that it will be more rewarding or enjoyable in the future. The grasshopper consumes today but suffers greatly in the winter. The ant is a saver. He delays today's consumption, which entails some modest suffering in the short run, in order to be able to consume during the winter. Another way to think about saving is that it is a form of *risk management*. As the fable goes, the grasshopper learns that "it is best to prepare for the days of necessity." Such days may never come, but a prudent person will reduce the risk of such a calamity by saving.

No one in Aesop's story is an investor. That is, the ant merely saves today's surplus in a hole for use in the future, just as folks used to save their money in a mattress just in case of a run on the bank. If the ant were an investor, he would figure out how to use today's surplus to generate far greater food production in the future, thus providing a surplus harvest just before or during the winter months. In nature, some ants actually are investors. Several species keep "domestic animals," such as aphids, leafhoppers, and caterpillars. They feed these "cows" on plants, then "milk" them later for honeydew as needed by the ant colony. Other species harvest leaves and flowers, chew them into a damp mash which they store in special rooms in the nest, and then feed off the spongy mushroom that grows on the decaying leaves.[1] Both practices are types of investment in that they use current work to produce a return in the future that is either larger or more valuable to the worker, or both.

If Aesop had known more about ant economics, perhaps his fable would have celebrated not just saving but also investing. Aesop would certainly have understood both concepts well. He was a Greek slave who lived from 620 to 560 B.C.E. One story had him serving as financial counselor to King Croesus of Lydia, perhaps the wealthiest nation in the ancient world at that time. Lydia did not come by its wealth because of natural resources or powerful armies; instead, it became a center of commerce and investment through its invention of coined money. Lydia was already a bustling trade center in the seventh century. Its monarchs were the first to realize that a small, standardized unit of money would help to encourage commerce by making possible both complex transactions among multiple buyers and sellers as well as the monetization of even small amounts of wealth, such as a week's labor or a small part of a farmer's harvest.

Precious metals, gold and silver in particular, were already a common medium of exchange in the ancient world, of course. However, the Lydian innovation was to issue small ingots in a standardized size and weight, clearly stamped to communicate their value even to the illiterate. The first coins were oval slugs several times thicker than today's coins and made of electrum, a naturally occurring mixture of silver and gold. Lydian kings had these slugs stamped with a lion-head emblem to signify their origin and authenticity. By stamping them, the Lydian government's mints flattened the slugs into the first true coins. During the reign of Croesus, the Lydians took the final step toward modern coinage and issued new money of pure gold and silver rather than natural alloy.

Because of their trusted status, Lydian coins dramatically expanded Lydian trade, particularly in the new open-air retail markets that began to supplant the old household-based trading system. To preview my thesis a bit: The Lydians were practicing an early form of Investor Politics. That is, their government purposely structured public services in order to maximize the trade and investment occurring within their jurisdiction. In this case, the service was a stable, reliable, and economical currency. The result was not only prosperity for merchants, workers, and consumers but also burgeoning government revenues. So much wealth flowed into and within Lydia, in fact, that its citizens did not quite know what to do with it. As Jack Weatherford tells it in his excellent 1997 book *The History of Money,* Lydian coins led to the invention of dice, the first "gambling district," and the first known brothels in the ancient world. They also helped generate the wealth Croesus needed to hire mercenaries and to outfit Lydian troops to conquer much of Asia Minor before foolishly attacking Persia and being over-thrown.[2] Aesop never knew the fate of his master, however. Croesus sent him to Delphi to satisfy some government creditors. But Aesop found the Delphians' claims to be fraudulent and refused to pay. An angry mob threw him over a cliff. It was a high price for Aesop to pay for faithfully managing his master's money.

AN ECONOMIC PREHISTORY

Money makes complex economic arrangements possible but is not required for saving and investment. Human civilization developed long before the advent of coins, but it was still always based on saving and investment. This is no exaggeration. Culture, art, commerce, religion, government—all presuppose that a community's immediate need for food, clothing, and shelter can be met without employing everyone. Only production in excess of one's immediate needs makes this possible. And only through the development of four closely related economic tools—savings, insurance, investment, and specialization—can these surpluses be generated. Increases in economic output per worker require increases in either the quantity or quality of capital available to those workers. Such capital can be physical (tools, buildings, and machines), human (labor skills and attitudes), or intellectual (inventions and industrial processes), just to name three.[3] To gain a clear understanding of the Investor Politics of the twenty-first century, we must look backward to human history and even to prehistory to examine the origins of capital formation. As we shall see, politics has always been intimately linked with investment, understood in the broadest sense of the word.

The earliest human societies that scholars can identify are the nomadic hunter-gatherers who inhabited various regions of Africa, Asia, Europe, and the Americas. Throughout most of their history, these hunter-gatherers traveled in small bands of twenty to thirty related individuals—a patriarch and/or matriarch, their children and grandchildren, mates from neighboring groups, and other assorted relatives. They worked together both to hunt animals for meat and to gather fruits, vegetables, nuts, simple tools, and other useful objects. Because these bands were frequently on the move, their shelter consisted either of portable artifices (tents, yurts) or structures they found or could construct quickly (caves, lean-tos).[4]

In this earliest of human societies, the line between political, economic, and spiritual institutions was blurred or nonexistent. Few of the tools future civilizations would use to draw such lines were available to the hunter-gatherers. Their nomadic lifestyle, for example, provided little opportunity to develop or enforce private property rights, not only over land but also over the products that land might produce. Private property rights are indispensable if societies are to separate the public from the private, the sphere of human activity over which political power is freely wielded and the sphere from which it is limited or excluded. Furthermore, the small size of these societies reduced the extent to which differences in knowledge or talent resulted in the development of markets or a division of labor beyond the most rudimentary sort.[5] Finally, because they lacked any practical means of saving and transporting more than limited quantities of food, these earliest human societies provided little reward or incentive for hard work. All that was hunted or gathered was consumed relatively quickly.

Even under these conditions, however, developments occurred in economic exchange and institutions that demand our attention. The earliest hunting and gathering humans cooperated with each other to derive sustenance from a sometimes-forbidding environment. They had to develop terms of trade and rules of work and reward in order to put members of the clan or band to productive use. A simple division of labor did evolve, based on age, sex, and physical prowess or infirmity. We know that these small societies, while primitive and sometimes brutal, also gave opportunities for those with different natural talents and skills. And while the invention of money was far in the future, these early humans engaged in mutually beneficial trade in valuable goods that sometimes spanned surprising distances.

Archaeologists and anthropologists divide human prehistory before metallurgy into at least two periods: the Paleolithic (Old Stone Age) and the Neolithic (New Stone Age). The names suggest a categorization based on stone technology, but the real dividing lines among these periods involve changes in geography and corresponding changes in economic technology and organization. To recognize the roots of saving and investing, one must go all the way back to the Paleolithic. It lasted from 2.5 million years ago until about 10,000 B.C.E. Humans during this period include *Homo erectus* and archaic *Homo sapiens*. Early in the period, humans used simple tools made either of the core of a stone after pieces had been flaked off or the flakes themselves. They used fire (discovered sometime between 1 million and 500,000 years ago) to drive or prod animals, to prepare food, and, of course, to keep warm.

Later, in the so-called "Middle Paleolithic Period," flake tools were developed into a wide array of scrapers, borers, and points used to manipulate animal kills and other materials. This was the period of Neanderthal *Homo sapiens* in Europe and of others even closer in appearance to modern humans. Their tools may have improved their hunting; more importantly, there is evidence of extensive social cooperation not only in hunting but in storing and exchanging food. As one writer has noted, hunting is not just about killing animals. Killing animals is the easy part, whether it is by using weapons, by traps, or by driving prey over cliffs. The difficult part lies in the organization of personnel so that they are in the right place at the right time and with the right gear to ensure a better-than-average chance of success.[6] Tasks that are even more difficult include coping with failure, weather, and the decline of animal stocks. Remember that earlier societies lacked effective technologies for storing food, and a diet of nuts, berries, and other gathered foods was not of sufficient quantity or nutritional value to tide families and clans over in the event of a seasonal decline of game.

THE INVENTION OF SAVING

It is here, in the Middle Paleolithic populated by humans whose language skills were limited or nonexistent, that economic behavior extending beyond kinship and simple, opportunistic hunting and gathering probably developed. More specifically, these Middle Paleolithic people pioneered the crucial economic behavior of managing risk—in this case, the risk of starvation. They did it with two rudimentary concepts: *savings* and *insurance.* In the former case, they learned to put stores of food in secure places in their hunting and gathering territory, then budget them to cover subsistence needs over the lean times. In the latter, nearby small kinship groups established social networks through alliance, intermarriage, visiting, and feasting that served as regional insurance policies. A group facing a decline in game (or lack of success in hunting) could make claims on the food stores of neighbors with whom they had previously invested time, attention, or their own food. This served to spread the risk of starvation over a broader number of hunters and gatherers, thus improving the chances of survival for all.[7]

The concepts of savings and insurance are closely related; indeed, one might think of insurance as a way of realizing the benefits of savings without having to develop technologies for saving food over a long period and without having to wait until a stock of savings is sufficiently large to tide a family or group over during hard times. The late Frank Knight, the University of Chicago economist and cofounder of the "Chicago school" of economics, defined insurance as a means of converting a large contingent loss into a smaller fixed cost.[8] In prehistoric times, insurance-type arrangements, if they were of large enough breadth for their members to escape simultaneous misfortunes, represented a reasonable technique for coping with risk under difficult technological conditions.

The Upper Paleolithic, beginning about fifty thousand years ago in various regions, represented the appearance of humans roughly identical to us today. It also brought two additional economic innovations of critical importance: *specialization* and *investment.* The Cro-Magnon and other advanced *Homo sapiens* of the Upper Paleolithic, unlike their predecessors, seem to have specialized in the hunting or gathering of specific species, rather than being purely opportunistic and pursuing whatever was visible in their range areas. Like savings and insurance, specialization was a form of risk management in the sense that it usually involved careful study of particular animals with the goal of predicting their behavior—and thus increasing the likelihood of catching them. Specialization took some of the risk out of hunting and gathering by allowing for the accumulation of knowledge with which small human societies could ensure a more stable and predictable food supply. It not only required study of animal habits and movements, but also a more detailed understanding of the climate and topography of their range areas.[9]

Accumulating such knowledge had a cost. It took a great deal of time and effort, time and effort that earlier human societies had probably devoted to less taxing recreational activities. Indeed, many people assume that economic progress throughout history has meant a progressive increase in leisure time, but until recently, the opposite has been true. In earlier Paleolithic groups, there was little to be gained by spending more time on hunting and gathering activities than on leisure activities. Simple hunting and gathering were such "hit or miss" strategies that increased time and effort invested in them would not have yielded much more in the way of results. The greater amount of leisure time available to these early groups was not a sign of prosperity, as we might think of leisure today. It represented the inability of these earlier communities to employ their labor effectively to improve their lot and take prudent steps against catastrophic loss.

However, with the introduction of specialization, increased time and effort devoted to the study of quarry and environment could pay off in higher return. So the more sophisticated hunters and gathers of the Upper Paleolithic discovered the value of investment—forgoing consumption or leisure in the short run for greater material benefit in the long run. Until it became practical to store information (through better language skills and specialization in a relatively narrow field of inquiry), investment would have had paltry returns.

This revolution in hunting and gathering had repercussions beyond just improvements in food supply. It was also associated with the development of larger, multi-family groups. For one thing, specialization and investment made population growth both feasible and desirable. Additional people meant additional opportunities to gather useful information and to carry out the complex strategies required to catch more game. At the same time, the improved food supply made it possible to support larger populations.[10] Specialization and the increased scale of human populations led to larger and more permanent settlements and to the beginnings of a territoriality that would eventually lead to concepts of private property in land and stock. Both the larger populations and the increased productivity of hunting and gathering made possible a greater division of labor within the groups, allowing some individuals the option of specializing in tasks other than hunting and gathering.

SAVINGS AND INVESTMENT CREATES TRADE

Finally, the development of larger groups with a higher level of specialization created the conditions required to inaugurate *trade* among unrelated groups. After all, if one group chose to specialize in a particular form of hunting and gathering, then the occasional acquisition of game or artifacts outside the specialty becomes more attractive. It represents variety and diversion. A coastal group specializing in catching fish and gathering shellfish would have something of value to offer an inland group specializing in hunting deer, horses, or other big game. This increased value of trade would apply not just to foodstuffs but also to other goods. In both western and central Europe of the Upper Paleolithic, for example, there is evidence that several species of seashells were traded or exchanged over hundreds of miles. Similarly, there is evidence of relatively long-distance trade in high-quality flints and other raw materials.[11]

The Upper Paleolithic Period ended with the end of the last Ice Age and the impact of global warming on the environment. The initial stages of this warming can be traced back to about 11,000 B.C.E., and affected different parts of the Old and New Worlds at different times. The oceans rose, forests expanded over the expanses left behind by the retreating glaciers, and portions of the globe saw climate change of cold to temperate or temperate to hot. These changes led either to human migration or to significant changes in the way humans lived in their home areas. One further note about the end of the Upper Paleolithic is that it coincides with the final settlement of every habitable continent.[12]

The key point for our purposes is that the development of multi-family societies, and later towns and cities, was based on the invention of economic practices based around delayed gratification. The habit of savings and investment paid its greatest returns once human settlements developed around new notions of private property. When families could work their own land or tend their own herds, the economic value of hard work soared.[13] After all, at a very basic level, agriculture and animal husbandry were the epitome of savings and investment. Rather than literally "eating the seed corn," farmers planted it in the ground, tended it for months (perhaps nearly starving the whole time), and then reaped a far greater bounty at harvest time. With herders, delaying gratification meant feeding scarce grains and water to stock animals rather than to their own families. It meant tending, not eating, the stock. Those who could learn to do this would, in the long run, be far better off than those hunter-gatherers who worried only about today's meal.[14]

If one considers the broad sweep of human history, this radical revolution in how human beings live has occurred only recently. It is said that of all the human beings who ever lived, 90 percent existed as hunter-gatherers.[15] The passage of time from the last Ice Age and early human settlements to the modern day is, geologically speaking, a blink of the eye. Yet consider how radically different our lives are compared with our hunter-gatherer ancestors. The key difference is the role of investment—not only private investment in the form of agriculture but public investment in the form of infrastructure. The construction of roads, bridges, and irrigation canals— long predating the existence of monetary markets and securities—is a form of investment to which most organized urban societies have devoted substantial resources throughout history. First by the practice of forced labor and much later with taxation, governments have compelled their citizens to "invest" a significant amount of time and effort in such public infrastructure, often with what we would consider to be a pretty good rate of return (economic in the case of city streets and waterways and defensive in the case of intercity roads, built primarily as a means of moving troops rapidly to their postings).

To say that investment is the critical component of civilization is not to say that more investment—or a higher savings or investment "rate"—is always better. The quality of investment, not its quantity, determines standard of living. Even as recently as the nineteenth century in America, most people still lived and worked on farms. They spent much of their waking hours working on projects designed not to make themselves better off that day but instead to make themselves better off over the course of a year or longer. They planted seeds, improved their land, tended livestock, converted food and other perishables into storable form, and contributed to public works projects with labor or taxes. Few could afford luxury items, vacations, feasts, or other forms of current consumption. They were frequently engaged in saving or investment activities, yet they had a demonstrably lower standard of living than even a poor American at the turn of the twenty-first century. Indeed, as chapter 3 explains, the genesis of modern financial investment—in the form of stocks, bonds, mutual funds, and other tools—has coincided with far greater productivity thanks to organizational and technological innovations. With proper public policies in place, this should allow us to defer *less* of our consumption, to live better now rather than later, and to still enjoy far higher benefits when our more productive investments mature.

Of course, there have always been some human beings who have found a way to fulfill their immediate needs without going to the trouble of saving and investing at all. They coped with declining hunting stocks, poor weather, or bad luck by marauding, pillaging, and enslaving. This was, despite its injustice, a fairly effective approach to "risk management"—as long as the potential marauders were militarily superior both to their prey and to competing marauders. At the same time, in order to keep from exhausting the supply of booty too quickly, the population of marauders as a whole had to be a lot lower than that of their prey. If the grasshopper, for example, simply provided for the winter by stealing the ant's stash, he might survive in the short term but the ant would starve and thus not be around to provide food for the grasshopper the following year. If, on the other hand, the grasshopper identified several ants as targets and stole or extorted smaller portions from each, he might eat well without consuming his "seed corn," so to speak. Unfortunately for him, if other lazy grasshoppers got wind of this, they might well muscle into his territory and reduce his take. Moreover, if some of the ants under his sovereignty got the idea of pillaging rather than working themselves, the system would soon collapse.

THE CREATION OF CITIES AND GOVERNMENTS

Agriculture inevitably led to permanent settlements. The first known cities developed in the Fertile Crescent that stretched from modern-day Israel through Syria and Southern Turkey to Iraq. The biblical city of Jericho on the Jordan River was one such early city, dating to about 8,000 B.C.E. and sheltering about two thousand people at peak times.[16] Another was Catal Huyuk in modern-day Turkey, where evidence exists not just of agriculture, herding, pottery, and long-range trade but also the beginnings of differentiation between political, economic, and religious activities.[17] Remember that Paleolithic bands were essentially extended families in which a patriarch, matriarch, or groups of elders probably wielded whatever authority existed. One or a small group would serve simultaneously as military leader, economic decision maker, and religious authority. However, with agriculture, bands found it economically beneficial to settle down. They also began to develop private property over land in the early cities, particularly as populations grew and the extended family no longer served as a useful framework within which to settle disputes or to allocate grazing land. It bears repeating that private investment is impossible without some semblance of private property rights. Farming or grazing takes hard work, careful planning, patience, and the ability to delay gratification. Human beings are not likely to choose such a difficult course unless they can be reasonably assured that they and their families will reap a goodly portion of what they sow.

Cities—surrounded by productive farmland and thus reflecting an unprecedented growth and concentration of population—allowed a greater division of labor than ever before. Someone talented at such skills as weaving baskets, making pottery, and performing religious rituals could now be spared from food gathering and encouraged to specialize. Two critical implications of this differentiation were the economic productivity associated with specialization and the increasing need to adjudicate conflicts among city dwellers engaged in a variety of occupations and market transactions.[18] A related problem was that the agricultural surpluses of cities made them far more attractive to marauders than previously wandering bands of protofarmers had been. In short, cities required a form of legal and political authority exceeding the loose confederations of hunting-gathering bands.

Inseparable from the birth of cities is the birth of government, well defined by Nobel laureate and economic historian Douglass C. North as a social institution enjoying comparative advantage in violence that extends over a geographic area whose boundaries are determined by its power to tax. Some use the term "monopoly on violence" to describe a government, but this is not strictly true. A monopoly suggests a lack of competition. Most governments, however, do face competition, either in the form of republican or democratic politics or, more common throughout history, the threat of outside invasion, internal insurrection, or the mass exodus of dissatisfied residents. The size and scope of a particular government depends on its comparative advantage versus alternative methods of providing public services. This comparative advantage is determined by such factors as the technology and prowess of a government's armed forces, the reliability of its courts and laws, or the cost of its tax system.

North divides all theories about the creation of government into two categories: *contract theory* and *predatory theory*.[19] The first suggests that Neolithic bands of human beings, previously lacking any concept of government as an institution separate from extended family, found it mutually beneficial to join together under a common ruler to accomplish ends that individual bands could not do on their own. Contract theories have a long pedigree; clearly, those of Thomas Hobbes, John Locke, and other Enlightenment philosophers live on in constitutions and governments today. But the social contract idea of government does not rely on some mythical period long ago when an entire society, by mutual consent, formed a contract to recognize a civil authority, as these philosophers have usually been interpreted to suggest. More useful is the idea of an *implied* social contract, developed pragmatically rather than formally. Over a period of time a relatively just ruler, providing useful services such as personal protection and law courts and a moderate tax burden, was likely to attract residents to his community and simultaneously avoid driving large numbers of his most productive citizens away. In addition, a fledging government that found a way to protect its constituents from outside attack was likely to survive to grow larger and more populous. Governments unable to fulfill this basic need got swallowed by marauders or melted away through emigration (though barriers to invasion and exit, such as deserts, oceans, or mountain ranges, allowed some monarchs to avoid a good bit of accountability[20]).

Finally, in areas where large public works were necessary to make farming or herding successful, a government administered well enough to build and maintain such projects would grow and prosper. Egypt is a classic case of such a government. Large-scale farming along the Nile without extensive irrigation and precautions against flooding would have been impossible. Individual bands or tribes, unable to exclude rivals downriver from benefiting from their irrigation projects, would lack the economic incentive to make such a significant capital investment. Furthermore, no private institutions capable of investment at such a scale yet existed. By compelling broad participation in waterworks, the Pharaohs (or, more probably, their appointees at the district level[21]) performed a service that allowed for increases in the number and standard of living of their subjects.

Of course, there is a less benign explanation for government: the predatory one. As stated earlier, the grasshopper can keep a good thing going indefinitely if he can extort food from a sufficient number of ants to avoid overtaxing them while simultaneously excluding other grasshoppers from horning in on his territory. Predatory governments are at least as common in history as are contractual ones. North argues that successful, long-lived governments usually mixed both sets of behaviors. "From the redistributive societies of ancient Egyptian dynasties through the slavery system of the Greek and Roman world to the medieval manor," he writes, "there was persistent tension between the ownership structure which maximized the rents to the ruler (and his group) and an efficient system that reduced transaction costs and encouraged economic growth." Because governments always find it difficult to keep these tendencies in balance, they inevitably falter and fail to maximize productive investment and growth. "Still," North concludes, "individuals given a choice between a state—however exploitative it may be—and anarchy, have decided for the former. Almost any set of rules is better than none, and it is not in the ruler's interest to make the rules so unpalatable that initiative is stifled."[22]

TRADE, MONEY, AND INVESTMENT IN THE ANCIENT WORLD

What we call the "ancient world" comprises the vast majority of human history in the West and Middle East, from the first large-scale states in Mesopotamia and Egypt in the period from 4500 B.C.E. until the fall of the Roman Empire in the fifth century C.E. The history of India, the Far East, and the New World developed along a different time scale, of course, but often exhibited similar patterns (it is in Europe's medieval period where the West's economic future diverged with that of the East). One ancient trend was nearly universal. Smaller states gave way to larger ones for a variety of reasons, including trade. Although luxury goods such as silks, spices, precious metals, and gems played a significant role in trade and in military history during ancient times, consumption items for commoners were also traded over significant distances. Greece relied on grain from Black Sea colonies and allies to sustain its economy, particularly during its wars with

Persia. The fields of Egypt and North Africa fed unemployed Roman ple-beians. In this time before true commercial law or international economic institutions, a larger scope for government meant some semblance of order, predictability, and protection from piracy. Of course, a larger, more bureau-cratic, and more expensive government, while reducing piracy and transac-tion costs in some ways, obviously presents the risk of hiking these costs it-self through taxation and corruption, as most ancient empires did before their decline and fall.

Important for our story is that the birth of long-range trade in ancient times allowed for a greater variety of agricultural investment. To use mod-ern financial terms, the ancients were able to diversify their portfolios. For example, some areas specialized in forms of agriculture or husbandry that had a short-term maturity, such as grain or vegetables. Others, supplied by grain-producing regions for much of their immediate needs, could dedi-cate less arable land to longer-term investments such as groves and vine-yards. Such products as olive oil and wine required many years of intense effort, while a field of barley or wheat might yield annual or even semian-nual returns. Still, millions of people, particularly those in Mediterranean cultures respecting secure property rights in land, chose to produce olive oil, wine, and other high-value goods requiring significant and often risky investment because consumers were willing to trade large amount of low-value goods for them. After the Lydians gave the ancient world its first real, standardized money during the seventh and sixth centuries B.C.E., trade ex-panded even more rapidly, opening up more opportunities for more prof-itable, long-term investment.

Monetary investment as we know it today—in which outside agents pro-vide capital and receive interest or a share of future profits—had its origins even before the invention of coins. At the risk of oversimplification: The Ancient Mesopotamians invented interest-bearing loans and equity invest-ment, while the Ancient Greeks invented banking. Of course, lending itself was far older than that. No doubt hunting-gathering societies and early set-tlements featured lots of borrowing and lending among relatives and friends of items such as tools, seed, rams or bulls for siring, and so on. Eco-nomic historians speculate that the invention of interest-bearing loans was stimulating by the growth of small settlements into true cities. In such places, one would find it advantageous to borrow or lend beyond just an immediate circle of family and friends. Without recourse to shaming or personal relationships to guarantee repayment, prospective lenders developed means of measuring the time value of money. Interest rates were born.

Merchants in Mesopotamian towns such as Uruk and Ur appear to have pioneered interest-bearing loans in the centuries before 2000 B.C.E. The lending of breeding stock was the most likely origin of this innovation. Indeed, the intimate connection between lending and livestock is easily seen in language. The ancient Sumerian word *mash*, which archaeologists identify as "interest," was also the word for "calf." The original meaning of the ancient Greek word for interest, *tokos*, was also "calf." The Latin root of the modern "pecuniary" is *pecus*, meaning, "flock." The ancient Egyptian word for interest doubled as "to give birth."[23] Perhaps the rate of interest in early contracts referred to the number of calves or lambs owed the owner of a stud. The concept of rate of return in breeding contracts later came to be applied to other business arrangements.

Certainly by the time of Hammurabi's reign in Babylonia, around 1700 B.C.E., lending must have been commonplace. We know this because surviving tables chronicle government regulations on the interest rate—a cap of 20 percent was frequently specified but just as frequently evaded by manipulating loan length and terms—as well as the use of interest to teach mathematics to young scholars. Other records dating to the same period from Ur, the biblical Abraham's hometown, reveal the existence of a financial district, a sort of ancient "Wall Street," where lenders congregated to make deals, compete, and finance long-range trade. These early financiers apparently experimented not only with lending at interest but also with business forms distinct from the traditional family proprietorship.[24]

One tablet tells the story of Ea-Nasir, a merchant from Ur who assembled a group of fifty-one investors. These investors provided either silver or trade goods, particularly baskets. Ea-Nasir conducted trade missions southward to Persian Gulf ports, where he traded for copper, precious stones, and spices. Ea-Nasir's business appears to be a rudimentary form of the limited-liability partnership. Investors were liable only for the money or goods they contributed up front. Losses beyond the capital investment were, it seems, swallowed by Ea-Nasir, as were the bulk of the profits to compensate him for this risk. In addition, the investors were compensated not strictly with interest but with a share of profits earned from Ea-Nasir's trips south. In other words, they were equity investors. Nor were they all large ones. Records show that ordinary citizens, investing a bracelet or two, could participate, anticipating the idea of mutual funds of small investors. "The effect of this business structure upon personal fortunes was profound," writes Yale University historian William Goetzmann. "People were able to 'insure' themselves against personal failure—if their own venture collapsed, then the investment in Ea-Nasir's might carry them through hard times."[25]

For all its intriguing innovations, however, the Mesopotamian financial system still lacked the independence that true banking required. Most of the lending, it turns out, was for "emergency needs" rather than for profitable investment—and the emergencies almost always involved taxes or temple requisitions, which were really the same things. More generally, Mesopotamian society simply did not allow for much large-scale economic activity outside of government, which officially owned large segments of the arable land and lorded over tenant farmers in ways more despotic than Europe's feudal barons would have ever dreamed. It took the individualistic, landowning ancient Greeks, particularly in Athens, to come up with private financial institutions more closely resembling banks. The Greek economy, more so than that of the Near East, featured long-term investment in such products as olives and wine. Stable private property rights and the decentralized, participatory government they engendered fostered long-term investment and made possible true private-sector banking, albeit on a relatively small scale.[26] Athenian lenders invested in overseas trade, providing maritime loans as well as opportunities for equity investment. Banks accepted deposits of money from natives as well as out-of-town merchants. One successful banker was Pasion, a former slave who lived in Athens in the fourth century. His masters were bankers, too, from whom he learned the trade. At his death, his was the largest bank of at least seven operating in the city.[27]

Still, it is difficult to separate ancient investment from government, since the same lenders financing international trade were also frequently government creditors, public officials, or hated "tax farmers." The latter, known in Jesus' day as "publicans," were contractors who bought the rights to collect taxes in a particular neighborhood or town, then profited by charging a higher rate, loaning money to debt-strapped farmers without other means of paying taxes, and in many cases by hiring goons to confiscate property on the flimsiest of pretenses. The ravages of the tax farmers and the financial insiders associated with rapacious governments who profited from public works and the sale of military supplies, coupled with the envy that lenders and investors have always seemed to engender in their fellow countrymen, gave ancient financiers a very bad name and paved the way for much government meddling. In both Mesopotamia and Greece, governments periodically issued debt amnesties and tried to regulate interest rates. Prophets and philosophers railed against the wealthy bankers in their midst. Socrates called government debt relief the tool of the "demagogue," but he compared moneylenders to wasps and parasites.[28]

Rome typifies the blended nature of ancient finance. By early Imperial days, Rome had developed a sophisticated financial sector, complete with lending, banking, (quasi) limited-liability enterprises, and the sale of "stock" in such enterprises among Roman nobles. Unfortunately, much of this financial activity revolved around lucrative tax-farming contracts in Asia Minor and other Eastern provinces. Even these nascent forms of monetary investment might have evolved into something more closely approaching international capitalism if the empire itself had not grown in size and cost. As economist Larry Reed, head of the Mackinac Center for Public Policy in Michigan, tells the story, swelling bureaucracies and armies led emperors to attempt ever more desperate ways of financing the government and paying debts. These included hiking existing tax rates, inventing new forms of taxation, inflating the money supply, and confiscation. Ultimately, the money economy itself was driven out of the West, not to return for several hundred years.[29] When it did, ironically enough in Italy, it set the stage for a new round of innovation in investment and finance, reviving the economic practices of ancient merchants in a far wider and more permanent fashion.

THE FINANCIAL REVOLUTION

Popular treatments of history often treat the Industrial Revolution as the turning point signifying the beginning of modern economics. However, the development of factory production was an effect, not a cause. It had important ramifications for productivity and the lot of the average person, of course, but previous as well as subsequent changes in business *organiza-*

tion—in institutions, not technology—deserve equal if not greater interest. The true birth of modern western economics can be found far earlier, in the eleventh, twelfth, and thirteenth centuries, during which enterprising Italian, Dutch, English, and other merchants, intellectuals, and political leaders developed a new set of institutions making the subsequent mercantile and industrial progress possible. We can properly call this period the Financial Revolution. The other institutional transformation, which Douglass North calls the Second Economic Revolution (the first being agriculture) and which involves the invention of corporations and the sale of their stocks and bonds, is the subject of chapter 3.

The Financial Revolution began with an innovation that makes few millennial history lists but—small as it may seem—sets the stage for capitalism itself. *Double-entry bookkeeping,* developed by Italian merchants in the eleventh century based on concepts borrowed from Arabic traders, was not the result of some esoteric pursuit of truth. It was a practical solution to a common problem—bookkeeping errors. Particularly before the widespread use Arabic numerals, maintaining accurate records of any large-scale operation, business or not, was a major challenge. Imagine having to keep books with Roman numerals and without the zero, an Indian concept introduced into Islamic culture by famed mathematician Al-Khwarizmi in the ninth century.

Al-Khwarizmi himself admitted that his interest in Indian numeration systems based on zero arose from the need for people to solve practical problems related to inheritances, wills, purchase and sales contracts, surveying, and tax collection. As what we called Arabic numerals began to spread throughout the Islamic world in the ninth and tenth centuries, the traditional, small-scale partnerships that characterized commerce early in Islamic history—a business form in which the Prophet Muhammad had himself participated—gave way to large-scale trading companies in which investors owned the equivalent of stock and around which a system of banking and credit evolved. Unfortunately, Islam's early trading institutions, though elaborate and the source of tremendous wealth, never developed into capitalism of a European sort. As was previously the case in ancient Mediterranean societies, Islam's rulers were heavily involved in business enterprises, rarely paid their own debts, and imposed excessive costs in the form of taxes, regulations, wars, and outright confiscation. Neither Islamic law nor Islamic rulers recognized the independence of trading cities or the enterprises that populated them. As historian Subhi Y. Labib has noted, other basic concepts such as commercial insurance "remained practically outside the scope of Islamic economic thought" during the period.[30]

However, Arabic innovations, particularly in mathematics and bookkeeping, would find fertile ground across the sea by the eleventh century. As merchant families from Venice and other Italian trading cities began to resuscitate long-range trade in the Mediterranean after the interruptions of the Dark Ages, someone armed with the new Arabic numerals hit upon a bright idea. To detect accounting errors in his business, he would enter all transactions twice, once as a debit and once as a credit. For example, the purchase of a new scale would require the entry of an asset (the value of the scale) and a liability (the cash withdrawal or debt incurred to purchase it). At the end of any recording period, typically a month, the merchant would total all debits and credits. If the two totals did not match, he would know to look for the flawed entry.

Double-entry bookkeeping became far more than an error-detection device, however. For the first time, it allowed managers to determine accurately the net worth of their business enterprises at any point in time. More importantly, it created a conceptual doorway to modern industrial organization. The only way for assets to equal liabilities is if the equity stake is itself considered a liability—an obligation to the owner. Double-entry bookkeeping is, in other words, based on the concept that a business is distinct and separate from its owning proprietor(s). In an eleventh century world of family businesses, this was revolutionary, to say the least. Such separation was necessary for the future development of limited-liability partnerships and corporations, the building blocks of a modern economy. Economic historian Werner Sombart sums it up well: "One cannot imagine what capitalism would be without double-entry bookkeeping."[31]

One further effect of this innovation was to make possible the creation of a system of international business finance far surpassing anything developed by the Mesopotamians, Greeks, Romans, or Muslims. After all, lenders in these societies had a major handicap. Outside their own circle of family and business acquaintances, there were huge transaction costs in extending credit. Independent information about a prospective borrower was nearly impossible to derive. Double-entry bookkeeping gave lenders a common accounting language and a useful way to distinguish the appearance of prosperity from the reality. The practice, write Nathan Rosenberg and L. E. Birdzell, Jr., in their seminal work *How the West Grew Rich,* "grew into an agreed-upon procedure for recording all economic events in a measurable and therefore calculable way. In a very real sense, economic reality became that which could be expressed in numerical terms in the books."[32]

In addition to double-entry bookkeeping, Rosenberg and Birdzell list several other innovative institutions of the period that facilitated the evolution of capitalism. *Commercial law* developed organically, based on Roman antecedents, as merchants groped for predictability in a world of petty tyrants, a patchwork of fiefdoms, and the ever-present threat of piracy. The ancient Greeks had pioneered the use of maritime loans to underwrite long-range trade, but by the twelfth century Italian merchants had invented more formal *insurance contracts* that guaranteed a trading mission against loss in return for a stated premium. Later, insurance markets in Italy, Amsterdam, and London differentiated *maritime* insurance, a risky product covering acts of piracy or of God on the high seas, from more marketable *commercial* insurance, which covered the profitability of the subsequent sales. "The division between specialists in maritime risks and specialists in market risks greatly facilitated the growth of maritime trade," Rosenberg and Birdzell write.[33]

True *bills of exchange,* in existence by the thirteenth century, permitted merchants to transfer the amounts they owed each other without having to exchange coin or goods directly. These early checks were themselves traded among far-flung traders, giving rise to a private system of paper money based on the credibility of the merchant families against whom the bills of exchange were drawn. *Deposit banking* was the next logical development, as lesser merchants deposited funds with prominent trading families whose drafts were credible money in faraway lands. The creditors found that they need not maintain the entire face value of their circulating notes and could use some of their deposits to buy other bills of exchange at discount—"that is, for lending money at interest despite the prohibition of usury."[34]

Also in the thirteenth century, some governments began a tentative but inexorable movement away from *arbitrary taxation* to a more predictable system for collecting revenue, controlled in England and later in Holland by the merchant class sitting in council rather than by kings or tax farmers.

Kings put up with their diminution of the direct power to tax in exchange for a steady flow of revenue.[35] One result in both England and Holland was that real capital assets such as vessels and trading stations could be owned and operated by private enterprises without fear of arbitrary seizure by sovereigns, a right that continental merchants—and, indeed, most of their counterparts in the Islamic world, India, and China—simply could not take for granted. This made large-scale private investment possible for the first time in markets previously the province of governments or small-scale merchants.[36]

The final innovation needed to pave the way for the mercantile revolution of the fifteenth, sixteenth, and seventeenth centuries was the development of truly *private property rights* and institutions. In England and in other regions of western Europe, increasing population pressures in the thirteenth century led to robust competition for arable land and pastures, increasing enclosure of range land and the evolution of laws governing alienation and transfers of land. States took over the administration of private property claims from feudal barons. At the same time, kings began to give exclusive franchises to private entities to operate certain economic enterprises or to monopolize certain trade routes. While hardly free market in nature, these franchises were not tax farms in the Roman or Muslim sense. They were honest-to-goodness trading enterprises that allowed private merchants to build up physical capital (ships and equipment) and human capital (skilled labor and knowledge of routes and markets) without as much fear of interference or confiscation of their ships or workers by governments.[37]

THE MERCANTILE REVOLUTION

From these early beginnings, western economics next expanded into large-scale international trade as explorers, conquerors, missionaries, and merchants ventured forth on the high seas. Historians such as Henri Pirenne observe that the motivation for the western exploration of the fifteenth, sixteenth, and seventeenth centuries was itself economic. While trade with the East, both overland along the ancient Silk Route and by sea from the Persian Gulf to the Indian Ocean, had continued during the Dark Ages and the rise of the Islamic empires in the seventh century, it slowed to a trickle as the Ottoman Turks thundered down from the steppe to conquer the Near East and Anatolia and swallow the last remnants of Byzantium. The fall of Constantinople in 1453 was a precipitating event for Western explorers, now charged with both a holy and a potentially lucrative task of finding alternatives routes around the Turks to the riches of India and China. Within the next half-century, western Europeans would sail around Africa, establish new routes to India, and discover America. By the end of the period, the general contours of the world had been explored and mapped and colonies planted in much of its fertile soil.[38]

One trend in this mercantile revolution was the development of governmental institutions that reduced the costs and increased the benefits of public investment. In theory, of course, governments can make investments that increase the productivity of workers. From Egyptian waterworks to Persian, Roman, Chinese, and Incan road networks, large-scale public infrastructure has always been a legitimate and valuable form of investment, albeit a compulsory one. The problem has always been that—lacking the incentives that private investors face to defer consumption only when the potential payoffs are worth it—governments frequently "invest" taxpayer dollars very poorly, costing their citizens dearly. The same pharaohs that irrigated the Nile Valley wasted their country's labor on pyramids. Ancient coliseums, treasure cities, monuments, shrines—all were costly public projects funded by forced labor better employed in productive pursuits. Wars of conquest also represented substantial public investment in men and materiel with uncertain returns, at best.

To constrain government investment below the point of diminishing returns, there must be institutional controls on the rate of taxation and the power of sovereigns. As Douglass North points out, these controls evolved in the West in the form of legislative control over taxation and an independent judiciary to protect property from excessive regulation or expropriation. Particularly in England and Holland, parliaments exercised increased power during this period with the result that kings were unable to finance their most ambitious and risky schemes. Nor were they capable of overturning judicial precedent protecting private property from encroachment. "The reduced cost of using the market to organize economic activity was the main source of productivity gains during this era," North writes.[39]

In the area of economic institutions, the mercantile revolution brought the *chartered trading company* and other government-created but privately run entities designed to facilitate overseas exploration, colonization, and exploitation of resources. England, France, and Holland all began chartering such companies in the 1500s, based on the older forms of Roman corporations and medieval guilds and in most cases providing monopoly grants of trading rights over particular regions or products. The British East India Company, chartered in 1600, was a good example of this institution.[40] While these were not really private businesses in the modern sense of the word, they were important way stations on the road to the invention of the private corporation in the mid-nineteenth century. Because of their government charters, these mercantile corporations felt secure enough to invest heavily in capital stock, particularly in ships and equipment, allowing commerce on an unprecedented scale, as well as dramatic reductions in the cost of trade goods due to the increased use of sea transportation (which, as economist Thomas Sowell observes, was many times more economical than land transportation during the period[41]).

Perhaps the most important legacy of the mercantile revolution was the birth, near the end of the period, of laws granting "monopolies" to inventors and innovators. In England, the pivotal moment was the passage of the Statute of Monopolies in 1624. Patents and copyrights were not really monopolies. They were the logical extension of property rights over intellectual capital, making possible for the first time significant and sustained private investment in industrial invention and innovation. As with previous economic transformations, institutional arrangements had changed by the seventeenth century to give private individuals new incentives to invest time, effort, and money for future gain. "Idle curiosity or learning by doing will produce some technological change," North observes, noting the steady but slow rate of technological change during previous periods of human history.[42] But once patent law had increased the private rate of return to industrial innovation, the result was a series of technological breakthroughs that, when combined with further progress in economic institutions, gave rise to unprecedented gains in living standards.

THE INDUSTRIAL REVOLUTION

Usually dated from about 1750, the Industrial Revolution is often considered the economic turning point for the Western world. Important as it was, however, it does not really deserve that description. The factory system of production did, indeed, gradually displace home production from 1750 to 1850 in most industries, with corresponding gains in scale and productivity. Much of the gains were due to the increased day-to-day supervision of workers that a factory system, as opposed to a home-based production system, allowed. Helping drive the movement toward factory production were two technological developments that had their origins in the intellectual capital formation of the mercantile revolution. One was the use of waterpower and steam in production and transportation. More so even than the division of labor inherent in factory production, it allowed new devices to be effectively employed to harness water and steam to produce immense quantities of goods. The second technological innovation involved the substitution of iron and steel for wood in fabricating machinery and other products. As Rosenberg and Birdzell observe, "this substitution changed the size, longevity, precision, and mechanical complexity of a wide range of products, from sewing machines to ships."[43]

The Industrial Revolution is also somewhat misnamed in that an important contemporaneous change in the West's economy was a dramatic rise in agricultural productivity. Although the population also grew, increasing the market for food, productivity based on new information and techniques grew still faster. Fewer people were needed on the farm to produce the same (or higher) quantities of food. So, they moved to cities, swelling the urban population and providing the labor needed for rapid industrialization. It is a myth that this movement from the farm to the factory brought drudgery, disease, and misery. The opposite is true; despite what we would today consider difficult conditions indeed for the new factory workers and their families, their standard of living almost certainly improved compared to what was available in the countryside.[44]

The western economy underwent fundamental changes during the period, I admit, as did the way the average person lived and worked. Yet, as Douglass North points out, the change was more in magnitude rather than in kind.[45] If an ancient Greek had been transported forward in time to 1750, he would have seen much that was familiar to him. Even in 1850, while he would have marveled at the standard of living of the average person, the world would still have been largely intelligible. If transported to 1950, however, our ancient time traveler would have been simply aghast, surrounded by what he could only interpret as magic and the luxurious lifestyle of an

Olympian god. These massive changes in human existence could happen in such a short time only because of changes in financial and social institutions that fostered the development of physical, human, and intellectual capital on an unprecedented scale.

CONCLUSION

Saving and investing, thought of in the broadest terms, are essential characteristics of human civilization. To delay gratification, to channel one's labors away from satisfying immediate desires to the accumulation and constant improvement of long-term, income-producing assets, is the core of economic progress. From the earliest human settlements to the creation of rudimentary capitalist institutions in the High Middle Ages and the development of large-scale maritime trade from the Renaissance to the nineteenth century, innovative merchants and governments fashioned the tools they needed to separate economic institutions from their political and spiritual cousins and to make possible both productive public investment and, more importantly, privately owned capital goods, eventually including patentable ideas. All that was missing to allow these investments to occur on a massive scale was a form of private economic organization. The greatest leap forward in economic innovation would occur in America after its bloody Civil War, with the rise of private corporations and personal investing in their stocks and bonds, the subject of chapter 3. At the same time, however, various social and political forces combined to radicalize the country's two main political parties and to set the stage for the advent of America's modern welfare state and the welfare politics it spawned. How this process came to unfold is the subject of chapter 2. The new Investor Politics is found at the intersection of these two trends—political welfarism and personal financial investment—one representing the gradual decline and death of limited government and the other the best hope for its rebirth.

CHAPTER 2

AMERICAN POLITICAL
REALIGNMENT AND THE ORIGINS
OF WELFARE

MERICA'S NEW INVESTOR POLITICS HAS THE
potential to transform significantly the relationship
between the public and private sectors, between citizens and the welfare state to which they have become accustomed.
There is nothing unusual about the American dilemma. Virtually
all industrialized countries at the beginning of the twenty-first
century face the very real possibility that the aging of the population—good news, of course, to anyone except government actuaries—will render false the promises they have made to their citizens
to finance higher standards of living with government "investment." I will focus on the American case for the remainder of this
book simply because I am more familiar with it. With some allowances for culture differences and the rates of personal investing
and long-term government insolvency, my analysis of the new Investor Politics can apply to just about anywhere.

The creation of the American welfare state is of such historic
importance that its story has been told many times from many
points of view. Much scholarship, particularly since the 1960s, has
treated big government as the product of an inexorable force of
history, the result of a natural social evolution toward a higher

form of social organization. Others have viewed the story through the lens of individual politicians whom they either canonize or vilify. But these approaches are inadequate. There was nothing inevitable about the rise of the welfare state, nor was it simply the creation of opportunistic or ideological presidents, as important as they were to its genesis. The welfare state was, instead, the result of decades of concerted effort by hundreds, then thousands, then millions of people who came to view government as the only answer to economic and social ills they perceived as intolerable. Their means were largely democratic, though they were not always candid about their ultimate goals and did not mind waiting until moments of national desperation—economic depressions and wars—to advance their agenda.

Too many critics of the welfare state cite the 1930s as the time of its birth. This is a poor reading of history. It is true that for most Americans the welfare state remained unthinkable until the onset of chronic, mass unemployment in the early 1930s. Still, some groundwork had already been laid, starting just after the Civil War. Farmers, who faced decades of falling prices and what amounted to unemployment or underemployment decades before the Great Depression, were persuaded of the need for ongoing government assistance far earlier than their urban counterparts. Those who, heeding the signals the market was sending them, left the farm to seek unemployment in the growing cities became a new political constituency of propertyless, anxious urban voters. Cultivating them, the Populist and Progressive movements led to expansion of "poor relief" and the beginnings of social insurance programs during the first two decades of the twentieth century. In addition, organized labor, which really became a potent political force during the First World War, sought to make disability, unemployment, and retirement programs universal so that businesses where they were already organized would not remain at a competitive disadvantage because of higher labor costs. Therefore, it is to the decades prior to the 1930s that one must look for the origins of American welfarism. Both the ideological and the strategic nature of entitlement legislation from the 1930s to the 1960s arose in the late nineteenth and early twentieth centuries. As an early staffer in the Social Security Administration admitted:

> The men and women I worked with, while they were Populists, while they were Progressives, while they were strong believers in social legislation, they were also strongly of the belief of the inevitableness of gradualism. In other

words, they felt it was more important to take one step at a time. Or perhaps I ought to put it this way—to digest one meal at a time rather than eating breakfast, lunch, and dinner all at once and getting indigestion.[1]

A TALE OF TWO LEADERS

A good place to begin is with the contributions of two nineteenth-century individuals to the movement that became New Deal welfarism. One was an American, one not. One was a politician who feared socialism; the other a writer who welcomed it. One remained famous while the other eventually faded from the popular imagination.

The first is Otto von Bismarck. An attorney and member of the Prussian parliament in the 1840s, Bismarck became the Prussian representative to the German Diet in the 1850s, maneuvering throughout the period on behalf of the Prussian King Frederick Wilhelm IV to create a national Germanic state. Later, as prime minister and secretary of foreign affairs, he engineered three Prussian wars—with Denmark in 1864, with Austria in 1866, and France in 1870 to 1871—that helped forge the German nation and define defensible boundaries. His political achievements were not just military and diplomatic, however. Bismarck was also instrumental in founding the first modern welfare state. His goal was not government aggrandizement per se. He was troubled by the rise of Marxist and labor union movements across the Continent and heavily influenced by the academic consensus of the day, which came to be known as the German Historical School of economics. These German thinkers sought a middle course between English-style laissez-faire and republican liberalism—which they viewed as socially turbulent and effete—and the Marxist dogma they viewed as vile, inflexible, and dangerous to the established order. They believed the answer was a kind of "state capitalism"—a set of regulations, programs, and institutions to blunt the sharp edges of capitalism and bind together the German nation, only recently a union of states long under the thumb of French, Austrian, or other European powers. In their minds, the only alternative to state capitalism was a Marxist revolution that would bring violence, discord, and national vulnerability.[2]

Bismarck, in other words, became the original political exponent of "the Third Way." He started out as an opponent to big government. From 1867 to 1877, Bismarck's government was allied with the German liberals who favored laissez-faire economic policies, including free trade and limited government. His main domestic agenda consisted of a *Kulturkampf* against the political power of the Catholic Church. But when a worldwide economic downturn led to a German depression during the mid-1870s, the capitalist consensus cracked. Bismarck's conservatives eventually broke with the liberals in favor of other, less market-oriented parties. He first signaled his policy shift with a high protective tariff. Then he got creative. In 1883, Bismarck established the first "social insurance" programs, consisting of sickness insurance and workers' compensation plans supported by compulsory "contributions" by workers and employers. The payroll tax was born. In 1889, an old-age pension program was added, again funded by payroll taxes as well as by other government revenues. At the same time, German schools were reorganized into a centralized government-run system and devoted largely to vocational training, an enterprise of which foreign visitors, including Americans, were much enamored. (Indeed, some American trade association executives and business leaders have continued to agitate for German-style education for more than a hundred years now, despite its utter incompatibility with freedom and individualism.) Bismarck's immediate aim, to ensure the loyalty of German workers to the crown, was achieved. Austria was convinced, and adopted welfare state policies in 1888. Hungary followed in 1891. Soon politicians throughout Europe, who faced the same stark choices, at least in their own minds, began to look to the German welfare state model as showing a way out of the capitalism-Marxism trap.[3]

Less grudging than these European statesmen in his enthusiasm for welfare programs was the American Edward Bellamy. Few readers today will immediately recognize the name, but in Bellamy's day, he was perhaps the most famous and successful American author of a new kind of speculative fiction that, before long, would be known as science fiction. Bellamy's profession, like that of many of his radical contemporaries in the late nineteenth century, was journalism. While a newspaper reporter in Boston, he began to write light novels on the side. In 1888, at the age of thirty-eight, he published his claim to fame, the utopian novel *Looking Backward 2000–1887*. In a plot reminiscent of Irving's Rip van Winkle, and subsequently ripped off by countless writers from H. G. Wells to Woody Allen, the hero of the novel falls asleep in 1887 Boston and awakens in the year 2000. He

finds that all industry has been nationalized, wages abolished, money converted into debit cards and distributed equally to all, and every human
need provided for by government welfare programs "from the cradle to the
grave," as one character memorably tells the sleeper.[4] Two years after its
publication, *Looking Backward* had sold 200,000 copies—an astounding
number for the time—and booksellers could not keep copies on the
shelves. Devotees of Bellamy, in another pattern to be repeated pathetically
at various points during the twentieth century, formed what amounted to a
cult to discuss and promote his ideas. They set up 162 Nationalist clubs (the
word socialist was taboo) in twenty-seven states and published a magazine
called *The Nationalist.*[5]

An unprecedented outpouring of fiction, journalism, and commentary
on social problems soon followed Bellamy's meteoric rise. The turn of the
century was the time of Wells, Frank Norris, Ida Tarbell, Upton Sinclair,
Lincoln Steffens, Jack London, Thorstein Veblen, William James, John
Dewey, Herbert Croly, and other writers of a muckraking, progressive, or
socialist bent. Never before had the popular culture been so suffused with
radical political agendas. It is impossible to understand the rise of the welfare state in America without recognizing the important groundwork laid
by intellectuals who believed passionately that a world of big business and
small government would be unjust, and most of its inhabitants destitute
and pitiable. During the four decades from 1892 to 1932, these intellectuals
and their followers would gradually seize control of both the Democratic
and Republican parties during times of economic and political crisis, setting the stage for the birth of the welfare state.

POPULISM AND THE DEMOCRATS

The socialist movement in the United States did not begin auspiciously.
Average Americans were without the class hatred, envy, and collectivist outlook of their European counterparts. They were not easily swayed by a
clever turn of phrase or thundering rhetoric in radical pamphlets. They
were practical people and conservative in the original sense of the word.
They eschewed radicalism of any sort—even the American Revolution
could claim only a plurality of popular support against Loyalists and a third
group of neutral frontiersmen. It was to the American sense of practicality,
not to ideology, that socialists of the nineteenth and early twentieth cen

turies had to appeal. Therefore, the most effective advocates of government expansion in the United States tended to be journalists who wrote about particular cases, companies, and people rather than theoretical or ideological questions.

For the forty years after the publication of *The Communist Manifesto* in 1848, revolutionary socialism consisted mainly of academic agitation and worker strikes on the European continent. Most Marxists knew they would not come to power in a sudden revolution. Indeed, many stayed away from politics altogether and waited for the state to "wither away." Eventually, it became obvious to most socialists that gradualism, not revolution, was the best bet to achieve power in the West. Had not Marx and Engels themselves not laid out a ten-point plan for achieving socialism, starting with graduated income taxes and government-run central banks and leading eventually to public ownership of the means of production?

In 1884, English socialists founded the Fabian Society, named after the Roman general Fabius who had battled Hannibal with delaying tactics, avoiding a pitched battle that, in all likelihood, would be lost. A common Fabian tactic was "permeation"—the infiltration of other organizations with a less radical, more mainstream reputation. Fabians also sought to wield influence in government, usually from behind the scenes rather than through elective office. However, even Fabian-style gradualism did not take hold in the United States. There was an American Fabian group during the 1890s that accomplished little and disappeared. The American constitutional system, said one Fabian leader, did not lend itself easily to the creation of new parties and social movements.[6] He was right. Separation of powers and checks and balances tended to "gum up the works," thus slowing the progress of reformist legislation. Also, the winner-take-all system discouraged—but, as we shall see, did not prevent—the creation of explicitly socialist parties to pressure the majority parties to move leftward. American advocates of welfarism had to use an even more indirect approach. They began to infiltrate the only legitimate movement seeking fundamental political change—that of the farmers.

American farmers in the late nineteenth century had numerous grievances, many legitimate. The post-Civil War consensus among Republicans and many Democrats favored a high protective tariff. It made the products purchased by farmers very expensive and led to retaliatory tariffs in other countries that limited farm exports. It was a double whammy, reducing their real incomes through lower earnings and higher prices. At the same time, farmers saw railroad companies and other big businesses as receiving special government assistance at their expense. For example, most state tax codes were still heavily reliant on property taxes. Yet, many states exempted rail lines and other property owned by railroad companies from these taxes, shifting the burden of public services—including those benefiting mostly industrial interests—to taxpaying farmers. Not surprisingly, political corruption was rampant as some big businesses maintained or expanded their favored status by giving out free train tickets to lawmakers, paying them cash under the barrel, or manipulating federal agencies to make millions in land speculation in the West and South.[7]

It should be noted that farmers were also led to political action for less justifiable reasons. New agricultural techniques and technologies were making farming increasingly productive, but markets for farm products were not growing apace. In short, fewer farmers were needed to produce what consumers desired. Prices fell. Many farmers were heavily in debt and without the means to get out of it. The market was sending a strong message: Get out of the farming business. Many did, swelling the nation's urban population. But many others did not heed the message. They began to hear the siren song of bimetallism—the idea that silver as well as gold should be coined as legal tender by United States mints. This was no trivial matter. Expanded coinage of silver would inflate the money supply, reduce the nominal value of farming debts, and increase demand for agricultural products—or so farmers were told (often by silver-mining interests).[8]

The first stirrings of agrarian activism began right after the Civil War with the creation of the Patrons of Husbandry, later known as the Grange. Some of the agenda of the Grangers was nonpolitical. They formed cooperatives, for example, and bargained for lower prices for seed, machinery, and rail transport while jointly bringing produce to market at a higher asking price. Grangers were, in actuality, attempting both vertical and horizontal integration of family farming. In the 1880s, a more political form of activism emerged with the Midwestern Farmers' Alliance and Southern Farmers' Alliance, plus affiliated local associations. These groups created newspapers, operated lecture bureaus, and encouraged local participation in Democratic or Republican politics. In 1889, the two largest alliances

merged at a meeting in Ocala, Florida, and came up with an agenda for political action that included direct government loans to farmers, inflation, a
lower tariff, strict regulation or government ownership of railroads, and a
graduated income tax.[9]

For our purposes, what is quite evident—even before this populist
movement became a party—is that socialists and other advocates of larger
government had already begun to attach their fortunes to the farmers'
cause and had in some cases imbedded themselves deeply in the Alliance.
When a slate of Alliance-backed candidates won election as Southern Democrats in 1890, but then almost to a man repudiated their populist ties, Alliance leaders joined with elements of the nascent labor movement to form
a new party, technically called the People's Party but commonly referred to
as the Populists. At their 1892 convention, the impact of Edward Bellamy
and other utopians and socialists was evident. One attendee wrote that Bellamy followers "were the brains of the convention. They were college professors, editors, artists, and authors . . ." They did not, in short, have muddy
boots. Many were longtime radicals who had finally found a political
home.[10]

The Populists won four states in the 1892 presidential election. Even
though Grover Cleveland, a traditional Democrat with free-market economic views, had been elected, Democrats began to wonder whether they
would be competitive with Republicans without the support of farmers and
other elements of the populist cause. Some were also genuinely worried
about social revolution. Shortly after Cleveland took office, the nation
plunged into one of its worst recessions to date (caused by profligate federal spending and the inflationary coinage of silver by Cleveland's Republican
predecessor, the incompetent Benjamin Harrison[11]). Unemployment rates
soared to record highs in 1893. For the first time, some began to think of the
federal government as the only solution to chronic economic problems. An
Ohio miner named Jacob Coxey led a march on Washington in 1894 to demand a huge public works program to create jobs. "Coxey's Army," as it was
called, suggested that the United States Treasury pay for the program by
printing more money. Police dispersed the crowd and arrested Coxey, but
similar protests spread nationwide. Democratic politicians in the South
and West began to clamor for Populist policies. At the 1896 Democratic
convention, they abandoned Cleveland and nominated William Jennings

Bryan. They adopted most of the Populist platform, including the income tax and a larger role for government in economic affairs.[12] The Populists as a separate party disappeared, their cause to be championed by a major party from now on.

PROGRESSIVISM AND THE REPUBLICANS

It was now the Republican Party's turn to be radicalized. This was accomplished through the rise of the Progressive movement shortly after 1900. If the Populist movement was an unlikely marriage of hardscrabble farmers and readers of utopian science fiction, the Progressives were an even more motley crew of reformers—former mugwumps (economic liberals who advocated civil service rules and an end to big-city corruption), suffragettes, temperance activists, trust busters, crypto-socialists, professors, self-styled intellectuals, and more than a few former Populists looking for something to do. Indeed, Kansas newspaper editor William Allen White joked that Progressivism was simply Populism that had "shaved its whiskers, washed its shirt, put on a derby, and moved into the middle class."[13] The key differences were sectional and tactical. Progressives were more urban than Populists, and more concentrated in the Northeast. In addition, they more aggressively sought systemic changes in American politics, such as the direct election of senators and the initiative process, which they viewed as means towards their large aims of government growth and business regulation.

One might view the rise of the more urban Progressives as the flip side of the decline of American farming employment. The distressed farmers who kept at it became Populists in frustration. Those who moved to the cities swapped rural homeownership for tenancy; they lived precariously as day laborers rather than agricultural capitalists and were, as Jefferson had warned, prime targets for conversion to a big-government philosophy. No longer were they spending their days in investment activities designed to build the long-term value of their farms. Instead, they spent their days operating machines and living in apartments owned by someone else. According to the available evidence from the United States Census Bureau, homeownership rates actually declined steadily throughout the late 1800s and early 1900s, as immigrants from rural America and overseas swelled the cities and reduced the percentage living on and working their own farms.[14]

In reality, the standard of living of these new city dwellers was usually better, particularly after a few years of adjustment, than what they would have enjoyed back on the farm. However, they no longer thought of themselves as owners, as direct investors in long-term assets. They came to see others—wealthy, aloof, corrupt—as the "capitalists" with whom they must have an adversarial relationship. It may have been the political equivalent of a psychosis. I believe, as Jefferson predicted long before, that the impact of urbanism on political sentiments and voting behavior was a very real and important factor in what was to come.

The first decade of the twentieth century was the golden age of the muckrakers. They turned their journalistic talents to uncovering corruption, poverty, and maltreatment of workers and consumers. Some of what they wrote was accurate. Some was well-meaning fiction passed off as fact. Still other writers nursed socialist sentiments and saw inflaming public opinion against big business and corrupt government as the first step to social revolution.[15] Perhaps the best explanation for the muckraking phenomenon was that, for the first time, there was a mass market for lengthy, in-depth journalism. Advances in printing and paper production led to the first nationally circulated magazines. The growing cities created a far larger market for daily newspapers, which in turn grew more sophisticated and their publishers more self-consciously "reformist" in outlook.

As an emerging philosophy of government, Progressivism got its toehold in journalism. As a political movement, it flowered in the statehouses. Two governors typify the trend. Republican Robert La Follette was elected governor of Wisconsin in 1900. Under his leadership, the state adopted electoral primaries, regulated railroads, created a graduated income tax, and instituted conservation laws. His administration brought in faculty members from the University of Wisconsin to sit on numerous state commissions and to draft social legislation. In 1910, a Democrat and former Princeton University President, Woodrow Wilson, was elected governor of New Jersey. Wilson pursued similar policies and created one of America's first government-run workers' compensation systems for private-sector employees.[16]

When people think of the rise of Progressivism, they equate it with Theodore Roosevelt. In a way, they are right to do so. His activist, interventionist tenure as president from William McKinley's assassination in 1901 to 1909 expanded the power of the chief executive and the federal government in general, increased regulation of business, and set the stage for additional government growth during the next two administrations. However, in the area of social welfare programs, Roosevelt did little as president. It was just before he relinquished control of the White House to William Howard Taft that Roosevelt began more forcefully to argue for a government role in safety net programs. In a 1908 speech, he had called for workers' compensation and income taxes. A small federal workers' compensation program was enacted. Two years later, approached by Republican progressives who thought Taft was betraying the reformist cause (even though Taft busted more trusts than Roosevelt had), the former president made a celebrated speech in Osawatomie, Kansas, to call for a "New Nationalism." His new agenda consisted not only of more extensive business regulations but also the enactment of an unemployment insurance to be funded, like the programs spreading across Europe, by new taxes on employment.[17]

Roosevelt's New Nationalism was essentially rewritten as the platform of the Progressive Party, which he and his allies formed in 1912 after a split with Taft Republicans. The presidential election of 1912 was one of those seminal events in American history about which too much can scarcely be written. A four-way contest between the Progressive Roosevelt, the Republican Taft, the Democrat Wilson, and the Socialist Eugene Debs, it was striking not just for the conflicting personalities involved but also for the ideas in common. By 1912, all political parties stood for "progressive" reform and, in one form or another, for increased government intervention in the economy. The two leading candidates, Roosevelt and Wilson, did explain their reform agenda differently. Wilson was, in fact, friendlier to competitive free enterprise and more suspicious of big government than was Roosevelt. Monopolies, the former president said, were inevitable. There was no need to break up trusts. Instead, government should regulate them for the public good. "A national industrial commission should be created," Roosevelt said, "which should have complete power to regulate and control all the great industrial concerns engaged in interstate business—which practically means all of them in this country."[18]

Wilson argued that it would be better for government to break up monopolies but otherwise to regulate with a lighter hand. He said that protective tariffs and other government intervention had actually caused some business monopolies to form and that competition was a better guarantor of public good than regulation, which he said might lead to excessive federal bureaucracy. "I do not want to be taken care of by the government, either directly, or by any instruments through which the government is acting," he said. "I want only to have right and justice prevail . . . and I will undertake to take care of myself."[19] Wilson sounded positively Cleveland-esque on the stump. Still, he endorsed much of the Progressive agenda, including income taxes. As president, he proved to be less than hostile to government growth than voters in 1912 might have expected.

In any event, Wilson won the election, albeit with only a plurality of 42 percent of the popular vote. Roosevelt won 28 percent, Taft 23, and Debs 6. Democrats also won control of the House and Senate and twenty-one governorships. Wilson's first order of business was tariff reduction. Unfortunately, his proposed alternative to match its revenue-collecting capability was a graduated federal income tax, made possible by the recently enacted Sixteenth Amendment. Two months later, he signed the Federal Reserve Act and created, in effect, the nation's first central bank in nearly a century. The act stemmed directly from the economic panic of 1907, which business leaders blamed on Roosevelt's corporation-bashing but many Progressives laid at the foot of Wall Street. Further Progressive legislation passed during the next three years, including a Workingmen's Compensation Act in 1916. It broadly expanded Roosevelt's limited workers' compensation program to provide federal payments to federal civil service workers who became disabled. It was the first real federal "safety net" program for nonveterans, but because it applied only to federal employees, it did not represent the federal government inserting itself into the compensation arrangements of private employers and employees.[20] It took a war and another economic crisis before the federal government would take that fateful step.

At this point, it is important to recognize how Progressivism, like Populism before it, had transformed major-party politics. It was not just that the most prominent Republican of the period, Theodore Roosevelt, had increasingly embraced Progressive ideas and warmed to a larger governmental role in economic life, permanently realigning the GOP as it attempted to woo his Progressive Party defectors back to the fold after 1912. At the grassroots level, both Republicans and Democrats in governorships, legislatures, city halls, and local party organizations had absorbed the Progressive philosophy with regard to numerous issues, including social welfare. This is easily seen in the swelling political momentum at the state and local levels for political process reforms, wider regulation, liquor laws, and the women's suffrage movement during the first two decades of the 1900s. The 1910s also saw the adoption of the first large-scale, nonveteran government safety net programs in the United States by Progressive-era governors and legislatures.

THE WORKERS' COMPENSATION FOOTHOLD

Workers' compensation is one of those issues that, while immensely important at the state level, rarely comes up in Washington political debates— unfortunately. It is impossible to understand the rise of the federal welfare state without paying attention to the sudden creation of state workers' compensation programs in the 1910s. It was one of the most rapid adoptions of a policy idea in American history, and helped to make the reputations of a number of Progressive politicians—including New Jersey Governor Woodrow Wilson. Furthermore, workers' compensation represented the first foothold in American politics of the idea that government should take steps to "insure" private-sector workers against some kind of calamity. Once planted, this seed would sprout into unemployment insurance, old age and disability pensions, and widow pensions in the 1930s.

Both Populist and Progressive ideologues had long envisioned compensation for injured workers as part of a comprehensive "social insurance" system that would, as Bellamy had put it, take care of Americans "from the cradle to the grave." But as with the other elements of their agenda, the idea sounded too radical, intrusive, and contrary to the limited-government principles of the Constitution to make much headway among rank-and-file Populist or Progressive voters and politicians, must less the general public. In the second decade of the twentieth century, however, the situation changed dramatically.

The issue of compensating injured workers had previously been hammered out in the courts. Near the turn of the century, the status quo ante placed liability on employers for injuries due to their negligence but established three common law defenses:

1) that the injured employee had knowingly assumed the risks associated with his particular job,

2) that a coworker had played a major role in the accident, or

3) that the employee himself had helped to cause the accident.

It might appear that this liability-based system was stacked against workers; to some extent, it was. Many workers were forced to wait for five years or longer for compensation. Others were unable to pierce those common law defenses at all. Many employers were also unhappy with the system. For one thing, it brought high administrative costs, even for a successful defense against an accident claim. Some business executives thought they would be better off providing immediate, predictable benefits to workers, regardless of fault, through some kind of company-based insurance system.[21]

With both employers and employees facing incentives to fashion a private workers' compensation system, why did it not happen? The answer is simple. Any private, voluntary workers' compensation system (like the government-controlled systems that states subsequently created) would have to be based on a "liability-for-compensation swap." Workers would sign a contract waiving their right to sue under the old liability standards in exchange for receiving benefits soon after an accident without delay or hassle. Unfortunately, state courts sent a very clear signal that they would not respect such contracts. Judges ruled that workers could not sign away their right to sue, even if workers did so freely with the expectation that they would gain through immediate, no-fault compensation.[22] These bizarre and illiberal court decisions made a private-sector solution impossible.

Some have argued that the courts' unwillingness to sanction a private, voluntary solution to workers' compensation reflected the influence of plaintiff bars that were even then beginning to exercise significant power among state legal communities and lawmakers. These attorneys did not want to see an end to the liability system. Instead, they wanted their state legislatures to pass laws that limited or removed the common law defenses against accident suits that employers had long enjoyed. Lending credence to this explanation was that, even as courts were disallowing no-fault workers' compensation contracts, state legislatures were, in fact, passing laws to weaken employer defenses. Their passage was due to skillful lobbying by attorneys in alliance with the growing labor movement. In 1900, only eight states had removed one or more of the three traditional defenses employers could use against lawsuits. By 1913, twenty-six states had such laws. At the same time, plaintiffs' attorneys were becoming far more aggressive in pursuing accident suits, either because of the changing laws or because of an uncertain legal environment, as state supreme courts began to show some Progressive tendencies. There were 154 accidental injury cases before state supreme courts in 1900 but an astounding 490 such cases in 1911. Not surprisingly, premiums for employer liability insurance skyrocketed during this period by 354 percent (after inflation).[23]

In short, by the early 1910s both legislation and common law standards concerning workplace accidents had changed so radically that employers, facing high insurance premiums and greater liability, became strong advocates of a government-imposed solution. So did labor unions. At first, the American Federation of Labor had worked with plaintiffs' attorneys to pass state legislation weakening employer defenses against liability. Labor leaders actually opposed direct government regulation of the workplace because they feared that regulators would be in the pockets of business and fail to protect worker interests. They thought litigation was a better solution. However, as their legislative agenda succeeded, union leaders discovered to their dismay that workers were not benefiting from the new liability laws. Lawsuits took time. Many injured workers could not afford to wait. Furthermore, attorneys seemed more interested in dragging out litigation and collecting fees and damage percentages than representing the true interests of their clients. The Ohio chapter of the American Federation of Labor, for example, stated that both insurers and lawyers involved in accident litigation were "parasites pure and simple, absolutely unnecessary in industry, yet demanding a part of its created wealth which they have no hand in creating, thereby raising the cost to both producer and consumer."[24] Unions, like their supposed adversaries among trade associations, changed their position around 1910 and became strong advocates of a government-imposed workers' compensation system.

There is no need to go into further detail about how these coalitions formed and passed workers' compensation programs. What is important is that states did so in a sudden wave reflecting the influence of Progressive politicians and ideas. New York began the trend in 1910 with the first workers' compensation law to withstand judicial scrutiny (courts had struck down previous laws in Maryland and Montana). Ten states followed in 1911, including California, Illinois, Massachusetts, New Jersey, Ohio, and Wisconsin. By 1920, forty-three states had workers' compensation laws. After that, there was a nine-year lull until North Carolina passed a law in 1929, the year the decade's shaky neocapitalist consensus finally cracked for good.[25]

In most states, lawmakers created a system that retained a private, competitive market for workers' compensation insurance but required most nonfarm employers to participate and set compensation rates and procedures. In a few unlucky states, lawmakers set up a government-run insurance system with lackluster results. In general, however, the workers' compensation movement, while made necessary only because of government's refusal to recognize voluntary contracts, nevertheless retained a component of market competition and pricing that serves as a useful counterpoint to later government unemployment and old-age insurance programs. States required employers to purchase workers' compensation insurance under rules set by law, but did not usually provide it. As we shall see, many free-market reformers today want to remake government welfare programs along the lines of workers' compensation; in other words, government would require employers to set up Social Security or unemployment insurance programs for their workers but allow them to use private companies rather than the government to provide the investment or insurance services needed. This is yet another reason why welfare reformers need to study the history and policy implications of workers' compensation.

PRELUDE TO THE NEW DEAL

Two other trends preceding the Great Depression helped to set the stage for the New Deal. One was the First World War. As numerous analysts have pointed out, the war had a significant impact on domestic policy in the United States—particularly on the size and scope of the federal government. First, shortly after the country entered the war, Congress amended the four-year-old income tax to double the basic tax rate, reduce the personal exemption, and create steeply punitive rates that topped out at 65 percent for individuals and 60 percent for corporations. Furthermore, the new Federal Reserve Board took steps to inflate the currency, leading to a painful postwar bust that served to further radicalize workers and labor leaders. The labor movement itself was expanded by wartime federal policy; between 1915 and 1920, union membership nearly doubled from 2.6 million to 5 million. Perhaps most importantly, various federal and quasi-federal boards and commissions arose to "govern" the country's wartime economy. These included the War Industries Board, War Labor Board, Grain Corporation, Sugar Equalization Board, Railroad War Board, Shipping Board, Bureau of War Risk Insurance, and War Finance Corporation.[26] Through their ability to regulate prices, wages, and labor conditions, these agencies expanded federal oversight into private areas previously viewed as off-limits to government tinkering. They were also staffed by up-and-coming politicians and activists who never forgot the experience, including future Republican President Herbert Hoover and a number of future New Deal administrators.

While the federal government's budget and authority dropped after the war, it never regained its relatively low prewar level. For example, the Republican administration of Warren Harding, elected in 1920, sought for years to reduce tax rates from their wartime levels. The maximum personal income tax rate was cut from 65 percent to 50 percent, then to 40 percent, and finally to 20 percent in 1926 during the highly underrated presidency of Calvin Coolidge, an advocate of limited government in both word and deed. This 20 percent rate was still substantially higher than the prewar rate, however, and applied to a larger share of Americans. Memories of the country's steeply graduated income tax during the war lingered, paving the way for a dramatic escalation of taxes to pay for the New Deal.[27]

Another way the war contributed to the creation of the welfare state was through the survival of some wartime agencies. One that had a significant impact on later New Deal legislation was the United States Employment Service. Some states and localities had operated public offices to match job seekers to job openings as far back as the Civil War. But these were small, inexpensive efforts until the early twentieth century. The economic panic of 1907 and continued high unemployment in some areas of the country, coupled with the growing Progressive movement at the state level, led some public employment offices to expand their services and budgets in the years prior to World War I. In 1913, the creation of the American Association of Public Employment Offices signified a full-fledged movement with its own lobby. It unsuccessfully sought federal funding and participation until 1918, when the Wilson administration created the United States Employment Service and sought funding from Congress to subsidize local jobs offices. At the time, the problem wasn't unemployment but the reverse. Companies were unable to find enough workers to staff their facilities, particularly in industries responding to high wartime demand. Federal involvement was designed primarily to benefit employers, so when the war ended and unemployment rose, one might have expected the employment service to go out of business. It did not, at least not entirely. States and localities retained many offices, sometimes with federal matching grants, during the 1920s.[28] The employment service was formally recreated out of this lingering system by the Wagner-Peyser Act of 1933, then integrated into the unemployment insurance system created in the 1935 Social Security Act.

The other trend contributing to the subsequent rise of the New Deal was the expansion of government welfare programs throughout the 1910s and 1920s in countries other than the United States. While the administrations of Harding and Coolidge represented the resurgence, however limited and precarious, of traditional limited-government precepts after the Progressive and wartime eras, no such "return to normalcy" typified the politics of European countries decimated by the Great War. Britain had already taken two critical steps toward a welfare state with the Old Age Pensions Act in 1908 and the National Insurance Act in 1911. The first gave persons over the age of seventy a guaranteed income—that is, if one's income fell below a certain threshold, the national government provided a weekly pension to make up the difference. Britain's old age pensions weren't social insurance; they weren't funded by payroll taxes but by general revenues. There was no sense that one had "prepaid" for the pension. On the other hand, the program differed from previous British poor relief because it created an entitlement to a guaranteed income. Previous welfare programs had never treated government assistance as something to which the poor had a property right. The 1911 National Insurance Act pioneered social insurance for unemployment and health care. Workers received national health insurance from ages sixteen to seventy and insurance benefits in the case of unemployment spells. Unlike the pension program, these were funded by payroll taxes on employers and employees.[29]

Another early example of welfare state-ism that influenced American policy was Sweden. Its government pension program, passed in 1915, was more like the later Social Security than Britain's program because it was funded by "contributions" from employers and employees. The country also created unemployment insurance, public housing, and other entitlements. A celebrated 1936 book by Marquis Child entitled *Sweden: The Middle Way* helped sell the New Dealers on the attractions of Swedish welfare state-ism as an alternative to full socialism, a case still regarded as persuasive by many American leftists today.[30]

CONCLUSION

By the 1920s, the stage had already been set for the modern American welfare state. All that was needed was a catalyzing event, a crisis so overwhelming as to weaken opposition to a broader federal role in the nation's economy and the lives of its citizens. The Great Depression was just such an event—a calamity caused in large part by government misuse of the economic tools already at its disposal, but blamed mostly on the failure of the market economy to maintain employment and provide Americans with the opportunity to build a future for themselves and their families. By 1935, the main elements of the welfare state were enacted across a range of programs, including price supports for farmers, government pensions for workers, government disability and unemployment insurance, and cash aid to women with dependent children. In an eerie twist of fate, historical events played out also exactly as Edward Bellamy had predicted in his novel, *Looking Backward*. In his story, a powerful leader had arisen in the United States in the midst of economic turmoil to recreate the federal government as a welfare state providing assistance "from the cradle to the grave." The only thing missing from Bellamy's account was the name: Franklin Delano Roosevelt.

CHAPTER 3

WALL STREET AND THE SECOND ECONOMIC REVOLUTION

N OT FOR DRAMATIC EFFECT DO I SUSPEND THE story of America's political realignment to briefly change the subject. No mystery will be revealed after intermission. That the welfare politics of the Populist and Progressive eras matured into the New Deal is a fact known to virtually every reader, and will be discussed in the next chapter. Understanding why the country's elected leaders addressed the economic crisis of the 1930s the way they did—and chose to satisfy the growing demands for income security with an unprecedented slew of federal welfare programs—requires that I backtrack to the same post-Civil War time period with which I began the last chapter and restart the story with a different focus. The previous drama began with the declining fortunes of many southern and western farms, the burgeoning factories and labor unions of the industrial heartland, and the teeming multitudes of immigrants streaming into eastern ports. This one begins on a far smaller but no less colorful stage: the floor of the New York Stock Exchange.

In the years after the Civil War, the stock exchange was the site of a series of financial conflicts known as the "Erie Wars" and the "Gold Corner" that were to have lasting effects on both the operation as well as the public perception of the nation's capital markets. The story begins with the rivalry of two powerful men: Cornelius Vanderbilt and Daniel Drew. Vanderbilt, who had created his vast fortune in canals before entering the railroad business, aided his associate Erasmus Corning in securing a franchise to create the New York Railroad in 1853. "Uncle" Daniel Drew, as he was known on Wall Street, owned a large share of the adjoining Erie Railroad and served on its board. In 1864, Vanderbilt and Drew first battled over the Harlem Railroad. Drew had bribed city and state lawmakers to help him take over the Harlem by first withholding, then approving, a petition to extend its rail line. Knowing their plans, he could sell Harlem stock short, buy it later at a low price caused by the legislative uncertainty, and pocket huge profits. It was a brilliant, if larcenous, plan. But Vanderbilt owned stock in the line, too, and stood to lose millions. Infuriated not only at Drew's attempt at stock manipulation but also at his successful bribery of politicians that Vanderbilt had once supported, the "Commodore" did a little financial magic of his own, employing agents complete with aliases to purchase Harlem stock and drive its price up, not down. Drew ended up owing Vanderbilt more than $1.5 million when he had to buy back his shorted stock. He plotted revenge.[1]

His opportunity came when Vanderbilt, through Corning, sought to combine the New York and Erie railroads in 1867. Drew resisted and enlisted the aid of two young, equally unscrupulous members of the Erie board named Jay Gould and Jim Fisk. The three oversaw the printing of tens of thousands of "phantom" shares of Erie stock, trying to make it impossible for Vanderbilt to buy control. They failed. Furthermore, Vanderbilt went to court to have the scheme invalidated. When Gould and Fisk ignored the court, Vanderbilt asked that the two be arrested for contempt. After fleeing to New Jersey and hiring armed guards and artillery to prevent extradition to New York, Gould and Fisk double-crossed Drew, settled their accounts with Vanderbilt, and voted to remove Drew from the Erie board. The following year, Gould and Fisk attempted their own manipulation of Erie stock, driving the price down 35 percent in an attempt to make millions from shorting it. While they were playing financial games with their railroad, Vanderbilt was building his New York Central into a safe, efficient, and profitable enterprise. By November, Wall Street had had enough of the financial chicanery of the Erie Railroad and similar enterprises. The stock exchange passed a resolution to require public registration of securities traded on the exchange, making it impossible to "water down" stock secretly as Gould, Fisk, and Drew had done. By 1869, even the Erie was forced to comply with the rule.[2]

Gould and Fisk were not finished. With the exchange clamping down on stock manipulation, the pair decided to try their hand at manipulating the commodity traded next door to the New York Stock Exchange—in the so-called "Gold Room" on Broad Street. They bribed Abel Corbin, brother-in-law of the new president Ulysses S. Grant, to discover the federal government's plans for selling its gold reserves. Convinced that Washington would not sell even if the price of gold were to rise dramatically, they bought large quantities of the commodity through third parties and then engineered a scheme to encourage rumors of speculation. Gold rose from $132.00 to $163.00 an ounce as investors sought what they expected would be an artificial price increase, generated by the federal government's unwillingness to add to the supply available for sale. Eventually, Grant ordered the Treasury to sell, popping the speculatory bubble—but not before Gould, again receiving inside information about the government's plans, pocketed millions in profits.[3] The "Gold Corner," so closely following the "Erie Wars," helped to reinforce the public perception of Wall Street as a den of thieves and charlatans that was to last for decades and contribute significantly to the Populist and Progressive movements. The financial manipulations also led America's emerging capital markets to restructure themselves. Through reform and self-regulation designed to make securities dealing a tool for business expansion rather than for stock manipulation, the New York Stock Exchange would soon grow to eclipse London as the center of world finance.

THE ANTEBELLUM FINANCIAL MARKETS

The New York Stock Exchange long predated the 1860s. Created in 1792 by twenty-four New York City merchants and brokers, it served primarily as a means of buying and selling government bonds for its first half-century. Revolutionary War debt was the genesis of the government bond market, but the ill-fated War of 1812 and increasing demands for funds by state and local governments to build canals and other infrastructure significantly expanded the exchange's activities into the 1830s. The trade in government bonds was almost totally an insider's game, controlled by a few financiers and the politicians who served, in a sense, both as their employers and their customers. However, in the 1830s, a new form of security arrived on Wall Street that would ultimately change the face of American finance: corporate stock.

The corporation has a long and somewhat complicated history. Its antecedents can be found in the Roman *collegium*, the medieval guild, and the chartered trading companies of the Age of Exploration. But these were creatures of government, empowered with state subsidies and protections and intended for tasks thought impossible to accomplish within voluntary markets. The revolutionary idea that took root in the nineteenth century—in England but even more deeply in America—was that individuals should have the right to organize themselves in corporate form in order to conduct profit-seeking business. It was a powerful idea, helping to lay the groundwork for the spectacular rise in production, efficiency, and real standard of living that was to follow.

The factories of the Industrial Revolution may have brought scale and specialization of labor to unprecedented heights; in organization, they reflected the older business forms of sole proprietorships and partnerships. As authors Nathan Rosenberg and L. E. Birdzell of *How The West Grew Rich* observe, the individualism and personal freedom that had characterized western economic progress since the fifteenth century were a necessary but insufficient foundation for the large-scale, integrated businesses that the latter half of the nineteenth century would bring into being. The introduction of new sources of power, of vastly different production methods, and of new ways to organize workers, required a means of attracting and employing huge amounts of capital. Investors required the security of knowing that the enterprise would be lasting, thus making it possible to earn a return from large-scale investment. At the same time, they desired a stable process for the sale of their stake in the enterprise to other willing buyers without having to renegotiate or seriously restructure it, as was the case with partnerships. As Rosenberg and Birdzell observe:

> For Western economies to develop . . . autonomous economic spheres within which authority over economic decisions was decentralized to multiple decision centers, it was no longer enough for individuals or even for small groups to enjoy the freedom to select their own ways of making a living. With the

growth of large-scale transportation, merchandising, and manufacturing, it became essential to extend a similar freedom to the formation and operation of larger groups. By the close of the nineteenth century, Western societies needed institutions in which large commercial groups could organize to engage in economic activity, and yet remain relatively free of political control.[4]

Corporations differed from partnerships in several respects (although the partnership form later evolved in ways that tended to blur the lines). Partnerships had developed over many centuries of experimentation by merchants trying to order their affairs not only for their mutual benefit but also to the satisfaction of their creditors and customers. Unless otherwise specified in contracts, partners comanaged their business, were fully liable for its decisions, and were personally responsible for its debts. Creditors probably insisted on the last point because they wanted to be sure that if they negotiated with a single partner, the resulting contract would be honored. Full personal liability meant that the partner was acting as a personal guarantor for the entire debt. Because partners could bind not only themselves but also their fellows in potentially costly contracts, they did not enjoy the freedom of buying and selling their shares of the business at will. After all, a partnership was a close, even intimate working relationship. Substituting a stranger for a friend or longtime associate could expose the other partners to great personal and professional risk.[5]

For the needs of commerce and industry during the mercantile revolution and the Industrial Revolution, partnerships and the joint-stock companies described in chapter 1 sufficed. However, they had significant limitations. Most partnerships did not allow for the separation of ownership and control that allows savers to invest their money but not their time or expertise in the success of an enterprise. Partnerships were also necessarily limited in scope because of the unfeasibility of taking on sufficient partners to oversee far-flung factories or lines of business. Joint-stock companies, on the other hand, allowed for the financial investment of many nonparticipants in a business; however, because they did not enjoy a firm legal status, their long-run viability was always in question, limiting their potential capitalization. Finally, neither partnerships nor joint-stock companies allowed for the liquidity that many average savers desired. There was no easy means of "cashing in" one's stake in a partnership if you needed the money.

The corporation offered a solution to these problems. Its long-term capital needs could be supplied by a steady succession of short-term investors. In effect, corporations were simply another variation on the old theme of specialization. Not all savers wish to, or are capable of, managing how their money is invested in capital assets. The advent of corporate securities allowed savers to specialize according to their own skills and interests—to produce a surplus in a job or profession of their choosing—and then "hire" corporate managers to transform the surplus into productive investment, thus boosting their future consumption or that of their heirs.

Furthermore, an ever-widening variety of corporate securities allowed individual savers to align their investments with their time horizon and tolerance for risk: short-term bonds, long-term bonds, nonvoting equity stakes (convertible bonds and preferred stock), and common stocks. Before the private corporation, financial markets primarily offered bonds issued by government or quasi-government institutions. Banks also offered the prospect of professional management of one's savings. But for a variety of reasons, financial assets held in bonds or banks simply did not generate the kinds of returns available from direct ownership of growing businesses. Sole proprietors or partners could realize the benefits of such ownership, of course, but savers—lacking the resources, skills, or knowledge to become entrepreneurs themselves—could not. Shareholding was the solution to the puzzle. "The corporate form flourished," historian Robert Hessen writes, "precisely because it split the atom of ownership in two . . . it is a mutually beneficial relationship for all concerned."[6]

In the early nineteenth century, incorporation statutes had proliferated throughout the American states, but they were not yet of a truly private nature. The statutes allowed for the creation of *franchised corporations*, which gave monopoly status and quasi-governmental powers like eminent domain first to highway and canal companies and later to railroads. States also licensed special banking corporations and gave them the right to print money. *Chartered banks*, like the utility franchises, were not considered private institutions in the modern sense. In order to receive a charter, bankers had to show that they were providing a public service in their areas, not just making a profit or financing their own businesses. Although outnumbered by unincorporated private banks operating in a free market for credit (but prohibited from issuing currency), the chartered banks became an increasingly important element of American finance. From 1790 to 1830, the capi-

tal stock in chartered banks grew from $3 million to $168 million.[7] Yet another category of private corporations were state-chartered insurance companies, once again closely regulated and given special powers and protections by lawmakers.

It was the stock of these quasi-public corporations—the transportation
franchises, the chartered banks, and the insurance companies—that began
to be traded on the New York Stock Exchange and other regional capital
markets in the 1830s and 1840s. Hundreds of franchise corporations formed
to build turnpikes in the northern states, for example, and raised millions
of dollars on the promise of cheaper construction costs per mile (because
the corporations were granted the power of eminent domain and could
thus compel the sale of the private land they needed) as well as significant
toll collections. Between 1812 and 1840, Pennsylvania alone chartered more
than eighty turnpike corporations that invested nearly $40 million to build
two thousand miles of roads across the state.[8] Still dominated by government bonds for decades, the New York Stock Exhange and other capital
markets changed only gradually to accommodate the needs of equity
traders. Even in the 1860s, when speculators like Gould and Fisk began their
shenanigans in earnest, there were only three hundred securities on the
stock exchange, most of them stock issued by railroad companies with significant government subsidies and political connections.[9]

Throughout the early and middle 1800s, in other words, most truly private enterprises were financed by means other than marketable stocks. For
both agriculture and commerce, the usual source of financial capital was either family resources or a short-term loan, typically for six months to a
year. Inland planters would, for example, issue a note bearing the loan
amount and interest to be paid and then endorse it to intermediaries such
as cotton brokers or "factors" who would then deposit them in private
banks in a coastal city like New Orleans, Savannah, Charleston, or Baltimore. The banks would hold the personal notes in reserve, issuing their
own notes to supply shorter-term credit for urban commerce.

During the 1840s and 1850s, America's early system for extending credit
began to evolve into a more formal market. Railroads and, later, telegraph
lines formed the backbone of an emerging national trade in bonds issued
by private enterprises. What was needed was a way for potential investors to

evaluate the likelihood that their loans to faraway companies would be repaid at the specific interest rate. In 1841, an enterprising businessman named Lewis Tappan founded the Mercantile Agency in New York City and began recruiting financial correspondents in cities across the growing republic. Tappan's plan was to gather information about major companies and sell it to domestic and foreign investors. In 1849, he decided to turn his growing business over to Benjamin Douglass, who added more correspondents, established true local offices, and professionalized his workers as "credit reporters" (an occupation that was to include among its alumni future presidents Abraham Lincoln, Ulysses S. Grant, Grover Cleveland, and William McKinley). That same year a competing firm headed by John Bradstreet opened its doors in Cincinnati. Two years later, it published the first book of commercial bond ratings. Investors grew more confident about the risks and returns of bonds, increasingly adding them to their portfolio of direct investment in the local businesses of their friends and acquaintances. Finally, in 1859 Douglass turned his company over to his brother-in-law Robert Graham Dun. The two credit-reporting companies would compete vigorously for the next seventy years before merging in 1933 to form Dun & Bradstreet, still a national leader in the field.[10]

A wide variety of personal and bank notes as well as bonds circulated through the economy in the decades preceding the Civil War but, contrary to the suggestion of some historians, the financial system was not particularly chaotic or unstable. The most dramatic events of the period surrounded the fight to reauthorize the Second Bank of the United States in 1832. Created in 1816 to help manage the federal government's huge war debts, the bank served as a sort of central bank in that, with reserves largely consisting of federal deposits, it acquired the notes of most of the nation's banks and used its resulting leverage to enforce what amounted to a standard ratio of outstanding bank notes to reserves. Like most central banks, however, it was susceptible to political manipulation and drew the ire of many who viewed it as an unelected, unaccountable arm of federal insiders. Its president, Nicholas Biddle, sought a new charter four years early, in 1832, without recognizing how unpopular the institution had become among many Americans. The bank particularly enraged activists of the Democratic Party under President Andrew Jackson, who saw it as a tool of his political enemies. Running for reelection that year, Jackson railed against "the elites" and "moneyed interests," blocked reauthorization of the bank's charter, and withdrew federal deposits.[11]

The Second Bank of the United States soon disappeared. A period of "free banking" ensued during which Washington kept its deposits in a variety of state-chartered banks. Some have alleged that Jackson's action, later ratified by President James K. Polk in the 1840s, led to rampant inflation and economic turmoil. But careful research by economist Richard Timberlake and others has shown that free banking worked fairly well, with institutions deterred from issuing too many notes or loans not by mandatory reserve ratios but by a desire to maximize long-term profitability. Those that debauched the value of their own notes soon lost depositors and borrowers. Banks also formed a variety of voluntary arrangements designed to ensure deposits and share information about money supply and demand. Furthermore, many of the bank failures that occurred during the period were caused not by a free market in banking but by regulations that required state-chartered banks to purchase often shaky state bonds as reserves. The era of free banking ended when Congress passed the National Bank Act in 1863, which established a national paper currency and federally chartered banks. Ironically, it was after the federal government decided to "manage" money and credit that rampant inflation and disastrous currency speculation appeared. "The final stripping of local banks of their power to control money came not because of financial failures," writes historian Jack Weatherford, "but as a result of political movements to centralize power in Washington."[12]

THE POSTWAR CORPORATION

The sheer size of the United States—coupled with the development of long-range transportation and communication networks and competition among states to promote economic development—led to significant changes in American finance after the Civil War. However, the economic benefits of these changes did not materialize immediately. Indeed, the war itself interrupted the pace of economic growth for at least a decade. Furthermore, one unfortunate consequence of the war from a financial perspective was the partial destruction of the southern banking system, which in many ways was superior to that of the North. Southern states such as

Tennessee, Georgia, Virginia, and the Carolinas had created excellent bank incorporation laws that allowed for diversification in both lines of business and geography. Unlike state-chartered banks in most northeastern and mid-western states, southern banks could establish branches across county lines, thus limiting their exposure to economic downturns in particular industries or communities. Some southern banks could even sell insurance. The war destroyed much of this financial infrastructure, and certainly inhibited its spread north and west. Economic historian Larry Schweikart argues that, had the southern model of banking proliferated, "it is possible that much of the banking collapse of the 1920s and 1930s might have been averted."[13] As it turned out, it took more than a century for southern-style banking to triumph, as banks bred to competition, such as Charlotte's NationsBank and First Union, capitalized on the development of interstate banking in the 1980s and 1990s to buy their larger and better-known rivals in Pennsylvania, Illinois, Texas, and California.

In another sense, however, the Civil War did give America's second economic revolution a nudge by setting up a truly national system for marketing securities. A key actor in the drama was Jay Cooke, whose experience as a business columnist for the Philadelphia *Daily Chronicle* during the Mexican War had introduced him to the potentially lucrative trade of federal bonds. As Abraham Lincoln's preinaugural statements appeared to move the country toward war in early 1861, Cooke created a new company to buy up all the government bonds it could. By the time the shells started to drop on Fort Sumter in 1861, Jay Cooke & Company had $200,000 in federal bonds to sell to patriotic Americans willing to pay top dollar to support the war effort. His bit of wartime arbitrage was hugely successful, even on margins as small as one-sixteenth of one percent. Soon even Treasury Secretary Salmon Chase was relying on Cooke to market federal securities. By 1863, more than a million citizens owned war bonds.[14] Although postwar money manipulations by the likes of Gould and Fisk soured many Americans on securities, Cooke's efforts had established the rudiments of a national network of agents, brokers, and marketers that soon turned its attention to corporate securities.

The first inklings that corporations might expand beyond their role of capitalizing quasi-public enterprises emerged in 1837, when the State of Connecticut enacted a "general" incorporation statute that allowed firms to obtain corporate charters by simple registration—without, in other words, the special permission of the legislature. This was a major change in policy brought on by competition, not persuasion. Earlier incorporation statutes had attempted to prevent corporations from competing in the private sector with partnerships, because the statutes' authors (wrongly, as we shall see) believed that the corporate characteristics of permanence and limited liability constituted an unfair advantage. But some corporations had already been exceeding the scope of their original charters by the 1830s because of the vague language of many existing statutes. Once Connecticut decided to cut the Gordian knot and encourage the new profit-seeking corporations to bring their business—and their incorporation fees and property tax payments—to that state, others felt the need to follow suit, particularly in the two decades following the Civil War. By the end of the nineteenth century, virtually all states had liberalized their incorporation statutes, while at least a dozen had enacted virtually unlimited laws.[15]

Still, while the constituents of the new financial structure were created during and after the Civil War, significant trading in corporate stock did not truly emerge until the 1880s. Even into the 1890s, many large-scale businesses, most notably Andrew Carnegie's innovative steel empire, were run as partnerships. For most of the period, stock exchanges continued to be dominated primarily by railroad and utility corporations, many predating the liberalized incorporation statutes and still operating with quasi-government powers and subsidies. An exception was the Boston Stock Exchange, which hosted a sizable trade in the stock of textile manufacturers. Even there, only a quarter of the spindles in New England textile mills were owned by incorporated firms and the number of investors remained limited.[16] Unlike in England, where the incorporation of manufacturing firms accelerated in the 1860s and 1870s, the American market for corporate stock required a catalyst—a reason why managers and investors would wish to incur the costs associated with setting up the larger-scale, more formal type of business for which securities markets were appropriate. The catalyst appeared in 1879 in the form of the business trust, created by an attorney for John D. Rockefeller.

Rockefeller had already amassed a considerable fortune by refining and marketing oil more efficiently that anyone else in the world. One secret to his success was a waste-not, want-not strategy that sought to use every by-product of the refining process. His chemists came up with three hundred different uses for a barrel of oil. Rockefeller also pioneered vertical integration. His partnership with Henry Flagler and Samuel Andrews not only refined oil but also harvested and dried timber, transported it to factories, and then produced the barrels necessary to haul the oil. Five years after the founding of their refining plant in 1865, the price of kerosene had dropped by 50 percent. Rockefeller's ceaseless pursuit of lower prices drove other refineries out of business, many of which he then acquired. By 1880, his company controlled 80 percent of the kerosene business. Contrary to the predictions of those with a simplistic view of markets, however, Rockefeller could not then rest on his laurels and run a high-priced monopoly. Kerosene itself had competitors, including whale oil and electricity. Furthermore, there was always the possibility of new entrants to the kerosene market. So Rockefeller pushed on. By the time the company reached 90 percent of market share five years later, it had driven prices down another 69 percent, to eight cents a gallon. There was still more to come. That same year, the Russians were drilling for oil in Baku. The American share of world oil production soon fell from 85 percent to 53 percent, with Rockefeller's share falling proportionately lower. He resorted to more vertical integration, including the construction of a shipping fleet, and more savings in the production process. The price fell to five cents a gallon and Rockefeller's share of the world market rose again to more than 60 percent.[17]

What helped Rockefeller react to the competitive threats from other industries as well as from overseas during the 1880s was the reorganization of his company, Standard Oil, into an Ohio-based trust in 1879. Trusts had long existed as a way for minors or others to have their assets managed for their benefit. Rockefeller's innovation was to use a trust to bind together all of his enterprises in different states. Owners of the businesses he acquired received trust certificates in exchange for the shares of stock they had previously owned in their companies. By 1882, the Standard Oil trust had integrated some forty previously separate corporations into a single whole. The managerial efficiencies he was able to derive from the new business form were significant, as were the bulk-buying discounts he wrung out of railroads and shippers. Other industries followed the lead of Standard Oil by reorganizing as trusts throughout the 1880s.[18]

With trust certificates, America's financial markets finally had a product they could sell to a wide base of (still largely wealthy) customers. Unlike the shares of smaller corporations, the trust shares could be evaluated practically by prospective buyers across the country, and there was usually a ready market for sale when liquidity was needed. Furthermore, trust shares typically allowed investors to buy a stake in manufacturing, which they viewed as having a lot of growth potential, instead of in the railroads that had dominated the exchanges for decades—and had so often failed to live up to their billing. At first, trust shares were sold as "unlisted" securities rather than on the New York Stock Exchange. However, when New Jersey changed its laws in 1891 to allow trusts to register as corporations, the market changed again. Most trusts were quickly incorporated and listed on the New York Stock Exchange and other major exchanges.[19]

POLITICAL REACTION AND RESTRUCTURING

During the 1890s, a series of related events occurred in rapid succession. First, in 1890 Republican Senator John Sherman of Ohio, younger brother of the famous general, succeeded in attaching his name to two key pieces of economic legislation and pushing them through Congress. If Grover Cleveland had remained president, both may well have been vetoed, but the dim-witted Benjamin Harrison signed and implemented them. They were the Sherman Antitrust Act and the Sherman Silver Purchase Act. Both reflected the growing uneasiness among lawmakers and the public about the role of big business in economic life, as well as the rise of the Populist movement as discussed in the previous chapter and attempts by some businesses to protect themselves from competition by integrated, efficient trusts.[20] To some extent, American business had brought the public's enmity on itself, since so many executives had sought and received special favors and subsidies from state and federal officials, shifting the cost of government services to cash-strapped farmers and filling the newspapers with stories of corruption.

Congress passed the Sherman Antitrust Act with a resounding 294-to-1 vote. This was not only because of the unpopularity of the trusts and the successful propaganda of Populist politicians and writers. Many members suspicious of Populists and friendly to business also voted for the act because of its vague wording. It prohibited any contract, combination, or conspiracy in restraint of trade and forbade any "person" to "monopolize, or attempt to monopolize, or combine or conspire with any other person or persons, to monopolize any part of the trade or commerce among the several states or with foreign nations." Neither the bill nor prior judicial decisions had adequately defined the term "monopoly." Business leaders and their congressional defenders chose not to oppose the Sherman Antitrust Act because they viewed it more as symbolic than as substantive. It remained so for more than a decade, with its chief short-term accomplishment being simply the elimination of the term "trust" from the business lexicon.[21]

Rockefeller and other entrepreneurs looked for alternative means of accomplishing the same task of integrating and capitalizing their businesses. He had a particularly compelling reason. In 1892, applying state law rather than the Sherman Antitrust Act, the Ohio Supreme Court began to unravel the Standard Oil Trust. Other trusts saw the handwriting on the wall. They found an answer in state laws allowing so-called *holding companies* to own part or all of corporations, even those in other states. New Jersey had already liberalized its holding company statute in 1889 and others followed suit. By 1899, Standard Oil itself reorganized in New Jersey as a $110 million holding company. Two years later, financier J. P. Morgan and railroad entrepreneur James J. Hill created the Northern Securities Company, also in New Jersey, with a capitalization of $400 million and control of Hill's privately built Great Northern Railway as well as the Northern Pacific line of his subsidized competitor, Edward Harriman.[22]

By 1893, investors on the major stock exchanges could buy shares in nearly thirty industrial companies, including the General Electric Company, formed in 1892 by the merger of Thomas Edison's Schenectady, New York, company with the Thomson-Houston Company of Lynn, Massachusetts. Further issuance of corporate stock was interrupted by the consequences of the other Sherman Act of 1890, which had ordered the federal treasury to make regular purchases of silver and had declared "bimetallism" the official monetary policy of the government. The result, as previously discussed, was a boom-and-bust cycle culminating in the Panic of 1893. Cleveland, back in office, persuaded Congress to end its silver purchases, but the damage was done. The country's liquidity crisis did not ease until additional gold mines were opened late in the decade.[23]

For all the damage it caused, the 1893 panic did give the market for industrial securities a boost. During the following four years of recession, investors saw industrial securities far outperform railroad securities. They clamored for more offerings. Furthermore, a number of smaller, less diversified enterprises were forced by economic hardship to merge or be acquired by trusts and holding companies whose stocks were then available on the major exchanges. From 1893 to 1897, the number of industrial corporations whose shares were listed in the financial journals grew from 30 to 170.[24] The merger movement accelerated dramatically after the depression ended in 1897. While some newly created enterprises failed to achieve economies of scale or resolve the managerial difficulties that accompany such growth, many others successfully reorganized their businesses as large-scale corporations offering marketable securities to investors. They were aided in this effort by a number of talented Wall Street financiers, led by Morgan. From 1898 to 1902 alone, more than 2,500 companies were merged or acquired.[25] The logic of merger rested on a variety of factors: the gains from scale, the introduction of electricity and other costly capital improvements, and the maturation of mass production. The bottom line, as explained by Rosenberg and Birdzell, is that "publicly held industrial corporations were very rare in the United States before 1890, and major industrial enterprises that were not incorporated and publicly held were almost equally rare after 1914. . . . These changes were of fundamental importance to twentieth-century capitalism."[26]

Another development of fundamental importance was the creation of the first practical index of industrial stocks in 1896. Journalist Charles H. Dow had tracked stock prices since 1884, starting with eleven railroad stocks. By 1896, however, he recognized that investors were showing much greater interest in industrial securities. He unveiled his twelve-stock industrial average in the spring of 1896, and in the autumn refashioned his old index to track twenty railroad stocks, which later became known as the Dow Jones Transportation Average. Dow's handy means of measuring the performance of major corporate securities caught on. It helped make the confusing world of Wall Street intelligible to the layman and promoted wider stock ownership in the decades to come.[27]

The bond markets also grew and matured during the 1890s. Business information companies, like those of early pathbreakers like Dun and Bradstreet, sprouted up across the country to gather and disseminate data on both existing and new firms. One innovator was John Moody. In 1900, he published the first *Moody's Manual of Industrial and Corporation Securities.* Many years of experience persuaded him, however, that savers required more than just raw information with which to make good investment choices. They needed analysis, simply and reliably communicated. By 1909, Moody had introduced the first bond ratings as part of *Moody's Analyses of Railroad Investments.* Ranging from Aaa to C, the ratings were applied to about 1,500 different securities based on public information. At first, Moody later recalled, the bond ratings "raised a storm of opposition, not to mention ridicule from some quarters." Before long, however, the idea "took hold with dealers and investment houses . . . and long before 1914 it had become an important factor in the bond trading and bond selling field."[28]

One last development in the frenetic 1890s helped create the country's first peacetime corporate income tax. Populists and other critics of big business had long sought an income tax on the wealthy—not as a revenue measure but as a conscious attempt to redistribute income. In 1894, as the depression deepened, Congress pandered to this "envy lobby" by enacting the first personal income tax since the Civil War. It was a 2 percent levy on incomes exceeding $4,000, which exempted 98 percent of the American population. But in 1895, the United States Supreme Court ruled that the tax violated the federal constitution's requirement that a direct tax be levied according to population rather than income. Enraged, advocates came up with what they considered an ingenious solution. Since most wealthy Americans owned stock in corporations, they could be taxed indirectly (and thus without constitutional challenge) by applying a federal tax to corporate income. Many income tax opponents, on the other hand, viewed a corporate tax as preferable to an individual one and made a strategic decision to support it. "I shall vote for a corporate tax as a means to defeat the income tax," said Senate Finance Committee Chairman Nelson Aldrich, a Rhode Island Republican and a millionaire himself.[29] The tax, finally enacted in 1909 as part of a tariff bill, confiscated 1 percent of the net income above $5,000.00 of every corporation. The fact that corporate taxation would ultimately be levied on top of individual taxation of the same income would have surprised not just its opponents but also its proponents, who were simply trying to circumvent the 1895 decision. Still, when the Sixteenth Amendment passed in 1913 and personal income taxes were levied, no one thought to go back and lift the extra layer of corporate taxes. By 1919, the corporate rate had already reached 12.5 percent.[30]

THE CAPITAL MARKETS WIDEN AND DEEPEN

Progressives, picking up the baton where Populists had dropped it in the late 1890s, did their best to stop the tide of mergers, incorporations, and stock transactions that were revolutionizing American business. In 1904, President Roosevelt prevailed in his first major application of the Sherman Antitrust Act as the Supreme Court ordered the breakup of Morgan and Hill's Northern Securities Company. Roosevelt later began an antitrust case against Standard Oil that culminated in a 1911 decision ordering that the holding company be broken into more than thirty subsidiaries (some of which, like Exxon and Chevron, still operate today). At the same time, however, both the Court and Republican Progressives like Roosevelt grudgingly admitted that the trust-busting model was flawed. As previously discussed, the former president ran in 1912 on a platform not of breaking up trusts but regulating them.[31]

The reality was that corporations with large capitalizations, national and international scope, and easily marketable stocks and bonds were here to stay. Regulators and tax collectors could hamper their activities somewhat, but were unable to kill them off. The number and valuation of stocks listed on the New York Stock Exchange rose fairly steadily from 1900 to 1920, and took off from there. Of course, economic progress during the first three decades of the twentieth century was not limited to the performance of existing big businesses. It was a time of technological innovation and organizational ferment, more often introduced by new companies that the young capital markets helped to form and grow. Products such as electricity, automobiles, aircraft, electronics, aluminum, and plastics tended to come from these new firms, many growing to a large size with a rapidity never seen before and not duplicated until the Internet-driven economy of the 1990s. What the older businesses contributed was the existence of the financial markets themselves, without which many of these enterprises would never have attracted the capital needed to transform their ideas into mass-produced goods for the burgeoning consumer market. Other capital flowed into new businesses designed to market these goods more effectively to consumers, such as supermarkets, department stores, and catalog companies.

The ratio of goods bought from intermediaries to those bought directly from manufacturers dropped by more than a third during the period.[32]

The early twentieth century also saw the birth of the middle-class investor, albeit at a relatively small scale. Although the available data are a bit spotty, a few numbers show the extent to which many Americans had added corporate securities to their savings portfolio. In 1900, according to one estimate, about 15 percent of American households, most of them wealthy, owned corporate stock. By 1929, according to a study using a different methodology, nearly 30 percent of households owned securities in some form—most apparently consisting of stocks.[33] Another indicator is the sales force devoted to selling stocks. In 1900, there were about 4,000 stockbrokers in the U.S. The sales force grew to 11,000 in 1920 and 22,000 in 1930.[34]

Of all those seeking to market corporate securities to the American middle class, there was none more successful than Charles Merrill. Together with partner Edward Lynch, a former soda equipment salesman whom he met while working at a textile mill, Merrill pioneered the sale of bonds to small investors. They used direct-mail solicitations and, ultimately, built a sales team at Merrill Lynch to market securities in branch offices across the country. The firm was particularly important in helping to finance the growth of supermarket chains such as Safeway. More generally, the firm called attention to investment opportunities in "emerging" industries such as autos and retail in contrast to the (relatively underperforming) railroad and utility stocks that had so dominated the exchanges. Other brokerage firms followed Merrill's lead, many with the same mixture of honesty and innovation and a few with a more duplicitous approach. Although the markets remained dominated by insider and institutional players throughout the 1920s—and even more so after the 1929 crash—Merrill's early innovations would lead to far greater democratization of capital markets in the decades to come.[35]

Not just the market for *private* securities widened and deepened during the first three decades of the twentieth century. State and local governments embarked on an unprecedented campaign of infrastructure investment with funds raised primarily on Wall Street. From 1918 to 1930, state highway spending grew from $70 million to $750 million, as public officials sought to put the popular new technology of the automobile to productive use.[36]

Investment in highways not only allowed individuals to enjoy their personal cars. It put new competitive pressures on railroads, both for freight and for passengers, and allowed communities far from rail lines to begin to participate in the nation's commercial life. The automobile had also provided highways with an economical means of generating revenues from its users, as states funded their bonds with excise taxes on the sale of gasoline. Earlier public and private investments in roads had struggled to provide a competitive return to investors because of how easy it was to avoid the toll collectors. With taxes on fuel, states had an excellent means of collecting revenues in rough proportion to a driver's use of the highway system. This user-fee system did not begin to unravel until the 1970s and 1980, when sky-high gas prices and federal regulations prodded auto manufacturers to increase fuel efficiency while state and federal highway funds were raided to finance other, non-highway programs (as discussed in chapter 7).

THE FED AND THE ROARING '20S

Theodore Roosevelt may not have been able to stop the growth of American business and securities markets, but his policies did have significant long-term consequences. After his reelection in 1904, he launched into a series of legislative and regulatory initiatives aimed at big business. These included capping railroad freight rates, instigating new antitrust cases, and imposing federal regulation on meatpackers, food processors, and makers of drugs and patent medicines.[37] Just months after these initiatives began, a banking panic began in New York and threatened to spread to other states. Whether justified or not, many business leaders blamed Roosevelt's bellicose behavior toward corporate America for starting the crisis. But the president convinced Congress to look elsewhere for causes and solutions. In 1908, lawmakers passed the Aldrich-Vreeland Act to encourage nationally chartered banks to increase the money supply. It also created a National Monetary Commission, which was to report back with a new plan for national banking in 1912. It did, leading to the creation of the Federal Reserve system in 1913.[38]

Once again, the United States had a central bank. Only this time, the federal government enjoyed more direct control over the officers and policies of the bank than it ever had over Hamilton's or Biddle's banks. Strictly speaking, the Federal Reserve was a system of twelve banks, in which private banks—both nationally chartered and state chartered—would be members. They were linked together under a Federal Reserve Board that provided the central control that President Woodrow Wilson insisted was needed. "The control of the system of banking . . . must be public, not private," he said, and "must be vested in the government itself, so that the banks may be the instruments, not the masters, of business."[39]

Whatever its origins, the Federal Reserve system has proved to be an uncertain regulator of the nation's supply of money and credit. When independent-minded chairs with significant financial experience have led it, the board has often kept inflation at bay and allowed for real growth in production, incomes, and standard of living. However, when chairpersons have attempted to achieve social or political goals by inflating the money supply, the results have often been disastrous. Any financial system based on fractional-reserve banking will likely experience some short-term business cycles, as banks create too much money (through notes or loans) and experience runs by nervous depositors. This is not necessarily an argument against fractional-reserve banking, with which America has had long experience. Contrary to the objections of some, the practice is deceptive only if its true nature is somehow obscured from borrowers and depositors. Even if the cyclical nature of fractional-reserve banking is inevitable (given a lack of perfect information on the part of market participants), the impact of these cycles can be relatively mild, and need not be national in scope. However, a central bank, if engaging in similar policies, can make the resulting booms and busts large and widespread, indeed.

Whether the stock market boom and bust of the 1920s was the result of the board's mismanagement of the money supply is a topic about which great tomes of scholarly research have been written for the past six decades. I will not attempt to settle the debate here, but I do strongly challenge the notion that the underlying economy of the "Roaring '20s" was built solely on excessive growth in debt and money. The gains in productivity and the introduction of popular new consumer goods, ranging from cars and aircraft to radio and refrigerators, undeniably reflected real economic progress. The fact that auto registration rose from 9.3 million in 1921 to 23 million in 1929 signifies a significant change in how Americans lived and worked. So does the fact that by the same year, some 27 million homes had 15 million irons, 6.8 million vacuum cleaners, 5 million washing machines, 4.5 million toasters, and 750,000 electric refrigerators.[40]

Still, something clearly happened in the mid- to late-1920s that caused stock prices to skyrocket and then fall to earth, prompting protectionist lawmakers and special interests to agitate for a higher (and disastrous) tariff, leading to a rash of bank failures. I am persuaded that the culprit was the Federal Reserve, which inflated the money supply in the mistaken belief that doing so was the best way of stimulating economic growth and helping Great Britain return to the gold standard after inflating its own currency during the Great War. Economists of the Austrian school of economics, including the late Murray Rothbard, have examined available data on the United States money supply during the decade to find evidence of an inflationary boom-and-bust cycle. One of the challenges of sorting out the conflicting claims of Austrians, monetarists, Keynesians, and other economists about the cause of the Great Depression is deciding how to measure the money supply. In an attempt to prove that the Federal Reserve followed a deflationary policy in the 1920s, Milton Friedman and other monetarists use a measure of the money supply that includes currency in circulation and commercial bank deposits adjusted for interbank holdings. They then show that the overall direction of board policy was to reduce the money supply from 1921 to 1929.[41] In his book *America's Great Depression,* Rothbard constructs what appears to be the better measure by including deposits in savings and loans and life insurance accounts, both of which were usually convertible to cash on demand and thus served as money in actual practice. His number shows a significant monetary inflation rate throughout the decade.[42]

The increased money and credit distorted the American economy in several ways. As economist Benjamin Anderson reports in his classic work *Economics and the Public Welfare,* it did help to finance some investments on Wall Street that would otherwise have not been made based on economic fundamentals. Because the increased credit reduced real interest rates— as individuals and business found themselves in a debtors' market—some speculators increased their use of "margin" buying of stocks, in which they paid only a fraction of the price of a stock and borrowed the rest. The result was a speculative bubble layered on top of what would otherwise have been more steady growth in values.[43] At the same time, the lower rates induced firms to invest more in plant and equipment with a lower potential payoff. According to the classic Austrian business cycle theory, such distorted price signals thus lead employers to put more labor to work producing capital goods demanded by business than can actually be productively used. The resulting misallocation of labor leads to unsold inventory, layoffs, loan defaults, and financial panic—precisely the sequence of events leading to the crash and the ensuing depression.[44]

One more factor was the political pressure to limit imports, motivated in part by the Federal Reserve's monetary policies. Inflation tends to encourage consumers to look for lower-priced goods from abroad. Although the available consumer price data for the 1920s do not indicate a general increase, it is wise not to treat them with too much deference. The proper measurement of consumer prices—involving the selection of a representative basket of commodities and adjustments for quality improvements—remains a tricky question today, and was certainly less precise eighty years ago. What we do know is that sentiment from a variety of quarters built during the later 1920s to increase the tariff. By 1928, many informed observers saw the passage of a new tariff bill as likely. By 1929, it seemed inevitable. Congress passed the Smoot-Hawley Tariff Act in 1930, further gutting international trade and the country's shaking economy, but the impact of its *impending* passage on investor confidence also probably played a role in the 1929 stock market crash.[45]

Crash it did. The Dow Jones Industrial Average began 1921 at just shy of 72. It closed 1924 at 121, a 68 percent increase. By 1929, the Dow reached a high of 381 before starting its death spiral. By 1932, the bear market bottomed out at 41.[46] Whether the stock market crash was truly responsible for the depression that ensued is the subject of the next chapter. It certainly had a lasting impact on the nation's securities markets. For one thing, it led to close regulation by the federal government. In 1933, Congress passed the Securities Act, which imposed new registration and disclosure requirements on the markets, and the Glass-Steagall Act, which severed lending from the securities industry and created a rigid separation between commercial banking, investment banking, and insurance. Most economists consider the latter to be an unjustified and counterproductive measure that unnecessarily weakened American financial institutions and complicated consumer access to financial products. The former arguably had a more salutary effect, in that it provided an information base with which average investors could evaluate companies and securities, encouraging their participation in the market.[47]

However, such an effect was long delayed. Americans already had a less-than-elevated view of Wall Street, left over from the high jinks practiced by the likes of Gould and Fisk. The stock market crash cemented the popular suspicion into orthodoxy. From a high of 22,000 individuals selling stocks and bonds in 1930, the ranks of brokers shrank to 18,000 in 1940 and 11,000 in 1950—and not because brokerages were getting more efficient. Americans simply were not interested in entrusting their savings to the market. In 1938, only 10 percent of Americans owned stock, less than half the rate before the crash. The number crept up slowly, indeed. In 1962, it had reached only 18 percent. As late as 1983, it was 19 percent.[48] Clearly, average workers and families took a long time to get over their fears about Wall Street. What finally made them change their mind?

WOOING THE AVERAGE INVESTOR

From the depths of the Great Depression through the early 1980s, average investors mostly stayed away from the securities markets. They put their money in the bank or in their homes. But a series of decisions—some the conscious actions of innovative entrepreneurs, others the near-accidental creations of nameless bureaucrats—set the stage for an explosion in personal investing in the last two decades of the twentieth century. The first decision lies in the latter, accidental category. In the years after the 1909 tariff bill creating the corporate income tax, Treasury officials began issuing rules for implementation. One involved the taxation of pensions. American Express had offered the first employee pension in 1875, but it applied to only a fraction of the company's workers, and the idea was slow to take root. By 1914, fewer than two hundred companies offered pension plans, and strict eligibility rules excluded most employees from participating. Given that no more than 5 percent of the labor force (most working for railroads or utilities) worked for companies with pension plans in 1914, and most of these were ineligible anyway, few observers noticed when the Treasury that year ruled pension contributions to be an "ordinary and necessary business expense" that could be deducted from a corporation's taxable income.[49]

The Treasury decision made little sense. Employee pensions were certainly not ordinary or necessary business expenses, given their rarity. Nor was the policy an early attempt to prevent double taxation of savings, which occurs when a government applies an income tax to the principal of an investment (thus reducing its returns over time by the same proportion) as well as to the interest, dividends, or capital gains from the investment. To treat consumption and investment equally, a government must either tax the principal of the investment or the return, but not both.[50] There is little evidence that this rule had yet occurred to federal officials. The personal income tax had been enacted only the previous year, and its implications for retirement income had yet to be realized. Furthermore, as Treasury later clarified in 1918, an employer's pension contributions were tax-deductible only if the pension trust or the worker had to pay tax on the contribution in the same year.[51] In other words, Treasury was treating a pension contribution as salary—as consumption rather than as investment—though it did not clearly say so.

Two tax bills in the 1920s helped to straighten out the mess. Once again, the bills' pension provisions attracted little notice. The Revenue Act of 1921 exempted employer contributions to trusts that were part of a stock-bonus or profit-sharing plan. Treasury officials had set the precedent the previous year by ruling that employer-paid premiums for group life insurance for employees were tax-deductible. They then applied the 1921 profit-sharing exemption to pensions, a move later codified in the Revenue Act of 1926. Finally, the proper mechanism for treating investment neutrally was clearly stated: the bill "exempted from taxation employer contributions to pension trusts and postponed taxes on the benefits of those trusts until they had been received by the employees" (119).

It would still take many years for a significant number of employees in the United States to participate in corporate pensions. After all, the tax deduction for receiving compensation in the form of tax-deferred pensions rather than salary wasn't worth much to the majority of Americans, whose income tax liabilities were minimal or nonexistent before World War II. Pensions mostly benefited corporate executives and professionals, along with a handful of unionized workers who formed pension trusts in the 1920s. From 1914 to 1929, the number of pension plans had doubled, but only to four hundred, meaning that about 10 percent of the workforce was employed by firms with pension plans. After dipping somewhat, it reached five hundred by 1938—but worker participation actually shrank, due in part to the creation of Social Security, which some employers saw as an excuse to reduce private pension coverage.[52]

The world war created the conditions for the growth of private pensions. The Revenue Act of 1942 dramatically increased both the rates and the base of the federal income tax. During the war, the percentage of workers paying income taxes rose from 6 percent to 70 percent (98). Suddenly most Americans, not just the wealthy, had reason to worry about taxable income. In addition, the act raised the corporate tax rate and imposed an "excess profits" tax on earnings above the prewar level, creating further incentives for companies to reduce their pretax profits. At the same time, the bill required that, in order to get the tax advantages of pensions, companies had to offer them to at least 70 percent of long-time, full-time workers. Finally, the next year federal officials ruled that pension contributions did not count towards federal wage and price controls. These policies pointed in a clear direction. Not surprisingly, interest in pension plans rose, uniting not only employers but also labor unions (greatly strengthened during the previous decade of New Deal legislation) and pension administrators in a powerful alliance of common interests. The percentage of private-sector workers covered by pensions rose from 15 percent in 1940 to 41 percent in 1960, then to 45 percent in 1970 (118–23).

The numbers dramatically overstate participation, however. Because of often-lengthy vesting requirements, only a fraction of "covered" workers in many pension plans actually received benefits upon retirement. Partly due to the vesting issue—as well as to perceived problems in the Social Security program and several well-publicized bankruptcies of corporate pension plans in the 1960s and early 1970s—Congress decided to revisit pension regulations in 1974 with a massive and complex piece of legislation entitled the Employee Retirement Income Security Act (ERISA). It imposed new minimum funding requirements on pension plans, shortened vesting periods, and required most employers providing defined benefit plans to purchase insurance from the new Pension Benefit Guaranty Corporation. Perhaps most importantly from the standpoint of Investor Politics, ERISA also created tax-deferred Individual Retirement Accounts (IRAs) into which workers could deposit their own funds and receive a deduction on their personal income taxes (131).

The Reagan administration placed the final big piece of the personal investing puzzle in 1981. Recall that, beginning early in the century, some corporations had chosen to provide retirement benefits in the form of stock-bonus or profit-sharing plans. The practice had originally received tax advantages that were later curtailed. In 1978, Congress changed the law to allow both employers and employees in these companies to deduct from their tax liability the compensation deposited in the latter's accounts. Three years later, the Internal Revenue Service ruled that not only stock bonuses or profit-sharing distributions are eligible for the tax exemption—so are simple wages. The 401(k) was born.[53]

Worker participation in both defined-benefit plans like traditional pensions and defined-contribution plans like 401(k)s, 403(b)s for nonprofits, and SEP-IRAs for small businesses grew dramatically during the period, particularly from the mid-1980s. By 1998, about one-third of all American families had at least one worker in a defined contribution plan, while 18 percent had a worker enrolled in a defined-benefit plan. Accounting for workers with both, some 41 percent were actively participating in private, tax-deferred retirement plans.[54]

DISCOUNT BROKERS AND MUTUAL FUNDS

Charles Merrill had pioneered the idea of pitching stocks and bonds to average investors more than a decade before the 1929 crash. His own firm was one of the few to play the crash correctly. In 1928, Merrill sent a letter to his customers counseling that they "take advantage of present high prices and put your own financial house in order." He even had a private meeting with President Coolidge, pleading with him to speak out publicly against speculation and buying stocks on margin.[55] It was to no avail; Coolidge viewed the idea as federal interference in financial markets. Disgusted by the travails of Wall Street, Merrill retired from the brokerage business for a decade to pursue other interests, both professional and personal. But in 1940, he returned to engineer a merger between Merrill Lynch and competitor Pierce & Co., which had acquired the Merrill branch network earlier in the decade. Merrill had another innovative idea: Why not woo investors, average or not, on the basis of price? Sounds like common sense today, but brokers had customarily added surcharges to the commission rate set by the big stock exchanges and had charged for such routine services as dividend collection. Merrill got rid of the extra fees. Indeed, he eventually decided to put his brokers on salary rather than compensate them through commissions, because the latter gave brokers an incentive to maximize trades that was incompatible with the interest of customers in maximizing real returns. Another part of Merrill's strategy was to spend heavily on promotion, advertising, and investor education to counter the negative perception of Wall Street that had lingered long after the market regained its footing.[56]

The strategy made Merrill Lynch the dominant brokerage in the United States, handling about one-fifth of trades on the New York Stock Exchange by the mid-1950s. But it did not significantly boost the ranks of middle-class investors. More affordable and accessible tools for individual investing than Merrill Lynch had yet dreamed up were needed. The first came in the form of mass-marketed mutual funds. Mutual funds pool the often-small deposits of individual investors to realize the advantages of diversification and the efficiencies of scale. They had long existed in the capital markets but played a minor role in total volume. Perhaps they would have remained a small and stolid corner of the market had not a corporate lawyer named Edward C. Johnson taken over a small Boston operation in 1943 named Fidelity Fund. Johnson saw mutual funds not just as conveniences but as ways to offer small savers the kind of professional investment savvy that large institutions and the wealthy already enjoyed. He also thought that the only way for mutual funds to "beat the Street"—to outperform the Dow Jones or broader stock averages—was if individuals rather than committees managed them. He was probably right about maximizing fund performance. The idea of solo managers, however, had a selling point beyond the numbers. It was exciting. When in the mid-1960s a brainy portfolio manager named Gerald Tsai started to make headlines for his impressive management of the Fidelity Capital Fund, mutual funds shed their conservative trappings. Managers like Tsai were young, rebellious, and seemed willing to challenge the establishment. It fit the *zeitgeist* of the times. Although there were some sizable dips along the way, the resulting marketing bonanza helped propel the growth of mutual funds over the next three decades.[57]

President Lyndon Johnson unintentionally stoked the growth of mutual fund industry in another direction. He simply sought to fund both his Great Society programs and the escalating war in Vietnam without raising taxes too much to threaten his or his party's political future. Johnson ran huge budget deficits and sought to inflate the money supply, intimidating the Federal Reserve into cooperating. After the 1968 election, President Richard Nixon's appointees continued the easy money policies and official-ly took the nation off the gold standard. Just about the time the Republican establishment in Washington had learned its lesson and began to tighten, Nixon's replacement, Gerald Ford, was defeated in 1976. President Jimmy Carter appointed yet another easy-money Federal Reserve chairman. After inflation surged again, in 1979 Carter had the sense to pick Paul Volcker, whose hard-money stewardship combined with Ronald Reagan's growth-oriented fiscal leadership to tame inflation in the 1980s.[58]

In the meantime, what this meant for the financial markets was that in-flation threatened the savings of millions of Americans. The tiny interest rates they earned on bank savings accounts (held low by federal regulation) were frequently offset by declines in the value of money. Clever money managers such as Harry Brown, Bruce Bent, and James Benham saw the fi-nancial markets as a way to offer Americans a more competitive return on their short-term savings. The result was the money market mutual fund, which emulated many of the features of savings and even checking ac-counts offered by banks as well as the higher returns available from pooled investment in Treasury bills, certificates of deposit, and short-term bonds. In 1973, only a year after Brown and Bent offered their first money market mutual fund, it had attracted $100 million from anxious savers. When Fi-delity added its own money market funds in 1974 and allowed investors to write checks against them, the revolution was complete.[59] In 1975, savers had moved $3.7 billion into nearly 210,000 money market mutual fund ac-counts. By 1998, there were 39 million such accounts—or more than one for every three United States households—containing some $1.35 trillion in household savings.[60]

At about the same time inflation had chased many Americans into the capital markets for relief, a number of brokerages, most of them far from Wall Street, had begun to seek ways of taking Charles Merrill's ideas of eco-nomical stock transactions for the average investor to a new level. When in 1975 the New York Stock Exchange removed its price floors on commissions—under pressure from the federal government—these would-be "discount brokers" saw their chance to compete with the big boys. The most successful was Charles Schwab, whose California-based brokerage pioneered low-cost, low-frills transactions made by phone operators and, by the late 1970s, with the help of computer networks. Through audacity, innovation, and effective advertising featuring Schwab himself, the company helped to reshape the way Americans bought securities. Furthermore, as financial journalist Joseph Nocera wrote in his excellent 1994 book on the transformation of middle-class finance, *A Piece of the Action:* "the creation of the discount business was, in hindsight, another of those moments that one could find from time to time . . . a moment when you could see a subtle shift taking place between buyer and seller."[61]

Still other developments were to follow: the maturation of the accessible "over-the-counter" market into the high-flying NASDAQ, the growth of investment newsletters and financial journalism, the impact of the Internet on investor information and day-trading, and the superstar status of money managers such as Sir John Templeton, John Neff of Vanguard, or Fidelity's spookily successful Peter Lynch. These and other factors vastly increased the participation of average savers in the financial markets. The number of mutual funds grew from 170 in 1965 to 7,314 in 1998. The percentage of American households owning mutual fund shares rose from 6 percent in 1980 to 44 percent in 1998.[62] Stock exchanges that conducted 15 billion transactions in 1980 were hosting hundreds of billions of sales by the late 1990s. The NASDAQ alone went from 27 million trades a day in 1980 to more than 544 million in 1996.[63] By 1998, nearly 17 percent of American households owned *taxable* mutual funds investing in stocks. In addition, about one in five households owned at least one stock directly—through neither pension plans nor mutual funds—and their median direct investment in stocks neared $18,000.00. Coupled with the nearly 20 percent of households with direct holdings in bonds or CDs and the aforementioned growth in retirement savings vehicles, these trends signified the achievement of Charles Merrill's dream of widespread personal investing. They also reflected a transformation of the role of corporations in the minds of an ever-increasing share of American families. Now corporate America was a source, not just of goods or of jobs, but of the wealth families needed to educate their children, tide them over during bouts of unemployment, fund a down payment on a first home, and help finance their health care and living expenses after retirement. The seeds of Investor Politics had been planted.

A FINAL NOTE ON CORPORATIONS

From the earliest days of general incorporation statutes, some politicians and social commentators have alleged that the corporate form of business amounted to a special favor from government. Some have argued that corporations enjoyed unfair advantages in the marketplace once they moved from the quasi-public sector of transportation to manufacturing and other industries. Others had said that corporations "owed" society for the right to conduct business in corporate form, and should therefore pay higher taxes and meet higher standards in wages and working conditions than their noncorporate competitors.

These arguments contain a number of fallacies. First, incorporation may have originated as a special grant from government to perform public tasks. During the nineteenth century, however, the role of the corporation in business and society changed—not because of corruption or as a result of special favors—but because both business leaders and policymakers, grappling with real-world issues like economies of scale and agency risk, found corporations to be a reasonable way to allow individuals to form voluntary contracts to meet their mutual needs. The old idea that corporations were "fictitious persons" gave way to a new concept, later called the "nexus of contracts" theory, in which corporations were merely default agreements that would have arisen from the bargaining of individuals in the market anyway.

Embracing this contractual definition of a corporation, Stephen Bainbridge of the University of Illinois Law School argues that state laws allowing incorporation are not special public favors to corporate shareholders, justifying special public expectations of social obligation from those shareholders. Instead, they are merely "default rules"—rules for establishing contracts between buyers and sellers of equity that would have come about in the marketplace eventually but at a high transaction cost. Rather than having every corporation and potential shareholder negotiate and sign contracts, the law recognizes a baseline corporate contract that everyone is presumed to agree to unless otherwise specified. "Refusing to hold shareholders personally liable for firm debts thus is the precise equivalent of enforcing a standard form sales contract, nothing more and nothing less," Bainbridge contends.[64]

In his seminal work *In Defense of the Corporation,* Robert Hessen demolished the arguments of corporate critics, most recently resurrected by "consumerist" Ralph Nader, who accuse nineteenth century politicians of corruption. The defining characteristics of corporations—that they extend rights to nonpersons, that they last indefinitely, and that they limit liability of shareholders to the value of their investment—are in fact all achievable without the corporate form. Despite the legal mumbo jumbo, corporations do not have legal rights because they are fictitious persons. Rather, they have rights because the individuals they represent have rights—the right to free speech, for example, or to be represented in court or in contracts. That these rights adhere to corporations is a convenience, nothing more. No one can reasonably argue that shareholders do not, as individuals, enjoy rights of free speech or contract. Similarly, perpetuity is possible in a partnership no less than in a corporation. It just requires a lot more work to hammer out rules for transferring partnership stakes and renegotiating the contract when necessary.[65]

Finally, limited liability, though a bit more problematic, is nevertheless explainable without recourse to a special government favor. For debt, limited liability was really an implied contract between corporate shareholders and creditors. After all, it was certainly possible for every business association to put a clause in any contract with a creditor limiting the liability of each member of the association to his or her initial investment. Creditors could take it or leave it. What the corporate form did was simply provide, in Bainbridge's phrase, a "standard form contract" to that effect. For torts, limited liability has a different justification, because it is impossible to form an explicit or implicit contract between a corporation and an as-yet-unidentified person who might be harmed by the corporation's employees or equipment in the future. Hessen traces the idea of limited liability for torts to the centuries-old concept of *respondeat superior*—let the master be answerable for the acts of his servant. Such a policy does, indeed, make sole proprietors and partners liable for the actions of employees under this supervision. But, he argues, it is wrong to extend the concept to corporate shareholders:

The tort liability of inactive shareholders should be the same as that of limited partners—that is, limited to the amount invested—and for the same reason; namely, inactive shareholders and limited partners contribute capital but do not participate actively in management and control . . . The proper principle of liability should be that whoever controls a business, regardless of its legal form, should be personally liable for the torts of agents and employees.[66]

So there was nothing nefarious about the development of industrial corporations over the past century and a half, or of exchanges and other means of marketing their securities in the 1930s.

CHAPTER 4

DEPRESSION AND THE NEW DEAL

S WE HAVE SEEN, THERE ARE A VARIETY OF PLAUSIBLE theories, unfortunately contradictory, about why the American economy and stock market soared throughout much of the 1920s, then crashed. Our concern in this chapter is the impact of these events on the adoption of entitlement programs. Regardless of the proximate cause of the Great Depression, it is highly unlikely that it would have progressed as it did if Calvin Coolidge had run for a third term for president in 1928. Coolidge, elevated to the White House at the death of Warren Harding and elected in his own right in 1924, was a successful president by almost any measure and would probably have won. Some believe he may have wanted to serve again, but preferred to be begged to run rather than seeming too eager. In any event, his terse statement early in the 1928 political season that he did "not choose to run again" was taken as a refusal of the nomination, while Herbert Hoover, his secretary of commerce, used his considerable charm and fame as a philanthropist and manager to run away with the Republican nod.[1] To those who subscribe to the "great men of history" theory, Coolidge's decision not to run in 1928 might be viewed as one of two pivotal individual actions in the creation of the modern welfare state—the first domino, as it were, in a cascade of events resulting in the Social Security Act of 1935. The other pivotal event would be the 1936 publication of *The General Theory of Employment, Interest, and Money* by John Maynard Keynes, which helped to cement a new consensus among politicians and intellectuals that markets alone were unable to provide sufficient investment, stability, and security for the average American.

WRONG PRESIDENT, WRONG TIME

As is often the case for public leaders whose reputations are made outside the legislative process, Herbert Hoover had a vague and internally inconsistent political philosophy. It reflected more of his interest in "doing" than a core set of principles that could be used to fashion concrete policy. So, for example, Hoover stated clear opposition to some of the welfare and social insurance programs proliferating in postwar, economically stagnant Europe. "Economic depression cannot be cured by legislative action or executive pronouncements," he argued. "Economic wounds must be healed by the action of the cells of the economic body—the producers and consumers themselves."[2] His rhetoric may have sounded like that of Coolidge, or even Cleveland, but Hoover was in practice an active Progressive. He had supported Theodore Roosevelt over Taft in 1912. His record in appointed government posts showed signs of an increasing willingness to regulate and to substitute federal for local action in such areas as infrastructure and fishing rights. As president, Hoover met the challenge of the Great Depression with a variety of federal responses strongly at odds with his preelection warnings about excessive government interference with markets.[3]

The first of these actually predated the stock market crash of 1929 that many see as the genesis of the Depression. Remember that for rural America, much of the 1920s already felt recessionary. The first shock occurred just after the war as European demand for American produce, which had spiked during the conflict, collapsed. During the following decade, increased harvests in countries such as Australia and Canada, plus increased productivity in American agriculture as farmers bought new machines and fertilizers, kept prices low.[4] Consumers benefited greatly from better-quality produce at lower prices, but many farmers found themselves unable to compete. Essentially, the market was now shouting: GET OUT OF AGRICULTURE! Some heeded the message, sold their farms, and began moving to cities to find work. Others did not. They saw farming not just as a business but as a way of life they did not want to give up. They attempted to gain more market power through cooperatives and farm bureaus but did not succeed in propping up prices. During previous periods, these farmers may have sought political solutions through a reduction of trade barriers, tax fairness for agriculture versus industry, or perhaps monetary inflation. But because they had been radicalized by the Populist and Progressive movements, they turned to Washington for more direct relief.

The first full-scale American welfare law for private citizens passed Congress in 1927. It was known as the McNary-Haugen bill, which set up what would later be called a "price-support" system for farmers. The federal government would guarantee a certain "parity" price for farm products regardless of the market price at the time of harvest. Federal revenues would be used to prop up the price as the government bought produce at the parity price and sold it for a loss on the world market. In effect, the bill offered farmers a guaranteed income by the federal government. But it was not to be. President Coolidge called the bill an unconstitutional expansion of the federal government's role in the economy and vetoed it. He did so again in 1928.[5] President Hoover, however, was not a stickler for constitutional niceties. After all, he was a doer, not a philosopher. America's farm economy was ailing, he thought, and so something must be done. Another farm-welfare bill passed Congress in 1929. Called the Agricultural Marketing Act, instead of setting up formal price supports, it offered federal loans to cooperatives to buy up agricultural produce, store it until the price rose, and then sell it at something close to a "parity" price. Hoover signed the bill into law. The program failed, however, because prices rarely rose. Federal loans became nothing more than direct payments to support higher-than-market prices, keeping marginal farms afloat and leading to a glut of unsold produce.[6]

Hoover's next challenge was far more serious but his answer was the same—try to prop up prices. The stock market crash of October 24, 1929, was, conventional wisdom to the contrary, not the cause of the Great Depression. It was a symptom of a decade-long credit expansion beginning to deflate. Hoover should have allowed the process to unfold, because it is self-correcting. Eventually, prices fall to such a level that production and consumption resume normally. Hoover and his advisors should have known this from their history. Only Andrew Mellon counseled patience and allowing the cycle to bottom out on its own.[7] But Hoover was no Cleveland—he wanted to act.

Just a month after the October crash, the president held a series of conferences with business leaders. He asked them not to halt planned construction programs, reduce wages, or lay off workers if business slackened. Unfortunately, at first they did what Hoover requested. The result was even more unemployment than the unfolding recession would have generated, because falling prices kept workers from generating enough return for their employers to justify their inflated wages. Americans who might have stayed employed at a lower wage were now jobless. Still, the president pushed price supports. In 1930, he called a special session of Congress to enact the Smoot-Hawley Tariff in order to keep commodity prices from falling. Tariffs were already high—38 percent for agricultural raw materials and 31 percent for other goods. The Smoot-Hawley bill jacked the tariffs up to 49 percent. As with Hoover's sessions with business, the policy was counterproductive. American farmers lost markets as foreign governments retaliated. And farm prices declined anyway—by half in the case of tobacco and two-thirds for cotton and corn.[8] Lastly, Hoover tried to prop up wages and prices by increasing federal spending. By 1932, spending on federal public works had risen by $500 million.[9] Much of it was financed by debt; the federal budget deficit ballooned from $500 million in 1931 to $2.7 billion in 1932.[10] The rest was financed by tax increases. Hoover signed a Revenue Act that doubled the income tax burden for most Americans while jacking up the top rate from Coolidge's 24 percent to a punitive 63 percent.[11]

These policies were disastrous. Overall, American exports fell from more than $4.5 billion in 1929 to less than $1.5 billion in 1932. Industrial production fell by half during the same period.[12] The ranks of the jobless grew to an unprecedented size. In 1929, the unemployed numbered fewer than 2 million, about 3 percent of the workforce. By 1932, the jobless numbered 12 million, about 24 percent of the workforce.[13] Never before, nor since, has the American economy undergone so huge a gyration in so short a time. Not surprisingly, the political fortunes of Hoover and the GOP collapsed as rapidly as unemployment rose. Democrats took control of the United

States House of Representatives in 1930. In 1932, Franklin D. Roosevelt, Progressive governor of New York, won a landslide victory with 58 percent of the vote and all but six Northeastern states. Actually, it was a surprisingly "modest" landslide, given the circumstances. Hoover had won an even larger share of the popular vote in 1928. Political winds shift quickly.

THE FIRST NEW DEAL

Despite what his champions and detractors would later claim, Franklin Roosevelt did not enter the White House with a coherent, well-planned agenda. The "New Deal" was never a policy agenda. It was a political slogan. Roosevelt may have been surrounded by a "Brain Trust" of politicos, professors, schemers, and rogues with ideological axes to grind, but his own economic platform, like Wilson's in 1912, sounded vaguely conservative during the presidential campaign. He accused President Hoover of "reckless and extravagant spending" and of thinking that "we ought to center control of everything in Washington as rapidly as possible."[14] His platform called for reductions in federal spending and tariffs, a balanced budget, removal of government from private enterprise, and a sound currency. "I accuse the present administration of being the greatest spending administration in peace time in all our history," he thundered. "It is an administration that has piled bureau on bureau, commission on commission."[15] Roosevelt's limited-government rhetoric was so strident that squaring his subsequent actions with his campaign promises requires that he be considered either a liar or a dupe.

The dupe hypothesis is, at least within the context of his first term, more credible. The fact is that Roosevelt's presidency, organized more around the mastery of the news media and political organizations than the supervision of subordinates, gave significant authority to his appointments to key administrative posts. His faith in advisors such as Rexford Tugwell, Adolph Berle, Harold Ickes, Frances Perkins, Harry Hopkins, and Henry Morgenthau—many longtime allies from his gubernatorial administration—led to disaster as they concocted scheme after scheme, commission after commission, in a vain attempt to use federal power to end the Depression. Author John T. Flynn, who wrote the classic work *The Roosevelt Myth* in 1948, called this early New Deal experimentation "the dance of the crackpots," an apt phrase.[16]

Most New Dealers had either Populist or Progressive pedigrees. As we have seen, these movements had previously radicalized both the Republicans and the Democrats, though the latter more thoroughly. The old Jackson-Polk-Cleveland tradition of low taxes, sound money, balanced budgets, and a limited role for the federal government had, among influential Democrats, almost completely died out. The election of 1932 was seen as a "changing of the guard," not unlike the way future activists viewed the elections of 1960, 1980, and 1992. A new generation of Democratic administrators and intellectuals, eager to implement an ambitious Populist-Progressive agenda, were ready and waiting for Roosevelt's call.

Other New Dealers drew inspiration less from prior political movements than from their own direct experience with government planning during World War I. One such Roosevelt appointee was General Hugh Johnson, picked to head the controversial National Recovery Administration. Fifteen years before, he had worked for the War Industries Board.[17] Still other members of the new administration, particularly the younger ones and those heading to Washington from academia, were transfixed by developments in Europe. Hard as it may be to believe today, many viewed Mussolini's Italy, Hitler's Germany, and Stalin's Soviet Union with awe and admiration. They may have disagreed with these societies' lack of political and personal freedom, but they saw as a modern economic necessity the central planning these regimes employed. The supposition that a larger, more powerful government was the "wave of the future" was reflected in the early policies of the new administration.[18]

The first involved money. Within hours of his inauguration, Roosevelt declared a bank holiday, closing all American banks for an indefinite period. Five days later, Congress approved the Emergency Banking Relief Act. It authorized the Treasury secretary to confiscate all gold and gold certificates in private hands. Owners of gold were given unsecured paper money in exchange, which was soon devalued by 40 percent. The act also set the rules whereby banks were allowed to reopen, with significant federal oversight. And it gave the Reconstruction Finance Corporation the go-ahead to use federal revenues to expand credit by purchasing the preferred stock of banks. A few months later, Congress would created the Federal Insurance Deposit Corporation (FDIC), the Home Owners Loan Corporation, the Farm Credit Administration, and the Commodity Credit Corporation—all attempts to use federal backing to prop up insolvent financial institutions, businesses, and households.[19]

The second thrust of the first New Deal was relief. Progressives had long argued for a larger government role in providing poor relief and unemployment benefits. Roosevelt had pioneered such policies as New York's governor. Now it was the federal government's turn. Congress passed the Federal Emergency Relief Act to provide grants to states and localities for welfare benefits to the unemployed. Roosevelt's welfare administrator in New York, Harry Hopkins, was tapped to dole out the funds. But Hopkins, a close Roosevelt confidante throughout his administration (and, unbeknownst to the president, a Soviet agent and sympathizer), was impatient with what he saw as cumbersome state and local administration of the funds. He believed that jobs programs were better than temporary relief. So later in 1933, Roosevelt authorized Hopkins to establish the Civil Works Administration (CWA). It directly employed some 4 million people, representing nearly 8 percent of the American workforce, to build roads, athletic fields, and airports. The CWA hired opera singers to entertain rural crowds and archaeologists to excavate prehistoric mounds. Even Roosevelt ultimately recognized the CWA for what it was: a "make-work" scheme with no economic rationale. He closed it down in early 1934 after only four months of operation.[20]

A similar federal employment program created in 1933, the Civilian Conservation Corps (CCC), was a little more successful. The CCC employed single men between the ages of eighteen and twenty-five to work in forestry camps across the nation. The work crews planted trees, dug reservoirs, built bridges, and developed parks. Some of the work was, in fact, valuable in rebuilding and maintaining public infrastructure. Of course, many of these projects diverted men and money from private investments that would have paid a larger return. In reality, the CCC was something like a volunteer army. Workers dressed in uniforms and lived under semi-military discipline. At its peak, the CCC employed half a million men.[21]

Interior Secretary Harold Ickes oversaw yet another jobs program called the Public Works Administration (PWA). It took longer to get going, apparently because Ickes took greater pains than Hopkins to spend taxpayer money with at least a modicum of care. The results were similar. Many useful projects were constructed. Other money was spent less on valuable infrastructure than on "pump-priming" activities designed to jump-start the economy. In 1935, Roosevelt put Hopkins in charge of the PWA and the make-work component of its budget grew. Total PWA spending during the Depression was $6 billion.[22]

The third thrust of the first New Deal was economic planning. Roosevelt's confiscation of gold was ominous, and the expansion of relief programs wasteful and sometimes laughable. But the Agricultural Adjustment Administration (AAA) and the National Recovery Administration (NRA), both created in mid-1933, mixed comedy and tragedy in a bizarre attempt to force the country out of depression. The AAA tried to prop up farm prices by paying producers to destroy food (even in the midst of hunger) and take arable land out of production. Federal agents fanned out across the countryside, trying to persuade reluctant farmers to plow their fields under for pay. They had an even harder time with the mules, who had been trained to walk between rows but now had to be made to pull the plows right across growing crops.[23] The spectacle gave rise to a popular joke about Roosevelt and his advisors being quite literally dumber than mules, who at least knew that destroying valuable goods was unlikely to constitute a path to prosperity.

The National Recovery Administration was even more objectionable. Created as part of a bill that gave labor unions special legal status, it set out to enforce "voluntary" industry codes regulating prices, wages, and working conditions. In a disturbing stylistic paean to European collectivists, the NRA mass-produced little stickers with a blue eagle insignia and the slogan "We Do Our Part," encouraging their posting in show windows, on factory doors, and on delivery trucks. "NRA days" featured parades, rallies, marching bands, games, and beauty contests. Most business executives (with the notable exception of Henry Ford) were cajoled into signing the codes, which dictated the production of dog food, hair tonic, and shoulder pads. In New York City, burlesque theaters were required to feature no more than four strip teases.[24]

The NRA and AAA were the most ambitious of early New Deal experiments. They were also short-lived and colossal flops. The NRA's industry codes were complex, counterproductive, and subject to special interest manipulation. In Detroit, for example, NRA codes did increase the minimum wage from thirty-five cents to forty cents an hour. Nevertheless, it simultaneously reduced the maximum workweek from sixty hours to forty, effectively reducing the weekly pay of workers.[25] Overall, the attempts to prop up wages and prices artificially did not alleviate unemployment or foster the productivity improvements and relocations, both physical and financial, that the economy needed to recover. Farm prices rose, mostly because of a series of droughts and pest infestations, but most farmers could not benefit from the price increases because they had little to sell. Still, Roosevelt and the New Dealers might have stuck with the NRA and the AAA if the Supreme Court had not intervened. But it did. In 1935, the Court unanimously struck down the NRA as unconstitutional. It did the same to the AAA in 1936.[26] In both cases, the argument was that the federal government had far exceeded its constitutional bounds. It was to be the last time the Court would so rigorously apply constitutional limitations on federal power over the economy.

THE SECOND NEW DEAL

It is during the second, more lasting period of New Deal legislation, from June 1935 through the election of 1936, that President Roosevelt demonstrated the political genius for which he is still respected. His political improvisation also laid the cornerstones of the American welfare state. On May 27, 1935, when the Supreme Court struck down the NRA, it must have seemed to Roosevelt that his administration might well be doomed, like Hoover's, to begin with a bang and end with a whimper. Opposition had grown from across the political spectrum. In addition to the Court's inconvenient reverence for constitutional limits, Roosevelt faced defections from his own ranks. Lewis W. Douglas, his fiscally conservative budget director, had resigned in 1934 complaining about growing deficits. "I see government expenditures piled upon expenditures, so that paper inflation is inevitable, with a consequent destruction of the middle class," Douglas said. "I see efforts to make the government the exclusive occupant of the field of credit. I see inferences that the government proposes and intends to plan for each individual economic activity."[27] Raymond Moley, who had served on one of Roosevelt's state commissions in New York and served as an assistant secretary of state, resigned even earlier, in late 1933, to edit *Today* and *Newsweek* magazines and to become an eloquent critic of the New Deal. A group of old-fashioned Democrats, including 1928 nominee Al

Smith, formed the American Liberty League in 1934 to combat big-government policies they said were undermining private enterprise. Among Republicans, there was a stirring, albeit a modest one, of the Coolidge-Mellon philosophy, no doubt inspired by the Court's dramatic decisions.

Roosevelt saw opposition from conservative Democrats, Republicans, and business leaders as shortsighted. "One of my principal tasks," he wrote in November 1934, was "to prevent bankers and businessmen from committing suicide."[28] Roosevelt was far more alarmed by opposition to his left, where demagogues fanned the flames of socialism and government redistribution of wealth. There were three leaders of this more radical side of Populist-Progressive agitation: Charles Coughlin, Francis Townshend, and Huey Long. Coughlin, a radio host with as many as 10 million listeners at his peak, was the latest in a long line of conspiracy theorists, blaming the Depression on international bankers and Jews, and often simply equating the two. Francis Townshend was an unemployed California physician and real estate salesman with a less-strident pitch. He argued that the federal government should pay a monthly pension of $200.00 to everyone over the age of sixty who would agree to retire and free a job for someone else. The pensioner would not be allowed to save any of his money, so that the resulting consumption would stimulate the economy. Soon there were Townshend Clubs across the country, like Bellamy's clubs before him, and politicians soliciting his advice and endorsement. The movement grew to number about 10 million and had success at the local level, including Colorado's adoption of a constitutional amendment promising a $45.00 monthly pension for the aged.[29]

Most radical of all was Long, Louisiana senator and blowhard, who touted an agenda called "Share the Wealth." He recommended that the federal government confiscate wealth with a 100 percent tax of all income over $1 million a year. The money would be redistributed so that every American would receive a house, a car, education for the children, pensions for the elderly, and a guaranteed annual income.[30] In early 1935, Long announced his candidacy for the Democratic presidential nomination. Roosevelt had reason to be concerned. Some business indicators had blipped up a bit, and the unemployment rate had fallen from its peak of 25 percent in 1933 to about 20 percent in 1935 (with much of the decline due to federal hiring, financed by increasing deficits).[31] For most Americans, however, the economic situation was not improving much if at all. Long had a constituency among disaffected Americans, one that threatened Roosevelt's political future. A secret 1935 poll for the Democratic National Committee revealed the magnitude of the threat. It suggested that Long might receive as many as 4 million votes in the 1936 presidential election as a third-party candidate, throwing several swing states to the Republicans.[32]

The opposition that developed on the right and left to the early New Deal forced Roosevelt to change direction. The so-called "second New Deal" began with the passage of the National Labor Relations Act on July 5, 1935. It represented Roosevelt's nod to growing left-wing unrest and gave labor unions unprecedented power. The National Labor Relations Board (NLRB) was established and given the authority to recognize labor union organization of individual workplaces. It was also a direct repudiation of the Supreme Court's decisions against the NRA two months before, which had struck down as unconstitutional government promotion of collective bargaining. As a direct result of the special status created by the act, labor unions mushroomed in membership from 3.8 million in 1935 to more than 10 million in 1941.[33]

Then, on August 14, Congress passed the Social Security Act. From a political perspective, it was a masterstroke. As public policy, it was poorly crafted and, as its more insightful critics noted at the time, financially unstable. The act created four bedrock programs of the welfare state: Old Aged, Survivors, and Disability Insurance (OASDI); a compulsory federal Unemployment Insurance (UI) program; Aid to Dependent Children, later renamed Aid to Families with Dependent Children (AFDC); and aid to the aged poor, which later became known as Supplemental Security Income. The Roosevelt administration set up the first two as "social insurance" programs on the European model, funded by payroll taxes on employers and employees (though they were careful, in those weeks after the Court's decision against the NRA, not to use the term "insurance" for fear it would be struck down on constitutional grounds). The other two programs were as much about bailing out insolvent state and local governments, as they were expansions of the welfare state. Both built on programs already in existence in most states. Federal aid for state grant programs to poor seniors remained modest for years afterward (though larger than OASDI payments until the 1950s), but grew rapidly after program expansions in the 1970s.

Aid to Dependent Children, originally intended as a small-scale relief program for widows with children, remained a general-fund item and consequently was never as secure from political attack as OASDI and UI proved to be (and, indeed, AFDC underwent major reforms in the early 1980s, late 1980s, and in 1996, when its nature as an entitlement was significantly curtailed).

For the purposes of the current chapter and the next one, we will focus on OASDI, which retains the original Social Security name. Part of the genius of the program was that it appeared so modest. The initial payroll tax was 2 percent of income up to $3,000.00 a year—half levied directly on employees, the other levied indirectly through the fiction of a tax on employers. Only those who had paid into the system would get anything out of it, and the retirement age was set at sixty-five, which was actually a little higher than the average life expectancy. Consequently, the number of beneficiaries remained very small for the duration of the Roosevelt administration. In fact, as late as 1953, about half of retirees remained ineligible for Social Security benefits.

THE ORIGINS OF SOCIAL SECURITY

Like much else of the New Deal, Social Security was an improvisation, a compromise fashioned on the fly from competing visions and factions. It was also a thoroughly political tool for the president, despite his clear support for the goals of the legislation. After Congress failed to pass two 1934 bills creating new federal grants to state unemployment insurance and old-age programs, the president created a cabinet-level Committee on Economic Security to draft a wide-ranging proposal for 1935. The committee, made up of administration officials, professors, and political activists, soon settled on two possible models for a federal welfare state. The "Ohio model," championed by welfare experts/activists Isaac Rubinow and Abraham Epstein, favored general government funding of aid programs. The "Wisconsin model," based on the work of University of Wisconsin economist John Commons and labor lobbyist John Andrews, advanced a more pure social insurance model based on dedicated payroll taxes. As discussed in greater detail in the next chapter, the original Social Security Act followed the outlines of the Wisconsin plan, but later the program, under attack from Roosevelt's critics among business leaders and GOP lawmakers, adopted some of the characteristics of the left-wing academics behind the Ohio plan.[34]

Roosevelt was not enamored of the Ohio plan. He did not view Social Security programs as an opportunity to advance European-style social democracy. He favored the Wisconsin plan, and indeed later vetoed changes in the program in the 1940s that appeared to weaken the idea of trust-fund financing. For him, the key aspect of the Social Security Act of 1935 wasn't philosophical but political. What Roosevelt was actually doing was getting himself reelected. The complicated scheme requires some explanation. The president and his administration had come to believe that the only way the nation would grow out of depression was if Washington "primed the pump" through government infrastructure and employment programs. But Roosevelt, despite his later reputation as a proto-Keynesian, didn't like the idea of a perpetual federal deficit. Neither did the American public, who in public opinion polls simultaneously favored increased government spending, a balanced budget, and no tax increase.[35] Roosevelt preferred to fund increased government spending with increased taxes. His 1935 program was designed to accomplish these goals with the least possible damage to his political future. The idea was to expand federal spending before the election, run a short-term deficit, juice the economy, and then raise taxes after the election to pay for it all.[36]

Part of the strategy relied on what became known as the "Soak the Rich" Act, also passed in 1935, which jacked up estate and income tax rates on upper-income households and corporations. When the new rates came into effect in 1937, they raised little additional revenue and squelched private investment, as discussed in greater detail later in this chapter.[37] Social Security, on the other hand, was an ideal tactic to advance Roosevelt's strategy. Like the Soak the Rich Act, it did not take effect until 1937. Furthermore, because the payroll tax applied to virtually all workers, but few retirees were eligible for benefits, Social Security would long generate far more in revenue than was needed for payout. The resulting "surplus"—another term consciously chosen by the New Dealers to imply, but not promise, an insurance benefit—wasn't saved in private banks or invested in private stocks, bonds, or real estate. To do so would have infuriated Roosevelt's enemies, who properly would have viewed private investment of the surplus as Washington owning and controlling private business. Besides, such a practice would not have served Roosevelt's short-term political interest. Instead, the surplus was held in federal treasury securities. In other words, it served to dramatically expand federal spending on programs totally unrelated to old-age benefits.

In the months after the passage of the Social Security Act, the administration expanded credit through its new alphabet soup of federal agencies, in effect inflating the currency and creating an appearance of economic growth from the end of 1935 through the 1936 election. The federal budget deficit, which in 1935 stood at about the same as in Hoover's 1932 budget ($2.7 billion), shot up to $4.4 billion in 1936.[38] Public works projects proliferated. Wages and prices rose, as did private employment in construction and related fields. And just before the election, Roosevelt's newest jobs program, the Works Progress Administration (WPA), again headed by Harry Hopkins, hired 3 million unemployed Americans, giving them make-work jobs and a pay check just in time for them to register their gratitude at the ballot box. As a 1938 Congressional investigation showed, some WPA expenditures ended up in the coffers of state Democratic parties, further aiding get-out-the-vote efforts for Roosevelt.[39] Overall, the unemployment rate dropped from 20 percent in 1935 to 17 percent in 1936 and 14 percent in 1937.[40] Only later, in 1937 and 1938, would Roosevelt's political strategy result in a massive recession that, in speed and severity, rivaled Hoover's, with unemployment rates soaring back to near-1935 levels.[41]

As it was helping to manufacture an economic upturn for the election, the creation of Social Security served to placate many Americans who might otherwise have been drawn to Townshend or Long. After all, they were desperate and wanted some kind of federal assistance. But most were still wary of the idea of being welfare recipients. Social Security was sold as something else entirely. Perhaps you would not receive immediate benefits, but by sacrificing a little now in the form of lower wages, you would eventually get what appeared to be spectacular returns in the future upon retirement. Here was a way for government to offer hope to suffering Americans without actually having to spend any immediate relief funds on them or weaken American self-reliance. In a twisted sense, the program actually appealed to traditional American notions of thrift, of saving for a rainy day. Only the federal government, not those banks so recently in threat of collapse, would be the agent of your savings. In a pattern later repeated in 1965,

Americans came to view a huge expansion of federal entitlements not as a "soak the rich" scheme or as welfare for the undeserving but as prepaid, "earned" social insurance benefit. This notion also served to soften the blow of Roosevelt's payroll and income tax hikes, since it appeared that average people would, over time, benefit from the programs they would finance.

Finally, Social Security was Roosevelt's way of placating his conservative critics. Given the subsequent development of the Social Security debate, this may seem implausible. But many Republicans and conservative Democrats came to view Social Security as the only means of heading off Townshendism, Long-style populism, or perhaps something worse, like socialism. This is a common theme in modern-day tributes to Roosevelt for having "saved capitalism from itself" by using government programs to smooth its rough edges and thus forestall revolution.[42] "If we do not get a contributory system started," warned one moderate Social Security advocate at the time, "we are in for free pensions for everybody with constant pressure for higher pensions, far exceeding anything that the veterans have ever been able to exert."[43] Roosevelt himself argued that Social Security would, in short measure, allow the federal government to "quit this business of relief"—meaning traditional welfare benefits that he argued sapped the initiative and self-respect of the poor.[44] Only a few prescient journalists and politicians, notably including an older and wiser Herbert Hoover, foresaw the financial insolvency inherent in Social Security. It might seem like a good deal for the workers of 1935, who stood to reap a huge windfall in twenty or twenty-five years at retirement. But it did nothing for the elderly poor in 1935. And for the next generation of workers, the ability of Social Security to deliver promised benefits without massive increases in the payroll tax was questionable at best. As we shall see, these critics erred only on the side of overestimating Social Security's solvency and not recognizing that its politically effective design would inspire new, expensive federal entitlements.

The aforementioned John Flynn was one of the few journalists at the time who understood the inherent fictional nature of Social Security's "trust fund" scheme. In a 1939 article, he compared the idea to a worker who saved $10.00 per week and put it in a box marked "Reserve." In a year, he saved $520.00 but from time to time borrowed money from the box, leaving IOUs in exchange that promised not only a face value repayment to the box but also 6 percent interest. Over ten years, the box would have an accumulated value of about $8,000.00. But the worker would have only IOUs making $8,000.00 worth of claims on his current income. He would actually have saved nothing, making the reserve "pure fiction." Anticipating today's Social Security debate, Flynn observed that the only way for Social Security to truly develop a reserve to pay future benefits would be to invest "in the bonds of some other government [for example, states] or some private corporations so that it could realize on the investment out of the earnings of some other entity than itself . . . But of course no one would suggest doing this."[45] Not yet, anyway.

In his excellent book *The Return of Thrift*, journalist Phillip Longman tells the story of one statesman who did see what the future held for Social Security. Carl Curtis was a Democratic county attorney in Minden, Nebraska. After the Social Security Act passed in 1935, he switched parties, won a seat in Congress, and became a relentless critic of the Social Security program. He warned that the program might last throughout the 1950s, but then it would collapse without a massive increase in taxes. Eventually, as a subcommittee chair in the 1950s, he called the founders and administrators of the program before Congress and got them to admit, under oath, that Americans were not legally entitled to Social Security benefits and that pay-as-you-finance could not last. But by then it was too late. As President Roosevelt confided to an aide in 1935, the long-term financing of Social Security was not part of the picture at its creation. "I guess you're right on the economics," he told his skeptical aide, "but those taxes were never a problem of economics. They are politics all the way through . . . With those taxes in there no damn politician can ever scrap my Social Security program."[46] Roosevelt had skillfully outwitted his opponents, regained his momentum, and assured his landslide victory in 1936. One additional stroke of good luck was that only a month after the president got his plan through, perhaps his most dangerous left-wing adversary, Huey Long, was assassinated in Louisiana.[47]

KEYNES AND THE INTELLECTUALS

As momentous as the passage of the Social Security Act was, one wonders whether the federal welfare state would have grown as large and as seemingly unassailable as it did over the next several decades if the views of the country's political and intellectual class had not been simultaneously transformed. Roosevelt was not a political philosopher. He did what he thought was expedient and what his advisors told him to do. The critical question is how his advisors came to discard traditional notions of limited government and economic freedom in favor of the New Deal agenda. As previously pointed out, many were former Populists or Progressives already predisposed to favor a more active and intrusive federal government. Furthermore, the neoclassical consensus among economists in America, Britain, and elsewhere was deeply shaken by the Great Depression, which had taken many business executives and leading economists such as Irving Fisher by surprise. Only a few observers had predicted the 1929 crash and subsequent depression. Among those farsighted enough to forecast events correctly were two economists with persuasively argued yet contradictory theories of the business cycle. Unfortunately, it was Cambridge University's John Maynard Keynes, instead of his sparring partner Friedrich Hayek, an Austrian émigré at the London School of Economics, who would first write an international bestseller and promulgate his economic theories to a broad audience of lawmakers, business leaders, academics, and journalists.

Keynes already had a large international following before the publication of *The General Theory of Employment, Interest, and Money* in 1936. His postwar bestseller *Economic Consequences of the Peace* had argued that the Treaty of Versailles went too far in burdening Germany with debt and might have dire economic and political consequences. At Cambridge, Keynes wrote and spoke about a variety of hot topics throughout the 1920s, dabbled (successfully, in large measure) in the British and American stock markets, and advised a number of candidates and officeholders. His influence on Roosevelt's administration may well have predated *The General Theory*. A previous work, *A Treatise on Money,* had outlined some of his views on savings, investment, and the need for government deficits to promote employment. In particular, it drew a sharp distinction between saving and investing that would later play a critical role in Keynes' economic philosophy:

> Saving is the act of the individual consumer and consists in the negative act of refraining from spending the whole of his current income on consumption. Investment, on the other hand, is the act of the entrepreneur . . . and consists in the positive act of starting or maintaining some process of production or of withholding liquid goods.[48]

As later (confusingly) laid out in *The General Theory*, the fundamental dynamic of the business cycle is, according to Keynes, whether investment will sufficiently approach saving to allow for full employment. Investment, he argues, is determined by interest rates, as businesses seek the highest possible return for the financial capital entrusted to them. Saving, on the other hand, is motivated by individual time preferences and projected future needs. To oversimplify a bit, Keynes praises investment but is skeptical of saving, which he derides as "thrift" and "leakage" and blames for causing unemployment. Unfortunately, his picture of the economics of saving and investment is better suited to an ancient or medieval world, without banks or money flows, where people saved by hoarding or stuffing money in their mattresses. In the modern world, where most people's savings are readily put to use in investment, even in checking accounts, Keynes' simultaneous fears of excessive saving and inadequate investment were bizarre, explicable only as a disguised brief for the old, bad idea of wildly inflating the currency to escape an economic recession. Henry Hazlitt, in a devastating critique of *The General Theory* from which I will liberally borrow, postulated that the economist may well have had the impact he did with *The General Theory*—despite its contradictory and ultimately useless arguments—because few actually bothered to read it. They relied on summaries, on press accounts, and on Keynes' public appearances. He was, by all accounts, a witty and congenial man as well as a persuasive speaker. He would have been great on *Larry King Live*.

That he was also more than a little off his rocker was, unfortunately, too little appreciated at the time. I think readers should have been tipped off by his suggestion that the government could stimulate a depressed economy by any form of deficit spending—including his notion of printing new money, putting it in bottles, and burying it deep in the ground for unemployed workers to dig for and find. This was either sheer lunacy or evidence of a shocking misunderstanding of basic economic facts, depending on how seriously he meant himself to be taken. If, as the journalists of the day put it, Roosevelt was literally dumber than a mule, Keynes, with all his erudition and academic degrees, was dumber than a ditchdigger. At least the latter knew the difference between digging a drainage ditch and filling it in. The two actions may consume similar amounts of time and effort, but one creates value—the other destroys it.

Hazlitt points out that, Keynes' protestations to the contrary, markets effectively coordinate saving and investment through changes in interest rates, which fundamentally reflect the intersection between the supply of savings and the demand for investment. In the long run, in other words, the average interest rate represents the average willingness of people to delay current gratification in anticipation of future benefit. It changes according to the productivity of capital assets, expectations of future need, and confidence in the security of property rights. Keynes spends a lot of time discussing the role of expectations in *The General Theory*, but, as Hazlitt correctly discerns, the English elitist actually thinks very little of the ability of the average person to form rational economic expectations. His recommendation is that government make up shortfalls in private investment by printing and spending money on virtually anything. Such inflation, he contends, will reduce unemployment. But as Hazlitt observes, a more direct route to reemployment is to allow wages to fall to market levels in times of recession, a policy against which Keynes argues intensely. Reducing real wages, through inflation, is Keynes' attempt to fool people into making economic adjustments they would not ordinarily make. "To try to cure unemployment by inflation rather than by adjustment of specific wage rates," Hazlitt writes, "is like trying to adjust the piano to the stool rather than the stool to the piano."[49]

Keynesianism was a detour that, until the monetarist and "new classical" corrections of the 1960s and 1970s, led economics into a fantasyland of double-talk and irrelevancy. For our story, perhaps its most pernicious effect was to provide a pseudo-academic rationale for an old bigotry—hatred of private bankers and investors. Keynes himself portrays his proposals for "the socialization of investment" as requiring "the euthanasia of the rentier, of the functionless investor."[50] Even today, when half the nation's population owns corporate stock, either directly or indirectly through pension plans, political activists and academics imbued with Keynesianism savage Wall Street for its greed and shortsightedness, despite the fact that one of Wall Street's primary jobs nowadays is to secure Mom's retirement, Dad's nursing home care, or their children's college education, by maximizing return on investment.

There is no evidence that President Roosevelt cottoned to Keynes' theories. Indeed, the two men met in 1934, and the president was not impressed.[51] But the impact of Keynes and similar thinkers in providing the intellectual justification for what actually happened under Roosevelt is hard to overstate. Protesting all the way about the importance of balancing the budget, the president did run huge deficits throughout his administration, inflating the money supply and, correspondingly, eroding the real value of worker wages in the aggregate, without allowing prices and wages in overextended industries to fall freely relative to the average. Roosevelt, in other words, committed Keynes' errors without reading *The General Theory* or even liking the man!

THE WAR AGAINST INVESTMENT

The reasons for the persistence of large-scale unemployment throughout the 1930s have, like the causes of the 1929 crash, been the subject of extensive academic and journalistic debate. Many conservatives have railed against Roosevelt's dramatic expansion of federal power without identifying the specific policies that kept the economy from a robust recovery. New Dealers and Keynesians have had to explain the inconvenient fact that years of deficit spending, government jobs programs, and social welfare programs failed to return the economy to a sound footing. History left them only with a fallback argument that World War II, by stimulating demand for materiel and other wartime goods, actually ended the Great Depression. But even history is suspect here, written as it has been primarily by those with pro-Roosevelt axes to grind and a simplistic, consumption-based model of how economic growth occurs.

The real answer lies, not surprisingly, in the available evidence. Government statistics do not come down from a mount, inscribed by a Divine Hand. They are vulnerable to a variety of errors of definition, correction, and interpretation. In the 1930s, the data problems were legion. Yet, the available statistics are all the intellectually honest observer has to go on, and they tell an important story about the role played by private investment, or the lack thereof. In a fascinating 1997 paper, historian Robert Higgs examines *net private investment*—the overall change in the nation's private capital stock—throughout the Great Depression. In 1929, gross private investment was $16.2 billion. Subtracting depreciation, net investment was $8.3 billion. After the crash, in 1930, net investment fell to $2.3 billion. From 1931 to 1935, net investment averaged a negative $3.7 billion. In other words, the stock of private capital available to produce goods and services actually shrank. In 1936 and early 1937, with Roosevelt's Social Security/ deficit spending gambit dramatically increasing federal purchases from private industry (at the price of resurgent inflation), net investment turned slightly positive. It flipped negative again during the 1937–1938 recession and reached the level necessary for sustained economic growth only in 1946.[52]

Remember also that investment is not properly measured only in quantity but in quality. Not all investment dollars are put to equally valuable uses. One proxy for the likely return on an investment is its term. Investors are more patient, willing to wait a long time, if they expect the investment to be highly profitable. Therefore, the *mix* of private investment is a key indicator. Higgs divides it into three categories: construction (long-term), durable producer goods (medium-term) and additions to inventory (short-term). In the last five years of the 1920s, construction made up an average of 62 percent of total private investment, compared to 32 percent for durables and 6 percent for inventories. Investors were thinking long-term, confident in their ability to realize (and retain) significant returns. But even during the rosiest three years of the Depression, 1935–1937, construction made up only 38 percent of total private investment. From 1939 to 1941, it averaged only 45 percent. Only after the war did long-term investment finally approach 1920s levels (584). A similar trend is observable in corporate bond yields. The spread between short-term and long-term rates grew wide as a chasm during the Depression years, reflecting investor unwillingness to commit financial capital to long-term investments without a significant risk premium. Not until the 1950s did the spread narrow, coming close to the precrash norm (585).

As discussed in previous chapters, there is no way for an economy to grow in a rapid and sustained fashion without significant private investment. Real per capita growth comes from gains in productivity, in the amount or quality of goods and services produced per worker. Productivity gains come from giving workers more or better capital to work with—be it physical (plants and machinery), human (education and training), social (teamwork, trust, and superior organization), or intellectual (new ideas, technologies, or applications). So why were investors so skittish throughout the Great Depression? Higgs provides several intriguing clues. Using the legislative and political history of the New Deal as well as findings from the public opinion polling industry that developed in the mid-1930s, he argues that "the insufficiency of private investment . . . reflected a pervasive uncertainty among investors about the security of their property rights in their capital and its prospective returns" (573).

The effect was especially pronounced during the second New Deal period from 1935 to 1940. One specific culprit was the aforementioned 1935 "Soak the Rich" tax act. It didn't just tack on an income tax surcharge of up to 75 percent for those making $50,000.00 a year, though that was bad enough; in this period before the advent of widespread stock and bond ownership, most financial investments were made by the affluent, whose skyrocketing marginal tax rate made such investments extremely unattractive. Perhaps an even more direct attack on private capital formation was the act's changes to corporate taxation. First, it created a graduated corporate income tax for the first time, thus punishing firms for making successful investments. Second, it levied income tax on intercorporate dividends, thus introducing another layer of multiple taxation on personal income earned from investments in corporate businesses. In 1936, another tax act made things worse. Congress approved a graduated surtax on corporate earnings, based on the percentage of earnings retained. In other words, it imposed yet another layer of taxation on the same income (573–74). Retained earnings—those not distributed to shareholders in the form of dividends—are used to make corporate investments to boost future income. They fund new machinery, technological innovation, or sometimes are held in other corporate securities when the returns promise to be better. All of these actions are investments that generate future, taxable income, either in the form of higher dividends or higher share prices at sale. To tax these activities—after already subjecting distributed income at the corporate level and at the personal level to tax—was to put a heavy burden on the very engine of productivity growth in a predominantly corporate economy. It is, in fact, amazing that corporate America continued to produce much of anything given Roosevelt's assault.

One last point deserves attention. Did America's entry into World War II serve finally to rejuvenate the economy? Many observers, looking at the timing of economic indicators such as unemployment and investment, believe the answer to be obvious. But Higgs urges caution. Wartime statistics are extremely suspect and are not comparable to those collected before and after. Business confidence did rebound after 1940, but an important nonwar factor appeared to be a contemporaneous "changing of the guard" within the Roosevelt administration as former corporate executives and other pro-business officials replaced true believers in key posts. Overall, Higgs concludes that:

> [T]he war years themselves witnessed a deterioration of economic well-being in the sense of consumer satisfaction either present (via private consumption) or prospective (via accumulation of capital with the potential to enhance future civilian consumption) and that the Great Escape [from depression] actually occurred during the demobilization period, especially during its first year, when most of the wartime controls were eliminated and most of the resources used for munitions production and military activities were returned to civilian production.(563)

CONCLUSION

If Social Security was a triumph of short-term political savvy in 1935, the president certainly paid the political bill in 1938. The new corporate taxes, when added to the new Social Security tax and increases in personal and estate taxes in 1937, led to a severe recession and significant Republican gains in the 1938 elections. The GOP continued its momentum into the war years, almost taking control of the House of Representatives in 1942. More importantly, a conservative coalition of Republicans and disaffected Democrats pretty much stymied any New Deal legislation after 1938. Overall, Democrats hit the high-water mark in 1936 with 76 seats in the Senate and 331 seats in the House. By 1944, Democrats enjoyed only a 56 to 44 majority in the Senate and a 242 to 193 edge in the House. After the war, Congress would go Republican. One wonders if it might not have happened far sooner had the president failed to engineer America's entry into what became a popular war.

To summarize, President Roosevelt's taxation, regulation, and entitlement policies led to reelection in 1936 and to political and economic losses afterward. Still, the dynamics of the Grasshopper Syndrome and the powerful attractions of the welfare state had been unleashed in America. Even during the Republican congressional regime of the late 1940s and early 1950s and President Dwight D. Eisenhower's otherwise successful eight-year tenure, GOP critics saw no practical way to roll back the welfare state or to reform its major programs. Indeed, many Republicans made peace with entitlements, content to look overseas for their signature political issues. The result was expansion, not contraction, of Roosevelt's legacy. The next four chapters will detail these expansions during the 1950s, 1960s, 1970s, and 1980s in the areas of retirement security, health care, and federal policy toward physical and human capital formation. They will also suggest ways that the new force of Investor Politics can be used to reverse this course and restore the principles of limited government and self-reliance so long in retreat.

CHAPTER 5

THE GREAT
SOCIAL SECURITY
DEBATE

T
HE REPUBLICAN SENATOR AND THE DEMOCRATIC head of the Social Security Administration had long been at loggerheads. In a magazine story, the senator had complained that Social Security surpluses weren't really being saved for future beneficiaries—they were simply fueling the growth of federal spending "while the [trust] fund gets a promise-to-pay which another generation of our grandsons and grand-daughters can wrestle with, decades hence."[1] The Social Security official strongly disagreed. Surplus funds, he promised in a subse-quent letter to the senator, were going to be used to reduce federal debt, not squandered on new programs, so that "future annual government expenditures will be proportionally lower."[2] Later, the two had a private chat. The Democrat suggested an idea. Instead of simply "investing" Social Security surpluses in federal treasury notes, why not allow the federal government to invest some of the money in the private stock and bond markets. "That would be so-cialism," the Republican senator snorted.[3]

It might sound like this exchange could have happened in 1999, with a Clinton administration official explaining to conservative senator and former economics professor Phil Gramm of Texas the president's plan to "save Social Security" by using surplus payroll taxes to reduce the federal debt and buy private securities. But the words were spoken over five decades ago.

The Democrat was Arthur Altmeyer, the first commissioner of Social Security. The Republican was Senator Arthur Vandenberg of Michigan, the program's most effective early critic. His prescient warning about Washington's plans to raid the Social Security surplus and saddle future generations with an unfunded liability was published in 1937—the first year of the program. It was wise that the senator rejected Altmeyer's half-hearted suggestion that the federal government invest Social Security funds in private securities. Unfortunately, Vandenberg apparently could not envision the alternative that now dominates discussion of Social Security reform—investment in stocks and bonds, yes, but in the form of personal accounts.

It is undeniably true that, in the last few years of the twentieth century, the idea of transforming Social Security from a government "social insurance" program into one of mandatory but individual private investment has received unprecedented attention. Several factors have contributed to the healthy debate now underway, including the success of reformers in countries such as Chile and Australia, the growth of personal stock and bond investing through mutual funds and 401(k)s, and the hard work of privatization proponents such as the Washington-based Cato Institute, which labored long and hard in relative obscurity to build the intellectual case for reform. However, no one should think that any of the insights about the insolvency, the unfairness, and the economic costs of Social Security are new ones. From the creation of the program in 1935, the great Social Security debate has raged in the corridors of power, in the pages of newspapers and magazines, and in the esoteric tomes of government reports. While there were many critics in positions of power, like Vandenberg, who understood the flaws of the program as originally enacted, they not only never came up with a privatization alternative but, in their own way, they contributed to the Social Security crisis that now faces us.

THE CRITICS FIND THEIR FOOTING

The Social Security Act of 1935, as we have seen, had both a short-term and a long-term purpose. In the short run, the Roosevelt administration sought to stifle increasing criticism from both the Left and the Right of the New Deal and ensure the president's reelection in 1936. By scheduling dramatic tax increases for 1937, the administration placated its more fiscal conservative members (including, it must be said, Roosevelt himself) with the notion that expanding credit and running an unprecedented peacetime deficit in 1936 would be followed closely by efforts to balance the budget after the election. Since Social Security benefits would remain miniscule for many years, the payroll tax would create large "surpluses" to fund the rest of the federal budget on a cash basis.

In the long run, Roosevelt saw the Social Security Act as "the cornerstone in a structure which is being built but is by no means complete."[4] He foresaw a comprehensive set of social insurance programs, introduced gradually, and financed by building up trust funds in emulation of private insurance. It is important to understand that the president and some of his top aides did not believe in a strictly "pay-as-you-go" system. That is, they did not believe that funding current benefits merely with current taxes was either economically prudent or politically wise. A pre-funded system, they thought, would avoid painful choices in the future while assuring the American people that they were participating in an insurance system, not simply a redistributive welfare program. Pre-funding through the buildup of surpluses was, in Roosevelt's words, "a protection to future administrations against the necessity of going deeply into debt to furnish relief to the needy."[5]

In retrospect, Roosevelt proved to be a fairly accurate fortune-teller. He was elected easily in 1936 during a government-created credit expansion. The subsequent tax increases then shrank the budget deficit from $4.4 billion in 1936 to $2.8 billion in 1937 and $1.2 billion in 1938.[6] At the time the act was passed in 1935, Social Security surpluses were estimated to total $47 billion by 1980. If such an accumulation of real assets (adjusted for inflation) had actually occurred, the program probably would not have faced the magnitude of fiscal problems it did in the 1970s and 1980s. Of course, nothing of the sort happened—or could have happened, given the initial structure of the program in 1935 and its revision only a few years later. Roosevelt understood the art of political maneuvering well, and had enough common sense to realize that Social Security represented an ambitious and expensive set of promises to future generations that needed to be properly financed. But his knowledge of economics and investment was faulty. In particular, he failed to understand that "pre-funding" Social Security was possible only if surplus funds were used to create real, income-producing capital assets. Entries on a government ledger did not count. Nor did his political luck hold out. By 1939, his critics, both liberal and conservative, had realized that the president's Social Security plan was vulnerable to challenge. Unfortunately, their joint approach to reform—to move the program away from a pre-funded insurance model towards pay-as-you-go—proved to be even more disastrous.

Roosevelt's short-run miscalculation was the 1937–1938 recession. Caused in large measure by the boom-and-bust credit cycle he had created and the imposition of costly new taxes on the already shaky economy, the recession led to a 35 percent increase in the number of unemployed Americans in just one year. In addition to the political problems this created (resolved in Roosevelt's favor only by the onset of war in Europe), the recession called into stark relief the problem of accumulating surpluses to pay future Social Security benefits. Liberals, including many within the administration, viewed it as unconscionable that the federal government would collect taxes but not provide more generous benefits to those in need. Influenced by Keynesianism, they argued that a higher level of government spending was needed to pull the country out of recession, financed not by raising tax rates but by running deficits (in other words, by inflating the money supply and thus raising taxes more surreptitiously). They disapproved of the new Social Security payroll taxes, believing them to be a drag on consumer demand.

On the other hand, conservatives such as Senator Arthur Vandenberg questioned how $47 billion in federal surpluses could realistically be "saved," given the nature of government finance and the temptation to spend every federal dollar that comes in. After all, in its first 159 years of operation, the federal government had accumulated only $27 billion in debt. Even if, as Roosevelt's officials promised, the government would effectively "save" Social Security surpluses by reducing the national debt and thus increasing private savings accordingly, no one expected that the federal government would, without Social Security trust funds, run up another $20 billion in debt by 1980. So there was not going to be $47 billion of government debt to offset. Inevitably, conservatives argued, Congress would not and could not "save" $47 billion, given that the surplus funds were to be immediately loaned out to the federal government. This argument may seen commonsensical, but even today, more than half a century later, defenders of the Social Security program continue to claim that surplus funds are safely "invested" in federal treasury securities.

Not just the principle of the thing horrified conservatives. It was the sheer magnitude of the projected, accumulated tax collections. To put the number in perspective: $47 billion was three times the total production of all gold in the world between 1900 and 1937. It was eight times the current money supply of the United States. It was enough to buy all the farms in America and leave $14 billion to spare. Vandenberg and several congressional colleagues stated in 1937 that a:

> . . . reserve is unnecessary in a compulsory tax-supported system; that its ultimate accumulation of a $47 billion reserve is a positive menace to free institutions and to sound finance and that it is a perpetual invitation to the maintenance of an extravagant public debt; that it will, in effect, transfer the burden of debt retirement from the shoulders of general taxpayers to the shoulders of the lowest-income group of the country in the form of a gross income tax on labor; and that it involves . . . a needless postponement of earlier and more adequate benefit payments.[7]

MAKING A GOOD DEAL A LOT BETTER

One of the most astounding aspects of the early debate over reforming Social Security was how quickly "conservative" critics of the program tried to run to the left of Democratic administrations by complaining about the regressive nature of the payroll tax and the stinginess of Social Security benefits. Politically, they may have seen no other option. Even in its first year, the program met with great approval by most voters. Throughout the 1940s and 1950s, support would grow even stronger. How were Americans, born to freedom and constitutional government, so easily persuaded that Washington should guarantee their retirement security and, later, protect them from disability and disease? Part of the answer is that, as shown in chapter 2, the earlier Populist and Progressive movements had already led to government expansion, particularly at the state and local level, into such safety net programs as workers' compensation, unemployment insurance, and state pensions for the aged, blind, infirm, and widows with children. The Great Depression of the 1930s served as a catalyst to activate public sentiments that had already been developing slowly over the past two generations. The Depression's magnitude was unprecedented. At the same time, the stock market crash and the rash of bank failures of the early 1930s weakened whatever support there was for private-sector alternatives to providing for retirement and other needs.

Contributing to this sea change in public opinion was, in a strange way, the fact that Roosevelt's plans for Social Security did not survive the decade. Keynesians of the Left, together with Vandenberg and the newly energized Republicans on the Right, worked together in 1938 and 1939 to fashion changes in the program. Vandenberg had already introduced a resolution in January 1937 calling for the abandonment of "full-reserve" funding of Social Security and either raising benefits, delaying scheduled tax hikes, or both. By 1939, there was enough support to pass amendments to the Social Security Act that:

1. moved forward the starting date of benefit payments from 1942 to 1940,
2. boosted benefits for new retirees by changing the benefit formula,
3. gave spouses far greater benefits than in the original bill,
4. created survivor benefits, and
5. postponed a scheduled payroll tax hike from 1940 to 1943.

The result of all these changes was a projected Social Security fund balance of $6.9 billion by 1955, instead of the previously anticipated $22.1 billion.[8]

The 1939 amendments were followed by subsequent changes that essentially put Social Security on a purely pay-as-you-go basis, not just in fact but in principle. Roosevelt had reluctantly agreed to the 1939 changes, fearful of continued recession. But Congress wanted more. In 1942, it delayed the payroll tax increase by a year, then again for three months. Roosevelt acquiesced, consumed by the demands of the war. In 1943, Congress delayed the tax again. This time, Roosevelt nixed the measure, using the veto pen for only the second time in his entire career, but he was overridden. After his death, the tax hike was postponed twice again, until 1950.[9] For the first thirteen years of the program, in other words, higher benefits than originally envisioned were financed without any increases in the payroll tax rate. Social Security recipients could not believe their luck. It was about to get even better.

Liberals in the 1940s, including those within the Social Security Administration itself, were happy with the erosion of the original pre-funded, insurance model for Social Security. But they didn't just want to maintain a level tax rate and gradually phase in larger pensions for retirees. Their plans for a federal safety net were far more grandiose. In 1942, Roosevelt's Social Security Board included in its annual report to the president a bold plan to expand entitlements from "cradle to grave," consciously employing socialist novelist Edward Bellamy's famous phrase. It called for an expanded Social Security pension system as well as disability insurance, increased programs for the jobless, and federal hospital insurance. As discussed in the next chapter, the drive for national health care, begun in earnest a few short years later by President Harry Truman, would culminate in the creation of Medicare and Medicaid in the Social Security amendments of 1965. The other ideas did not take so long. In 1950, Congress reformed the core old-age pension program of Social Security again by significantly expanding coverage and benefits. The average retiree saw his monthly benefit increase by 80 percent, as did widows and orphans. The 1950 amendments did revisit the tax issue. The payroll tax, levied at 2 percent of the first $3,000.00 of wages since inception, would go to 7 percent of $4,800.00 in covered wages by 1965, with the first percentage-point increase scheduled for 1951.[10]

The Social Security Disability Insurance (SSDI) program was added to the benefits package beginning in 1957. SSDI is one of those hidden corners of the welfare state that has grown into a huge federal expenditure without attracting much notice. In dollar terms, the SSDI program is twice as large or larger than programs attracting far more attention from the news media and from the general public, such as Food Stamps, cash welfare, the federal school lunch program, or the Earned Income Tax Credit.[11] It is designed to provide long-term, rather than short-term, disability insurance. That is, eligibility for benefits begins no earlier than six months after developing a disability serious enough to preclude significant employment. When adding the SSDI benefit to Social Security, Congress and administration officials viewed short-term disability to be the proper object of savings, investments, and private workers' compensation insurance. But they considered long-term disability benefits to be a logical extension of retirement benefits. After all, the theory behind the earlier Social Security retirement and survivor benefits was that workers faced the possibility of losing the ability to provide for themselves and their families due to the infirmities of age or death. Disability before the age of sixty-five (after which all disabled workers are eligible for retirement benefits) represented a similar risk.

The problem with this argument is that unlike aging or death, "disability" has no straightforward definition. Nor is it necessarily an irreversible calamity. In practice, the SSDI program has found it difficult to exclude beneficiaries with debatable claims of disability, nor has it devoted much attention to moving beneficiaries off the rolls by treating their physical or mental conditions, retraining them, and finding them jobs. The result has been a skyrocketing caseload and unforeseen expense. In 1994, after a decade in which disability benefits grew by 75 percent in real, inflation-adjusted terms, Congress had to transfer funds from the retirement and survivors' trust fund to the separate SSDI trust fund just to keep it solvent.[12] But in its early years, SSDI was yet another goodie added to the Social Security basket, apparently without significant cost to taxpayers.

Throughout the 1960s and early 1970s, the Social Security gravy train just kept chugging along. Through a series of income-replacement and cost-of-living adjustments, benefits rose by 93 percent from 1965 to 1972.[13] During the same period, several new social welfare programs were added to the mix. Medicare and Medicaid, created in 1965, are the subjects of the next chapter. In 1972, Congress and the Nixon administration agreed to expand dramatically a parallel system of joint federal-state welfare payments to disabled and elderly Americans that had existed for many decades. The new federalized program, called Supplemental Security Income (SSI), guaranteed an income floor under which no eligible recipient would be allowed to fall. SSI would supply monthly checks to supplement wages, savings, or Social Security retirement and disability benefits up to the income floor. Furthermore, you could be eligible for SSI even though you lacked the work experience necessary to receive Social Security. Though funded by general revenues rather than by payroll taxes, SSI is operated by the Social Security Administration and, like its other programs, has ballooned far beyond original expectations. Its budget for fiscal year 2000 was about $29 billion, with nearly 6.3 million adults and children on the rolls.[14] Most state governments also supplement the federal SSI program, either by chipping in extra money for federal payments or administering their own "special assistance" programs for needy elderly or disabled residents in rest homes. So the total cost of SSI programs is, once again, far larger than more celebrated "antipoverty" programs such as Food Stamps or Temporary Assistance for Needy Families (TANF), formerly known as AFDC.

AN INVESTMENT TOO GOOD TO BE TRUE

What all this meant was that to the average American of the 1950s, 1960s, and early 1970s, Social Security seemed nothing less than a magical money machine. In their 1999 book *The Real Deal: The History and Future of Social Security,* Sylvester Schieber and John Shoven ran some numbers to compare the rate of return enjoyed by early Social Security recipients with what they would have realized from private investments. Basically, retirees born before the year 1915—who became eligible for full Social Security benefits in 1980—enjoyed a real rate of return from the program that far exceeded what they would have received had they invested the same amount of money in private, large-company stocks.[15] No wonder the program became so firmly established in American culture. It was a great deal. To the extent that voters thought of Social Security in terms of Investor Politics, they had little reason to question the program's design, fairness, or economic impact. Coupled with the fact that mass participation in private capital markets was still many years away (as discussed in chapter 3), few had the personal experience or economic insight necessary to consider private-sector alternatives. Nor did even skeptical politicians, be they Republicans or Democrats, feel it wise to question Social Security or stand in the way of its further expansion.

Unfortunately, it was all a mirage. The spectacular return on investment that Social Security appeared to provide was not the result of government bonds being safer than the stock market. It is true that the period in question included the tail end of the Great Depression, small economic dips in the 1950s and 1960s, and the oil shocks and rampant inflation of the 1970s. But while the real rate of return on stocks was about 6 percent a year from 1940 to 1980, lower than the average return for earlier and later periods, the return on government bonds, adjusted for inflation, was actually negative. Social Security was, and is, a horrible way to promote investment—to build real, income-producing assets. Nor is it really a form of national saving, as its defenders proclaim. As Bill Styring and Donald Jonas of the Hudson Institute humorously put it, Social Security trust funds do not fund "warehouses filled with retirement condos, jars of Roquefort dressing, and health-care professionals labeled 'for future retirees.'" The real reason why Americans seemed to do so well under Social Security during its first four decades was that most retirees received huge, unearned windfalls. They received generous payments even though they had paid relatively little into the system during their working years. Those who retired between 1945 and 1975, for example, received a net transfer of wealth from younger generations of roughly $7 trillion in today's dollars.[16]

This is the aspect of Social Security that has earned it the epithet of "Ponzi scheme." Charles Ponzi was a con man who ran not the first but perhaps the most successful pyramid scheme in the nation's history. A pyramid scheme is designed to enrich its originators by adding ever-wider layers of contributors. If you promise someone a 100 percent return on an investment, receive $100.00 from that person, and then convince a second person to do the same, you can repay the first, keep your promise, and then advertise your financial wizardry. As additional people take you up on the offer, you can satisfy a growing list of investors. Eventually, however, the pyramid collapses. It becomes impossible to find enough suckers to pay the initial $100.00. Because the money is never actually invested, never used to create capital assets in order to produce something of value, it does not take long for the scheme's liabilities to far exceed its revenues. Those at the "top" of the pyramid, who get in early, often do very well. Those at the bottom are left holding the bag—literally, in the case of some unscrupulous multilevel marketers more skilled at selling memberships than at making and distributing products consumers actually want for their own sake.

Ponzi ran his popular scheme for a few months in 1920. On August 13, he was arrested and charged with fraud. He served two prison terms and was released, in a twist of fate, just as President Roosevelt was assembling the committee that would draft the Social Security bill later in the year.[17] Like Ponzi's fraudulent scheme, Social Security's early success was because far more people paid into the system than were making claims on it. When the first retirement benefits were paid out, the ratio of taxpayers to recipients was forty to one. In 1950, when benefits were expanded, it was sixteen to one—still a large, gently sloping pyramid. But by the time the Nixon administration was trying to outbid Congressional Democrats in Social Security generosity, the handwriting was already on the wall. Rapid inflation, coupled with slackening wage growth and the stubborn tendency of elderly recipients to stay alive in record numbers, put an end to the Social Security mirage. The dependency ratio was approaching three to one. The question soon became not how many new benefits could be added to the program, but how to pay for promises already made. The answer to that question was a series of payroll tax hikes and benefit reductions that invited a different question: why Social Security turned so quickly from a good deal to a horribly bad one.

"RESCUING" SOCIAL SECURITY

It wasn't long after the 1972 amendments hiking Social Security benefits another 20 percent that the system's precarious finances began to manifest themselves. The first problem was that employment and real wages weren't growing as rapidly as projected, exacerbating the extent to which the dependency ratio was not moving in the system's favor. Secondly, the 1972 amendments included a flawed inflation adjustment. "The 1972 indexing approach created huge actuarial deficits for the system over the 75-year horizon, roughly four times as great as the shortfalls we now face," Schieber and Shoven write. "It caused the benefits for initial retirees to go up faster than inflation, faster than wages, and faster than the system itself could withstand in the long run." They also argue persuasively that Social Security administrators knew very well the implications of the 1972 amendments, even if Congress did not, and may well have viewed the resulting crisis as an opportunity to lock in higher taxes and benefits.[18]

Whether engineered or not, a deficit in Social Security appeared as early as 1975. By 1977, the annual deficit reached $5.6 billion.[19] After rejecting a reform package, including a tax hike, proposed by President Ford in 1976, Congress passed a similar package pitched by the Carter administration the following year. It reformed the indexing formula, increased the taxable wage base, and accelerated and increased previously scheduled increases in the tax rate. At a signing ceremony, President Carter said that the bill had guaranteed fifty years of "sound" finance for the Social Security system.[20]

It was not to be. The 1977 amendments, though substantially hiking taxes and thus shrinking the return to future retirees, were themselves based on rosy economic forecasts. A few months after taking office, President Reagan and his advisors fashioned another painful reform package. It reduced early-retirement benefits, phased out the "earnings test" that discouraged those over sixty-five from working, and tightened other benefits rules. The result of Reagan's honest appraisal of the long-run shakiness of Social Security was a political bloodletting in Congress and in the court of public opinion, which had not been prepared for the reality of the program's insolvency. In September, the administration regrouped, calling for a high-level commission. Democrats agreed, but delayed any substantive work until after the 1982 elections, during which they used the Social Security issue to make substantial gains in Congress.[21]

The commission, headed by future Federal Reserve Chairman Alan Greenspan, finally reported out a reform package in 1983. Tense negotiation between Senator Patrick Moynihan of New York, Senator Robert Dole of Kansas, and officials from the Reagan administration led to a compromise later in the year. It again accelerated previously scheduled payroll tax hikes, while also taxing benefits and the self-employed, delaying cost-of-living adjustments, and expanding coverage to include government and nonprofit employees previously exempt.[22]

Needless to say, the 1983 reform package has failed to rescue Social Security from insolvency, while simultaneously making the program even less rewarding to today's young workers. At this writing, Social Security's unfunded liability over the next seventy-five years totals $19.8 trillion. This is the amount, adjusted for inflation, that currently projected benefits exceed projected collections from the current 12.4 percent OASDI payroll tax. The first year that benefits will exceed collections is 2016. After that, the federal government will have to either scale back Social Security benefits in some manner, raise the payroll tax rate, or chip in subsidies from general revenues, itself requiring either tax hikes or spending cuts. These changes will be painful. Balancing the system would require either a 53 percent increase in the payroll tax rate or a 33 percent reduction in benefits. As economist Daniel J. Mitchell of the Heritage Foundation observes, such large tax hikes or benefits cuts would "make Social Security's already meager rate of return even worse."[23]

Meager is right. According to an analysis by the National Bureau of Economic Research, Americans born before 1915 and retiring before 1980 received an impressive 7 percent average rate of return, after inflation, on the payroll taxes they paid into the system. Those born in 1930 and retiring in 1995 received only a 2.5 percent return. Those now retiring can expect less than a 2 percent return, while those born in 1990, retiring in 2055, will be lucky to get a positive rate of return at all.[24] The forecasts differ by sex and race, though there is some disagreement about in which direction. Some argue that minorities will suffer more than whites because of their lower life expectancies, which shorten the period during which they collect benefits. But blacks and Hispanics also earn less on average than whites do, so the progressive nature of the benefits formula works to their advantage. Women also do somewhat better than men because of lower wages and higher life expectancies.

Overall, according to John Goodman of the National Center for Policy Analysis in Dallas, a twenty-year-old black male in the year 2000 can expect to pay $40,979.00 more in Social Security taxes than he receives in benefits. A comparable white male will lose $44,831.00 on his Social Security "investment." A twenty-year-old black woman will lose $31,913.00 compared to $34,920.00 for her white peer.[25] No matter how you look at it, the return will be negative for virtually every young person entering the workforce today. The iron laws of demography, the tax hikes and benefit cuts of the 1970s and 1980s, and the lack of any real assets in the Social Security trust fund have effectively erased Roosevelt's promise of social security to all working Americans. It cannot be honored.

TRUST FUND MYTHOLOGY

At this point it is worth taking a closer look at the issue of government trust funds. More ink has been spilled on this topic in recent years than in the first six decades of the Social Security program, yet the quality of the arguments hasn't improved since Senator Arthur Vandenberg and Social Security Administrator Arthur Altmeyer first employed them in 1937. Both sides of the debate are guilty of using imprecise terms that lead to confusion. For example, defenders of the system say that excess payroll taxes are "invested" in federal treasury bonds. They are correct only if an imprecise definition of investment in employed. Purchasing a federal bond—and in this case not even a transferable, general obligation bond but a "special obligation bond"—is not necessarily an act of investment in an economic sense. It depends on how the resulting federal revenue is spent in the current operation of the government. There are some federal expenditures that one might call investments in that they create capital assets, such as highways or college educations, that generate future economic growth and consequently growth in federal revenues. Whether the return on such investments is higher than alternatives, such as state highways or private educations, is more problematic; if federal spending supplants state or private spending on such items, it represents disinvestment. More importantly, a great deal of federal spending is simply a transfer of money from the people who earn it to those who will consume it. The nation's capital stock does not grow, so neither do its productivity rates or future tax revenues.

Even intelligent, experienced lawmakers and economists continue to mistake any holding of federal treasury securities as a secure form of investment. Henry J. Aaron, for example, is a senior fellow in economic studies at the Brookings Institution in Washington. In a 1996 article in *The Washington Post*, Aaron challenged the idea that the Social Security trust fund is a myth:

> Every dollar of Social Security reserves is invested in special Treasury securities. One way to see the value of these assets is to imagine yourself the financial manager of a large insurance company. You are in charge of a portfolio that includes U.S. government bonds like those held in the trust fund. Far from regarding these government bonds as mythical, you would recognize them as the safest asset in your portfolio. You can sell at any time or hold to maturity for redemption at face value, without the slightest default. Anyone who suggested that such assets were a "myth" would be dismissed as a financial ignoramus.[26]

Aaron is correct that government bonds have long been considered a safe form of financial investment. There are two serious problems with his analysis, however. First, his example bears little relationship to the investment of Social Security trust funds. Specifically, *it matters who the investor is.* A more proper analogy would be to assume that the private insurance company wants to expand its market share by offering benefits that are more generous but without increasing premiums or projecting higher returns from its portfolio. To do so without reducing the financial value of his portfolio, the manager issues bonds from the company to itself, adding their value to the portfolio. His company has an excellent track record of paying its debts. The bonds might include a promise to pay a market interest rate. But they are not real investments. The selling of the bonds does not generate revenue with which to build a valuable physical or human asset. They do not improve the company's ability to earn future income, and thus to pay back the bonds at maturity. Indeed, the only asset the company would build with such a policy would be customer satisfaction at getting more for less, although accomplishing this would create a corresponding liability of at least the same value.

In reality, any insurance company filling its portfolio with its own securities would be running a Ponzi scheme. Early in the game, subscribers would pay only moderate premiums and receive generous coverage. The price, however, would be larger and larger piles of IOUs in the trust fund— not IOUs from some other, income-producing company, but from the insurer itself. These unfunded liabilities would accrue in the portfolio until some future date at which the company's ability to cannibalize its other assets to cover its obligations would disappear. At that point, the pyramid would collapse and someone would probably go to jail for fraud. The situation is no different for Social Security. Its trust fund is full of IOUs that the government has written to itself.[27]

The second problem with Aaron's analysis is his premise that government bonds are "the most dependent asset in [a] portfolio." The big difference, of course, between corporate bonds and government bonds is the form of repayment. The former are repaid if and when the corporation issuing them generates sufficient revenue through economic activities. The latter are repaid with taxes, by definition collected involuntarily. Corporations must use the proceeds they receive from selling bonds to create real capital assets with which to earn future income. Technically, governments need not do so. Their ability to repay is backed by force. Keep in mind, however, that ultimately all bonds, even those issued by governments, are repaid from business earnings collected as taxes, either levied on business profits or on worker wages. If the economy has grown sufficiently between the time a government bond was issued and the time it must be redeemed with interest, then the taxes required to pay the bondholder are not particularly onerous. They might even be levied at a lower rate than when the bond was issued. If the economy has not grown enough, the taxes are quite burdensome.

Furthermore, even guns are not necessarily a guarantee of sufficient revenue collections. When governments are in competition—city against city, state against state, country against country—excessive tax rates can chase productive businesses and individuals away, thus shrinking the economy and requiring even higher rates to collect the same revenue. High tax rates can also lead to reduced work effort and elaborate tax evasion strategies. In other words, even the ability to issue government bonds is still effectively constrained by economic factors. The long-term creditworthiness of a government depends on how much it borrows and how it uses the money it receives.

Later in his *Post* article, Aaron appears to recognize the problem of government "investment" but draws what appears to be a strange conclusion:

> In one important sense, the [Social Security] trust fund has been "spent." So have the life insurance premiums that were invested in government securities. In both cases, saving that might have gone for investment in new buildings or machines goes instead to pay for current expenditures of the federal government. Because saving was spent on current public consumption, not on real capital assets, the nation lost the added future production that real capital assets could have produced. But the diversion did not occur because Social Security is poorly managed or because private saving was unwise. It occurred because the federal government does not collect enough in ordinary taxes to pay for expenditures on activities other than Social Security.[28]

Aaron's suggestion that Social Security funds are spent because the federal tax burden is too low invites a giggle. The real problem is not inadequate federal taxation, but how the current federal budget reduces real investment in the economy, both on the tax side and on the spending side. As we shall see, there are a variety of ways to rectify the situation.

Just as defenders of the current Social Security system mistake government bonds as equivalent to investment, advocates of Social Security privatization also err in complaining that trust funds are not real assets because they are just claims on future income—the income the government will have to tax to pay benefits when the trust fund obligations are redeemed. This is true but beside the point. All securities, whether issued by government or private companies, are "just" claims on future income. A corporate stock is only as valuable as the corporation's ability to generate income in the future. A bond is only as valuable as the ability of its issuer to pay interest and principal from future income. The real problem with government trust funds is not that they are only promises to pay in the future. All financial assets are. The problem is that government trust funds do not, on balance, fund productive investments that generate economic value in the future. They fund current consumption, including Social Security benefits and other transfer programs, as well as "investment" activities that provide subpar returns compared to those available at lower levels of government or the private sector. They do little, in other words, to expand the economy over time so that future Social Security beneficiaries can live comfortably without putting an excessive burden on the future workers who must, inevitably, create the income required to support retirees.

SOLVING THE SOCIAL SECURITY CRISIS

There are five possible ways to reorganize the finances of Social Security and the federal government to alleviate the system's unfunded liability and to give workers a better, more secure return in their retirement. All involve creating a higher rate of growth in the private economy over time, so that the economic pie is far larger in the future when the Baby Boomers start eating their slices. All center on investment. However, they have varying political and economic implications. Practitioners of Investor Politics would be wise to consider them carefully and choose the options with the highest possible returns in the long run.

OPTION 1: PAY DOWN THE DEBT. Some policymakers want to use Social Security surpluses the way Arthur Altmeyer promised to use them in 1937—to pay down existing or projected federal debts. As of the 2000 fiscal year, total federal debt was $5.5 trillion, $3.7 trillion of which was held by investors (the remainder reflects obligations to Social Security and other trust funds). It is a big number. The investor-held debt accounted for 23 percent of the total credit-market debt owed by the nonfinancial sector of the United States economy. In addition, the annual cost of servicing this debt is also significant. In fiscal year 2000, the federal government paid $215 billion in interest on this publicly held debt, about the same amount spent on

Medicare and more than half the total expenditure for Social Security benefits that year. At this writing, federal debt service represents about 2 percent of the gross domestic product. The number is expected to decline to $173 billion, or 1.6 percent of the gross domestic product, by 2004.[29]

According to economic theory, federal government debt reduces productive investment in several ways. First, the cost of servicing the debt represents budget authority that the federal government cannot spend on federal investment (such as infrastructure improvements) or encouraging private investment through tax reduction. Without the debt, for example, the federal budget could easily accommodate a nearly total abolition, at least in the short run, of the current double taxation of capital gains, corporate income, and inheritances.[30] Ending these aspects of the tax code that punish savings and investment would, needless to say, have salutary effects on the economy.

Second, the theory goes, federal debt supplants private investment. Most of the dollars that investors spend to purchase federal treasury securities would, in the absence of that option, be invested in corporate bonds and stocks, bonds, real estate, or other private assets. To the extent that these investments are more productive uses of money than federal expenditures are, the size of the economy over time would be far larger than the baseline. Furthermore, many economists project that interest rates would decline if the debt were paid off. David W. Wilcox, assistant treasury secretary for economic policy under President Clinton, defended his administration's debt-reduction approach to Social Security reform as "the most pro-growth, pro-saving fiscal policy that we are aware of."[31]

Third, to the extent that investors seek security and stability over long-term return, in the absence of federal bonds they might choose to purchase more state and local bonds, which typically finance far more productive assets than do their federal counterparts. Most states have balanced-budget requirements that forbid borrowing just to finance current operations budgets. Bonds are issued to finance state transportation projects, water and sewer facilities, school buildings, and other public assets that at least offer the prospect of boosting economic growth over time. Furthermore, it is likely that borrowing costs for state and local governments would decline, as demand for their securities pushed down interest rates, further expanding the pool of revenues available for public investment activities.

Advocates of paying down the federal debt over the next two decades argue that it would address a significant portion of Social Security's unfunded liability. A 1999 study by four Urban Institute researchers estimated that if the federal government followed a strict debt-reduction policy throughout the first two decades of the twenty-first century, the federal debt would be eliminated by 2016 and the resulting interest savings would cover about two-thirds of the increasing costs of Social Security through 2022. After that point, however, "benefits will continue to grow," requiring that "more must be done to reform the system."[32] Even proponents of debt reduction do not view it as a long-term solution for Social Security's finances. Those who question the debt-relief strategy are even less sanguine. An analysis by the National Center for Policy Analysis found that retiring existing federal debt would leave more "room" for the federal government to borrow when the Social Security trust fund runs out of money. But the resulting obligation would still be astronomical. The payroll tax would have to rise to 20 percent or more by 2050 to cover Social Security benefits.[33]

There are other problems with relying on debt reduction to address Social Security insolvency. For one, there is no guarantee that future Congresses and administrations will stick to a debt-reduction plan lasting the better part of two decades. The pressures to spend federal surpluses on new programs to reward favored constituencies would be great, while few effective lobbies exist for annual debt reductions (groups like the Concord Coalition, despite their good intentions, are simply outgunned). Also, if the goal is to maximize productive investment in the private sector or at lower levels of government, a quicker path than paying down existing federal debt would simply be to invest surplus dollars immediately in the private or state and local capital markets. Paying down low-interest federal treasuries in order to free up money for private investment in the future would be like paying off a low-interest loan today instead of investing in the stock market today, in order to free up money to invest in the stock market tomorrow. Given that the stock market grows at a historical average of 7 percent in after tax, after inflation terms, such an investment strategy would usually prove costly. You would sacrifice a higher rate of return in stocks in order to pay off a lower-rate loan.[34]

Not that reducing the size of the federal debt is a bad idea. Unlike private debt, or even state and local debt, federal debt does not necessarily facilitate the creation of valuable assets. There are good reasons to run federal deficits—winning World War II, for instance. Much of the current debt owes its existence to far less admirable causes, such as the failed "War on Poverty" or the proliferation of wasteful, pork barrel projects. But debt is best measured in percentage terms. Microsoft chairman Bill Gates has personal debts that far exceed my own, yet somehow I doubt that he finds it as challenging to pay his monthly bills. A $250,000.00 mortgage is highly burdensome to a family making $70,000.00 a year, but is of little consequence to someone earning $700,000.00 a year. Similarly, the proper way of measuring federal indebtedness is its share of the economic base from which taxes are raised to finance it. Publicly held debt stood at about 40 percent of gross domestic product in 2000, compared with more than 100 percent during World War II and 50 percent in 1992.[35] The United States can continue to reduce this debt ratio by issuing little or no additional debt, paying off existing debts on time, and focusing on expanding the denominator of the fraction through economic growth.

OPTION 2: REFORM THE TAX CODE. In particular, debt reduction deserves a low priority as long as the current tax code retains its bias against corporate equity, savings, and physical and human capital formation. John Stuart Mill, writing in the nineteenth century, had it right:

> In a country advancing in wealth, whose increasing revenue gives it the power of ridding itself from time to time of the most inconvenient portions of its taxation, I conceive that the increase of revenues should rather be disposed of by taking off taxes than by liquidating debt, as long as any very objectionable imposts remain.[36]

Later chapters of this book examine the impact of the current tax code on such investment activities as building plants and equipment, pursuing an education, training and maintaining a quality workforce, buying a house, building private retirement assets, and rearing healthy and productive children. Simply put, federal taxes either discourage these activities or distort them in inefficient ways. So do the tax systems of most states and localities, taking their lead from the destructive federal income tax and adding their own quirks, such as imposing sales taxes on goods but not on services and using property taxes to fund government programs whose benefits bear little relationship to property ownership in a community.

By remedying these defects of the tax system—and furthermore, by reducing marginal tax rates on income through across-the-board tax cuts—policymakers would create far higher rates of economic growth in the future, thus alleviating some of the financial burdens that entitlement programs like Social Security will impose on future generations. Estimates of the impact of taxes on economic growth rates vary widely, depending on the assumptions and ideological biases of those conducting the studies. Suffice it to say that, as Milton Friedman once wrote, economists may not know much, but they know that if the government sets the price of a product below the market rate, a shortage will result. If the government sets the price above the market rate, a glut will result.[37] If the tax code creates a bias against savings and investment, either through double taxation or sky-high tax rates or both, the economy will suffer from a shortage of productive investment. If the tax code punishes work with high marginal taxes on income, the economy will suffer unemployment and underemployment. Both will lead to lower growth in production and living standards.

History bears this out, as discussed in the previous chapter. Presidents Harding and Coolidge cut income tax rates. The economy grew. Presidents Hoover and Roosevelt, misdiagnosing a depression caused by monetary manipulation, hiked income tax rates. The economy faltered. Kennedy cut the top income tax rate from Roosevelt's 91 percent to 70 percent. Real gross domestic product grew 4.6 percent a year for the next five years, compared with 4.2 percent during the previous five. Reagan's tax cuts, with the top marginal rate falling to 50 percent in 1983 and 28 percent in 1986, fueled a real annual growth rate of 3.5 percent compared to 0.7 percent previously.[38]

OPTION 3: REFORM THE FEDERAL BUDGET. This option receives far less attention than it deserves. As stated earlier, proponents of continued "investment" of Social Security trust funds in federal securities often exhibit very little interest in what the federal government does with these funds. Because all financial assets are claims on future income, the operable question is whether the issuer of a stock or bond is putting its revenues to productive use in developing real capital assets. The federal government is not doing so. It may be possible to change this, at least a little.

For example, if Congress and the president were serious about addressing Social Security's long-term viability, they would excise wasteful federal expenditures that squander federal bond proceeds. They would abolish foreign aid programs. They would aggressively combat Medicare and Medicaid fraud, end special subsidies and loan guarantees for favored constituencies, and eliminate entire departments, such as Commerce and Energy, that serve little useful purpose other than boosting federal employment and giving candidates "goodies" (jobs, contracts, and favors) to promise to aides, donors, and supporters. As currently constituted, however, federal policymakers have few incentives to economize. Whether controlled by Democrats or Republicans, Congress has preserved pork barrel politics. Whether liberal or conservative, presidents have made budget policy on the margins, leaving the departments and agencies of the government largely intact despite the vestigial nature of many of them.

Investor Politics, as described in this book, does not mean an end to government. Far from it. There is such a thing as public investment. Highways, bridges, and other infrastructure can clearly facilitate economic growth, and their maintenance and expansion generate more of it. Public expenditures on education can allow for higher levels of human capital formation and, consequently, higher productivity. Basic functions of government, such as national defense and a well-functioning system of law and courts, are preconditions for productive, long-term private investment. Unfortunately, the federal government does a poor job of many of these functions.

One way to improve its performance would be to reform the federal budget along the lines already adopted by most states and localities. The budget should be divided into three categories: a General Fund representing current operations; a Capital Fund encompassing long-term investments ranging from office buildings to nuclear submarines; and a set of Enterprise Funds, within which self-financed programs, such as airports and other infrastructure, can be operated without user fees being stolen to fund unrelated programs in the federal budget (as currently happens with gasoline taxes). The General Fund, comprising the government's payroll and most welfare and transfer programs, would have to be financed with general tax revenues; it could never run a deficit. The Capital and Enterprise funds, on the other hand, would be financed by a combination of bonds and current revenues. This would allow for long run financing of some federal assets for which the costs should properly be spread across years and generations. Such bond issuances would rarely be more than modest in size, and should in fact be limited by a constitutional amendment that either submits them to public referendum or that caps total debt to a quarter or so of total gross domestic product. As explained in greater detail in the following chapters on physical and human capital, the federal government is rarely the most efficient means of providing needed investment, even of the public sort.

Finally, one or more of the funds in this reformed federal budget would, on occasion, collect more revenues than needed for a given year's expenditures. Under the current practice of "investing" federal surpluses in federal obligations, the money is often squandered. The best way to prevent that would be to require excess funds to be parked in "cash"—one or more deposit accounts or money market mutual funds, selected by competitive bidding. In any event, if the surplus amount exceeded a small percent of a fund's annual budget, say 3 or 4 percent, an immediate tax rebate or user fee reduction would be required until the surplus was eliminated.

OPTION 4: ALLOW GOVERNMENT TO INVEST TRUST FUNDS. Under the budget reform I suggest, the federal government would do a small amount of "banking" with private money managers. But some politicians and policy analysts would go much further. They recognize the limits of "investing" large Social Security surpluses in non-negotiable, low-yielding federal treasury bonds, yet they resist the idea of creating individual accounts in which to invest the funds in private stocks, bonds, and other securities. Instead, they believe that the federal government should do the investing itself.[39] In his 1999 State of the Union Address, President Clinton proposed that one-fifth of Social Security surpluses be invested in private securities offering a higher rate of return.[40]

Henry Aaron and Robert Reischauer, former director of the Congressional Budget Office, made the case for government investment in private securities and against private retirement accounts in a *Washington Post* essay. First, they argued that private accounts, in which workers would exercise choice of investments for their own money, would weaken the "social insurance" aspect of Social Security, by which they mean the redistribution of income inherent in the program. They argue that some would inevitably lack either the earnings or the financial acumen to accumulate significant retirement assets, and would end up reliant on SSI or some other explicitly welfarist program "requiring a demeaning means test." Second, they argue that private stock markets, while offering high rates of return over the long run, contain large gyrations in value. "Market volatility may be an annoyance to the wealthy, but it is potentially catastrophic for the majority of Americans who have few financial assets other than Social Security."[41]

These first two objections are easily dismissed. If a public assistance program is desired for those who earn little during their working years or invest their savings poorly, then by all means it should be explicitly redistributive and labeled as such. I would wager that virtually no one outside the community of Social Security analysts and policy wonks understands the redistributive nature of the program, hidden as it is in the income replacement rates. Aaron and Reischauer seem to be suggesting that continued public confusion about this issue is a good thing. Advocates of true self-government must disagree.

Second, there are, admittedly, periods of declining stock market returns. For them to decimate a worker's retirement funds, however, three things would have to occur. First, the decline would have to happen just before a worker's retirement. Second, that aging worker approaching retirement would have to have a significant portion of his assets in stocks, even though any money manager worth his or her salt would be recommending a shift to bonds and cash to protect past gains in anticipation of withdrawals. (The design of a privatized Social Security system might seek to prevent these two factors from converging by setting diversification and asset allocation guidelines based on age). Third, the market decline would have to be significant enough to erase previous gains. This is unlikely. As analyst Peter Ferrara points out, even at a rate of return on stocks of half the historical rate, Social Security recipients would receive two or three times what the program currently promises, but cannot pay.[42] Overall, one study found that even a decline, starting on the date of retirement, equal to the worst quarter in the stock market's history, would still give virtually all depositors greater returns than Social Security can provide.[43]

Also, in every privatization plan I have seen, a means-tested minimum benefit for the elderly poor is always included, presumably replacing and expanding the current SSI program. The risk of a lengthy downtime in the stock market and the economy at large is a given in any retirement program, government-controlled or not. The revenues required to pay benefits must still be taxed from current workers. If the economy tanks, leading to business losses and unemployment, these revenues will slacken. With Americans investing their own money, rather than expecting the federal government to do it for them, they will have huge incentives to make sure that their political leaders avoid fiscal or regulatory mistakes that damage economic growth. The necessary relationship between a healthy economy and the value of retirement savings is a strength, not a weakness, of a personalized system.

Finally, Aaron and Reischauer make a somewhat more persuasive argument:

> If Social Security . . . was freed to invest in private assets, it would earn even higher returns than the average private account. The reason for this is straightforward: Brokerage fees for buying and selling stocks and bonds and for sales and management fees charged by mutual funds chomp away at the return from private accounts. On average, these expenses are likely to take 1 percent to 2 percent out of accounts' balances each year before retirement. Such charges would reduce, by 20 percent to 40 percent, the amounts the workers would ultimately accumulate in their accounts. If Social Security hired private managers to invest its large reserves in private assets, the costs would be negligible, less than one-hundredth of a percent of the funds under management each year—leaving more of the total return to support pensions.[44]

Based on their assumptions, the authors are making a valid point about the impact of administrative expenses on private account returns. Even so, the extra expense might be worth it. The risk of federal ownership of private assets through direct Social Security investment were concisely summarized by Senator Vandenberg's reaction to the idea as posed by Altmeyer: "That would be socialism." Advocates of the idea claim that, through competitive bidding and profit-maximization rules, a federally run system could promote private investment of trust funds without inviting direct government control of private industry. Such a benign result would fly in the face of experience and common sense. Over time, the Social Security trust fund could have several trillion dollars in the capital markets. Politicians would find it next to impossible to resist playing politics with such a large stake in the private economy. They could reward individual companies or entire sectors that followed "social responsibility" rules such as paying union-level wages, providing health insurance, meeting racial hiring quotas, or adopting "green" production processes.

Many state pension plans already sacrifice return for social or political objectives. They favor in-state companies, avoid investments in "socially irresponsible" companies or those located in undesirable foreign countries, and impose cultural or ideological standards. In 1998, a Texas education pension fund disinvested in Disney based on complaints from a pro-family lobby. That same year, New York yanked its pension fund's 11 million shares of tobacco company stocks. In 1993, the pension fund of Kansas lost $185 million after lawmakers steered pension assets into a failed scheme to promote state economic development. Missouri, Pennsylvania, and Connecticut have experienced similar failure with so-called "economically targeted investments" in their state economies while Illinois, New York, and California raised their pension plans to balance their government budgets.[45] Harvard University economist Martin Feldstein warns that, regardless of their promises now, politicians simply could not be trusted to invest Social Security dollars free from bureaucratic bungling and politics.[46]

As someone who has viewed the machinations of pension politics up close at the state level, I would agree. Some states, like my own, have avoided most of the pitfalls of political investing, but only because of the stubborn resistance of a handful of politicians. It is doubtful that the electoral system can consistently generate such leadership. Federal Reserve Chairman Alan Greenspan certainly seems to agree. In January 2001 testimony before a Senate committee, he remarked that allowing Washington to acquire private stocks and bonds would pose significant risks. "The federal government should eschew private asset accumulation because it would be exceptionally difficult to insulate the government's investment decisions from political pressures," he told the senators.[47]

In any event, Aaron and Reischauer are basing their argument on what are probably invalid assumptions. Far from taking 1 to 2 percent of account balances a year, private managers of individual retirement accounts would likely consume between 0.2 and 0.5 percent of assets a year. One Standard and Poor's (S&P) 500 Index fund run by Vanguard cost 0.19 percent of assets in 1998. The average administrative cost of such funds was 0.38 percent. Even adding in the cost of collecting worker contributions and routing them to their selected funds (costing, in current defined-contribution plans in the private sector, about 0.17 percent of assets), the total administrative costs of a personalized Social Security system would likely start out small—

say, one-half of one percent—and then shrink over time as experience and technology suggested greater efficiencies.[48] William Shipman, both a published author on Social Security and the head of a private investment company, estimates that a private system could be administered by between 0.10 and 0.35 percent, depending on how aggressively the private system were phased in.[49] David John of the Heritage Foundation puts these numbers in perspective by observing that a simple personal retirement account plan would probably cost no more than $7.00 a year annually. "Many people pay more than that each month for just a checking account," he writes.[50]

The option of direct federal investment of Social Security funds is a flawed one. It does, however, reflect an Investor Politics mindset. It grants that Social Security and other government entitlements are, ultimately, unsustainable as secure and successful guarantors of the public welfare without a means of increasing productive private investment.

OPTION 5: CONVERT SOCIAL SECURITY INTO PRIVATE, MANDATORY SAVING. As should now be obvious, this option forms the core of a realistic Social Security reform strategy. There are a variety of such plans on the table, carefully designed by analysts with far more knowledge and expertise than I have and published by such think tanks as the Cato Institute, the Heritage Foundation, and the National Center for Policy Analysis. In 1996, the idea got a major boost when a majority of the members of an advisory council on Social Security appointed by the Clinton administration endorsed one of two versions of the idea of personal accounts.[51] Readers interested in comparing and contrasting different models should visit the web sites of these and other groups advocating privatization, starting with SocialSecurity.org (Cato's informative site). For the purposes of clarifying the major issues involved, let me summarize perhaps the most far-reaching of the reform proposals, penned by Peter Ferrara and Michael Tanner for Cato:[52]

• Current beneficiaries and those about to retire would see no changes in their Social Security benefits.
• Workers would be given the choice of whether to stay in the current Social Security program or to opt for a new private system. For those choosing the latter, the worker and his or her employer would each deposit 5 percent of the worker's wages into an individual account owned by the

worker. Because the current combined payroll tax rate is 12.4 percent, this would leave 2.4 percent of income to help pay for Social Security benefits already promised to current beneficiaries.

• The choice of investments and account managers would be constrained by federal regulations but would include a variety of institutions, investments, and account designs.

• Participants in the private system would be required to purchase private long-term disability insurance and life insurance meeting minimum federal standards.

• At retirement, workers could convert their accumulated assets into annuities or take periodic withdrawals, preserving the balance of their accounts for their heirs.

• The federal government would retain a minimum-benefit system, modeled on SSI and funded from general revenues rather than from payroll taxes. Retirees whose low earnings or poor decisions left them with insufficient private savings to buy an annuity worth the minimum necessary to avoid poverty would receive supplemental federal funds with which to purchase such an annuity.

• Workers opting into the private system after years of paying into Social Security would receive "recognition bonds" equal to their previous contributions. These would be placed in their private accounts and redeemed upon retirement.

• The costs of transition to the new, private retirement system reflect the unfunded liability of Social Security, and are thus not new. It is inevitable that the federal government will have to pay benefits to current retirees while allowing workers to accumulate private assets with most of their payroll taxes. These costs can best be borne by selling unneeded government assets, reducing other government spending, or spreading them over the generations through additional bond issuances.

CONCLUSION

Other plans phase in personal investment more slowly or finance transition costs differently. My own view is that a more gradual approach, beginning with only a few percentage points of the payroll tax, is more likely to be enacted than is Cato's purer approach. I also think it does not much matter how small the initial private stake is. Once the system begins, and workers get a taste of owning and managing their own accounts, a new interest group will be created. Workers with private Social Security accounts will lobby for expansion. As discussed in the final chapter of this book, investors already represent a large and growing voting bloc. They have clearly discernible views about a variety of related economic issues, but their highest priority is likely to be the continued growth and safety of their private investments. The dynamics of Investor Politics will kick in. The politicians will be stunned.

A little noted advantage of a privatized system like Cato recommends is that it will significantly improve the disability and survivor components of Social Security. SSDI is pretty good at paying benefits—although its generosity and inability to police fraud has led it to bankruptcy even more quickly than the retirement system[53]—but it is lousy at getting the disabled back to work. Only about 1 in 500 SSDI beneficiaries return to work each year, and not because the caseload is too old, infirm, or uninterested in work. During its period of most rapid growth, between 1985 and 1995, disability benefits grew by 75 percent in real terms and the caseload grew from 4 million to 6.6 million, with the growth disproportionately among younger and less-severely disabled workers. One in three SSDI recipients is under the age of forty, and 35 percent expressed interest in returning to work in a 1993 study by the Social Security Administration.[54]

There are good reasons to believe that privatization will increase the job placement rate significantly above the current system's miniscule level. Disability insurers in the private sector are far more aggressive in assessing claimants' ability to work, linking them up with rehabilitation and job placement services early in the process so they do not become dependent on monthly benefit checks.[55] They have strong incentives to encourage self-reliance, which also happens to be the long-run interest of recipients. If privatization of disability insurance is included in Social Security reform, it will have positive effects on the quality of life of the disabled and likely be significantly less expensive as a result of more job placements and less fraud, thus boosting the rate of return of the private retirement accounts.

Similarly, the survivor benefits from Social Security are paltry compared with alternatives available from life insurers. Requiring the purchase of term insurance for young workers with dependents, income splitting between spouses in savings account deposits, and the ease of inheriting account balances will give most Americans coverage equal to, and in most cases exceeding, the current system. The experience of three Texas counties that opted out of the Social Security system in the early 1980s, before that loophole was closed, is illustrative. Their employees receive a life insurance benefit worth three times salary (capped at $150,000.00).[56] In Chile, survivor benefits in its privatized Social Security system are 50 percent higher than under the country's previous government system.[57]

One final issue deserves attention. Remember that the only way that future workers can afford to sustain the living standards of future retirees, given the fact that by 2030 there will be only two workers for every retiree, is for them to have more physical and human capital with which to increase productivity. Making sure no one gets a smaller piece of pie, and indeed that most get more pie than their parents and grandparents ate, means *baking a bigger pie.* No other solution is possible—unless we raise taxes, reduce benefits, or both. Would Social Security privatization increase productive investment? Some say no. They make at least three arguments. First, if money currently collected as payroll taxes and deposited in the Social Security trust fund were instead diverted to private accounts, the federal government would need to borrow an equivalent amount to maintain current non-Social Security spending. The result would be no net gain in private investment.[58] This scenario begs the obvious question: Why maintain current non-Social Security spending? If preserving retirement security for today's workers is such a high priority, surely it is worth doing even at the expense of current, wasteful federal expenditures. Furthermore, the objection is irrelevant if the balanced budgets achieved at the turn of the twenty-first century are maintained. They were balanced even if the Social Security trust fund had not existed.

Secondly, some critics charge that as Social Security funds move into the stock market, equity prices would rise in the short run but the return on those assets would be reduced in the future. Furthermore, a shift from bonds into stocks would drive down the price of bonds and raise interest rates, thus leaving the total amount of capital in the economy little changed.[59] These forecasts exaggerate the magnitude of the new funds flowing into the market. While large in absolute terms, daily Social Security collections routed into the stock market would represent only a small percentage, 6 percent or less, of current market volume. Over time, this number would shrink further as wealth generated by previous investment of retirement savings was reinvested.[60]

The third argument is that if workers opt for mandatory private savings and begin accruing significant balances in their accounts, they will feel less of a need to ensure their retirement security and reduce voluntary savings by a similar amount, resulting in little or no net increase in private investment. A variant of the argument is that an increase in the value of privately held savings will result in higher consumer borrowing, thus offsetting gross savings and limiting the real increase in net private investment.[61] This is Keynes' old idea of the lack of connection between savings and investment. Savings, the theory goes, is motivated by concern about the future. A worker's propensity to save is determined by how much he perceives he will need to tide him over during a future spell of joblessness, disability, or retirement. It is not motivated by the potential rate of return of the investment financed by his savings. Therefore, when times are good, he will tend not to save as much as may be needed for productive investment. Indeed, if by receiving higher investment returns from a growing economy he increases the total value of his savings, he may reduce future savings in favor of current consumption.

Martin Feldstein has written extensively about these issues, especially since the Congressional Budget Office in 1998 accused his version of Social Security privatization of failing to increase net private savings and investment, the economic benefits of which Feldstein and other proponents count on to help finance the transition to personal accounts. Feldstein points out that few workers currently have much voluntary savings other than their homes, which most will continue to buy regardless of how much their savings accounts grow. So there is not much room for workers to offset mandatory savings with reduced voluntary savings.[62] Feldstein predicts that the present value of the economic gains from increased net private savings could be as high as $10 trillion over a seventy-five-year period.[63] Other analysts agree with him. Boston University's Laurence Kotlikoff estimates that privatization could add 0.5 percentage points a year to the gross domestic product, a big gain to a rate that averaged 2.3 percent for much of the 1990s.[64] In 1996, the National Taxpayers Union Foundation conducted a study concluding that Social Security privatization would boost the savings rate by 2.6 percent of the gross domestic product.[65] Testing a similar proposition about the impact of expanded IRA accounts on the propensity to save, researchers from Harvard, Dartmouth, and Massachusetts Institute of Technology analyzed data for families contributing to IRAs after participation rules were expanded in 1981. The data show that the increase in IRA saving far outweighed decreases in savings in non-IRA assets for these families. Higher real rates of return (from reduced double taxation of savings) motivated these families to save more, not less.[66]

More generally, this argument about net private savings reflects Keynesian suppositions about the behavior of savers and investors that have long been challenged by free-market economists of the Austrian, Chicago, and supply-side schools of thought, who argue that interest rates do affect the decisions of individuals to consume or save. Their views are validated by the explosion of personal investment described in chapter 3, the result of technological and organizational changes that have made it easy for average people to access financial markets. They are also validated by the actual behavior of workers in Chile, Australia, and Singapore—all countries that have private, mandatory savings for retirement. All three countries have seen large increases in net savings, not decreases. After Chile privatized its Social Security system in the early 1980s, the savings rate rose 150 percent. Singapore has the highest personal savings rate in the world.[67]

Still, it is fair to say that the magnitude of the increase in net private savings and investment from Social Security is difficult to predict. Some people will undoubtedly do as the critics predict—end their annual IRA contributions or borrow more as their Social Security accounts begin to grow. Such behavior need not be widespread, however, nor is it inevitable. The fact is that, by building a comprehensive set of entitlements and punitive tax policies since 1935, the federal government has fought a long and somewhat successful war against the natural human impulse to save. Americans are under the impression that the government has provided not just for their retirement but also for their future nonretirement needs, such as medical care, disability, housing, and the education of their children. As subsequent chapters will show, these promises will soon be exposed as empty. With the proper mix of tax and entitlement reforms, Americans will increase their savings in these areas as well, more than offsetting any "wealth effect" from Social Security privatization that would otherwise shrink the nation's pool of voluntary savings.

CHAPTER 6

THE NEW
HEALTH-CARE
IMPERATIVE

W HAT SENATOR ARTHUR VANDENBERG WAS TO the early Social Security program, Representative Wilbur Mills, a Democrat from Arkansas, was to the birth of Medicare—an able critic but a poor legislative strategist. For much of the 1950s and 1960s, the powerful Mills, who headed the House Ways and Means Committee, viewed proposals for national health insurance with great skepticism, appearing on several occasions to embrace the American Medical Association's position that government insurance would lead to socialized medicine. In 1964, a year before the creation of Medicare, he warned that hospital costs were already increasing at a rate of 6.7 percent a year, compared with 4 percent growth in average earnings. Such a trend, if continued, would force the system to continue to raise taxes to keep up with claims. "Clearly," he said, "this would be the case of the tail wagging the dog." Wilbur Cohen, a longtime Social Security official and one of the architects of the 1965 Medicare legislation, observed that Mills was "probably the only man out of the 535 people in Congress who completely [understood] the actuarial basis of Social Security."[1]

In one of history's great ironies, it was Mills' own House Ways and Means Committee that fashioned the Social Security amendments of 1965 creating Medicare and, in an afterthought, Medicaid. Apparently motivated by huge Democratic gains in 1964 and the belief that precautions in the bill would prevent his worst fears from being realized, Mills helped create a set of health-care entitlements that, in the first two decades of the twenty-first century, imperil the federal government's finances to a far greater extent than does Social Security and has subjected most of America's health-care expenditures to federal finance and regulation. "Although people justifiably worry about Social Security," said Stanford University researcher Victor Fuchs in 1998, "paying for old folks' health care is the real eight-hundred-pound gorilla facing the economy."[2]

HEALTHCARE GROWS UP

The story of Medicare is but the climax of a longer story, stretching back across the twentieth century, of the constant efforts of Populists, Progressives, and other advocates of national health-care insurance to overcome the natural tendency of lawmakers, lobbies, and the American people to recoil from the idea. As with other elements of the welfare state, the medical entitlement was advanced in fits and starts, in some cases seeming to benefit from political accidents more than persuasive argument or popular groundswells.

The concept of health insurance was itself a twentieth century creation. The practice of medicine predates the period, of course, but its ability to provide useful treatments for serious or life-threatening ailments was limited. To the extent that people availed themselves of the services of doctors and other medical providers, they paid with cash, bartered, or "ran a tab." Around the turn of the century, however, medical care began to take some giant leaps forward. It was a period of invention and scientific progress across the board. In health, advances in anatomical understanding as well as pharmaceuticals led to new treatments for many illnesses. Not only were doctors now able to successfully treat far more conditions than before, but there were also other health care services available to consumers. With the advent of antiseptics and aseptic practices in the latter nineteenth century, for example, hospitals transformed themselves from asylums and hospices for the disabled or terminally ill, respectively, into places of healing. "Americans began to view hospitals not as places to die," writes economist and medical historian Terree Wasley, "but as facilities for meeting the health needs of the public."[3]

The two world wars also served as catalyzing events for medical breakthroughs. World War I sparked the invention of a variety of drugs, including aspirin. World War II created the modern practice of employer-based health insurance. The idea predated the war. Large railroad and mining companies were the first to experiment with "company doctors," group health plans for employees, and contractual relationships with hospitals and physician groups in the early twentieth century. These industries had high accident rates, so it paid for companies to invest in medical prevention and to keep providers on contract to assure workers of timely care. These companies also had many employees deployed in remote locations, further increasing the need for the employer to make sure health care was available. Another source of early innovation in health insurance came from the so-called "fraternal orders" and "benefits societies" that arose in the late nineteenth century to provide life insurance, disability aid, and other benefits to their members. Based around churches, lodges, or ethnic groups, these organizations began the practice of employing doctors to examine prospective members so that accurate prices could be charged for life insurance. Later, fraternal orders engaged their services to treat existing members on contract.[4]

By 1930, most of the elements of the health-care marketplace as we now know it were in place. Many large employers had some kind of group health insurance, though the number of American workers enrolled was still miniscule. The Great Depression stimulated further variations on the theme. Shaky finances led hospitals to attempt to lock in steady business by contracting with employer groups to provide care. In 1932, several hospitals in the Sacramento, California, area formed a community-wide health plan. Subscribers paid premiums to the plan, rather than to individual providers, and received insurance coverage not just for unforeseen catastrophic illnesses but also for routine services provided in hospital clinics. Other struggling hospitals quickly adopted similar arrangements, which became known as Blue Cross plans and were organized as nonprofits. Commercial insurers followed their lead, charging prices for coverage based on age and health differences (as life insurance was and is priced). They also added coverage of doctor bills to the mix. In response, doctors formed their own nonprofit plans, analogous to the hospitals' Blue Cross plans, which became know as Blue Shield plans.[5]

As the 1930s continued, these new health insurers began to jockey for position in state legislatures (Congress was not yet in the picture). Lobbies for physicians and hospitals were already among the most powerful interest groups in state capitals, the former successfully excluding all but members of the American Medical Association and its state affiliates from the practice of medicine. Now the competitive threat from commercial health insurers cried out for action. State insurance commissioners had earlier expressed interest in applying reserve requirements and other regulations to health insurers, whose parent companies were frequently already subject to such regulations on their life insurance products. Doctors and hospital officials, who dominated the boards of Blue Cross and Blue Shield plans, convinced state lawmakers to impose these regulations on commercial insurers—but to exempt nonprofit plans. They also secured exemptions from income, premium, and property taxes. In exchange, the Blues pledged to provide insurance to anyone who wanted it and to subsidize premiums for those with low incomes or serious medical conditions.

Not surprisingly, the Blues gained and maintained a sizable market share from these cozy arrangements, which benefited not only the employees of the plans but the doctors and the hospitals that controlled them. Why? Because of the way the Blues ran their payment systems. Most for-profit insurance companies took claims from their members and sent them reimbursement checks. It was a familiar model. Commercial insurers already paid automobile owners after receiving and examining repair bills. They paid life insurance beneficiaries directly, rather than the creditors of the deceased to whom much of the money would eventually go. But the Blues did things differently. They made direct payments to hospitals and physicians for services rendered. Patients rarely received checks themselves, and often did not see complete bills for the services they consumed. The result of this "third-party payment" system was inevitably a higher rate of consumption of medical services. "Hospitals approved of those procedures," Wasley writes, "and because of the domination of the market by the Blues, other commercial insurers were forced to adopt the same policies to remain competitive."[6] Once health insurance became widespread, this "cost-plus" reimbursement system was to contribute to a huge increase in health-care spending up until the present day.

THE HEALTH INSURANCE EXPLOSION

For all the early glimmers of activity in health insurance, only a tiny percentage of Americans had any form of health insurance in 1940, and the share of total medical bills paid by insurance was but a sliver. World War II changed all that. Widespread employer-based health insurance was the accidental side effect of two factors: wartime controls on wages and prices as well as changing definitions of "income" at the Internal Revenue Service. Federal caps on wages made it difficult for employers to compete effectively for scarce workers. Business owners, particularly in industries producing arms and materiel, began to think of creative ways around the controls in order to attract sufficient labor. They found the answer in non-wage benefits paid to workers in lieu of cash salary increases. In 1942, the War Labor Board decided that fringe benefits up to 5 percent of wages would not be considered inflationary and thus would be exempt from their price controls.[7] Shortly thereafter, the Internal Revenue Service declared that fringe benefits were a legitimate cost of doing business, rather than a form of compensation analogous to salary, and would thus be exempt from taxation.[8]

Not surprisingly, these two decisions had a tremendous impact on the health-care market. While the Blues and other insurers had slowly been gaining a foothold, most Americans in the early 1940s still paid for health care with their own wages, savings, or installment debt. But from 1942 to 1945, enrollment in group hospital plans grew from 7 million to 26 million subscribers. After the war, the dynamics of continued high levels of taxation and collective bargaining by unions seeking to capitalize on the special status of employee benefits led to further growth in health insurance as a form of compensation. By 1956, about 70 percent of the population of the United States had some type of hospital insurance and more than half had insurance for some physician charges, compared with less than 10 percent enrolled in hospital insurance and virtually no one with physician coverage in 1940.[9] This number continued to grow during the next four decades, though not nearly as rapidly.

Another way to measure the trend is the extent to which insurance began to supplant the old ways of paying doctors and hospitals. As late as 1948, even as hospital insurance was growing rapidly, patients and their families still paid about 95 percent of all medical bills. By 1956, insurance was paying nearly a quarter of medical bills.[10] With the advent of Medicare and Medicaid in 1965, and continued growth in the coverage of employer-provided insurance, the trend lines reversed. By 1990, only a quarter of medical bills were paid by patients, with the rate of third-party payment for hospital charges reaching 95 percent.[11]

The impact of third-party payment on the provision of goods and services has long been understood by economists. It increases consumption. People who do not perceive the direct cost of buying something often buy more of it, either in quantity or in quality. Travelers, for example, who are paying their own way, are usually far more frugal in their selection of rental cars, airline tickets, and hotel rooms than those on an expense account. For health insurance, a common analogy involves automobile insurance. Required for most drivers, it typically pays for repair costs in the case of major accidents. It does not pay for routine maintenance, such as getting an oil change or rotating the tires. Nor does it offer drivers a "gasoline benefit" to cover the cost of filling the tank. Consequently, drivers tend to be very sensitive to price when shopping for gas or routine services.

The impact of third-party payment on health-care consumption has been dramatic. By the late 1990s, medical expenditures accounted for about 15 percent of the gross domestic product, up from 4 percent in 1940 and 6 percent in 1965.[12] Some of this increase would have happened anyway. For one thing, the growth of knowledge, skilled providers, and treatments made medicine more valuable for both investment and consumption. As discussed below, health care services such as immunizations, checkups, and preventive care are one means of building and maintaining human capital. With the creation of "miracle drugs" for polio and other childhood diseases, incentives for families to devote more resources to their children's long-term health multiplied. Ditto for employers, whose interest in healthy, long-lived employees was heightened by a shift in the economy toward service and knowledge industries. On the consumption side, health care will tend to grow at the expense of other goods. As economies develop and family incomes grow, the percentage spent on bare necessities such as food, clothing, and shelter is bound to shrink. Once basic needs are met, increasingly affluent people will seek other areas in which to improve their standard of living. Health care is a particularly enticing place to spend extra dollars. Who would not want to live a longer, more active life with less pain? Who would begrudge his or her child the constant attention of skillful medical professionals, or elderly parents the latest drugs and devices to alleviate chronic illnesses?

The use of insurance to pay routine, small-dollar medical bills is an important reason why health care costs have risen so rapidly. Furthermore, the current structure of health insurance—obtained either from one's employer or from the government—is not the result of some evolutionary process. It is a social norm propped up by huge government expenditures and regulations. In fiscal year 2000, federal and state tax breaks for the purchase of health insurance totaled about $136 billion, or nearly 40 percent of total health plan premiums paid. Direct government expenditures for Medicare, Medicaid, and other health entitlements added up to $443 billion—about 53 percent of total health care expenditures in 2000.[13] The health insurance entitlement, including both government spending and tax breaks, is far larger than the Social Security entitlement, and more immediately imperiled by rapid growth, shaky finances, and promises that cannot be met.

CREATING AN ENTITLEMENT, STEP BY STEP

As we have seen, turn-of-the-century Progressives and Populists had already included access to health care as one of the rights they believed government should guarantee. As with other welfare benefits, many advocates were inspired by developments abroad. Otto von Bismarck's 1883 social insurance program for Germany had included a health benefit, rapidly emulated by other nations. Great Britain created its compulsory national health program in 1911. In 1906, American activists formed the American Association for Labor Legislation to lobby for a variety of welfare measures. One of their key priorities was a national health program. During the 1910s, they attracted a variety of Progressive and other politicians to the cause.[14]

Congress rebuffed their first attempt at federal legislation on health care during World War I. During the 1920s, Progressives had better luck in state capitals than in Washington, but the Depression changed the political calculus. In 1934, when Roosevelt appointed his Committee on Economic Security to fashion social welfare legislation, advocates saw an opportunity to add health benefits to the mix. The Committee's final report heightened the hopes of advocates within the administration even more (while alarming no one outside the administration, since the report was kept secret). "A health insurance plan will be forthcoming," the report promised, with the president's approval. But Social Security proved more difficult to enact than initially expected. The administration saw national health insurance as too controversial to include in the 1935 Social Security Act, so the idea was tabled. Even an early version of the bill, establishing a "Social Insurance Board" and authorizing it to study proposals for health benefits, mutated into a provision creating a "Social Security Board" and making no mention of health.[15]

The absence of statutory authority did not worry the national health insurance lobby at all. In 1937, the administration formed a "Technical Committee on Medical Care." Its members ultimately developed a report stating that "it would be desirable to formulate a comprehensive National Health Program," including health insurance funded via general revenues or payroll taxes, direct federal support for hospitals, disability insurance, and federal support for public health and medical assistance programs run by states.[16] Each of these elements of the Roosevelt administration's "National Health Program" was accomplished, in one form or another, within thirty years.

As we have seen, the 1940s was the decade that widespread health insurance was born. Advocates of national health insurance welcomed the trend, but saw private provision of insurance as only a transitional phase. Beginning in 1943, a series of bills named for Senator Robert Wagner, Senator James Murray, and Representative John Dingell were introduced to create compulsory national health insurance for all workers and their dependents. The bills had been drafted by the Social Security Board, and were subsequently introduced again and again. Harry Truman flirted with the idea of aggressively pursuing their passage, but recoiled once he realized the extent of political opposition. It was sizable. The American Medical Association was implacably against the idea. So was the American public. A *Fortune* poll in 1942 found that 76 percent of voters said the government should not provide free medical care.[17]

By the early 1950s, activists within and outside government made a fateful change in strategy. Direct advocacy of national health insurance had failed. Many of its proponents in Congress had lost reelection in 1950, and the overall Republican trend did not bode well. A gradual approach, granting the legitimacy of a private (but increasingly regulated) insurance market, would have a better chance. They settled on the idea of limiting their national health proposals to the aged and infirm, believing that the public would view them as more appropriate beneficiaries of government largesse than workers. Once national health care for the elderly and disabled had taken root, activists could push for expansion to broader and broader segments of the population. Led by future Health, Education, and Welfare Secretary Wilbur Cohen and others, they recrafted their proposals. The first success was in 1956, when Congress and the Eisenhower administration agreed to add disability benefits to the Social Security package. As a Brookings Institution analysis later observed, advocates viewed SSDI as "a necessary prelude" to the passage of Medicare. "Incremental change . . . has less potential for generating conflict than change that involves innovation in principle," the report argued. Social Security executives, "even when undertaking an innovation in principle, tried to cut and clothe it in a fashion that made it seem merely incremental."[18]

The next step was to create comprehensive health insurance for retirees. Labor union officials, together with officials of Social Security and other agencies, crafted a bill that, after two years of deliberations, was rejected by the House in 1959. Here is where Wilbur Mills, the colorful congressman from Arkansas, enters the story. Mills and other opponents of national health insurance believed that, despite its initial defeat, the new retiree-insurance bill had a good chance of passage. Pictures of destitute seniors, suffering from serious ailments and lacking any hospital insurance, were worth far more than a thousand words about "socialized medicine." States already had small-scale programs to assist the aged or disabled needy with chronic conditions. Mills and his ally in the senate, Oklahoma Democrat Robert Kerr, fashioned a bill to create a new federal program, called Medical Assistance for the Aged, to provide support for state relief efforts. Congress passed the Kerr-Mills bill in 1960.[19]

PRELUDE TO MEDICARE

The Kerr-Mills strategy failed. Such attempts to "co-opt" a movement by giving it small victories often fail, because they ignore the extent to which small victories create "rising expectations" on the part of movement sup-porters. If the growing public sentiment for national health-care programs had been due merely to sympathy for the elderly poor, Wilbur Mills might have proven right in his judgment. But the real source of political momen-tum for Medicare was the apparent success of Social Security, in which al-most everyone was a participant. Once the idea dawned that Washington might be a good steward of Americans' retirement funds, the leap from So-cial Security to Medicare was not really that large. It seemed an expansion of a proven model, not the radical departure that Mills, the American Med-ical Association, and other critics had long alleged.

During the early 1960s, the push for comprehensive old-age health in-surance strengthened at the federal level. What developed were the con-tours of a debate that continues to this day. On the one side were the ideo-logical heirs of Roosevelt's Committee on Economic Security, who had proposed that health benefits be part of the original social insurance sys-tem. Democrats Cecil King of California in the House and Clinton Ander-son of New Mexico in the Senate began to introduce bills in 1961 to create a compulsory health insurance plan for the elderly to be run by the federal government. The other side, recognizing the political appeal of retiree health care, fashioned a bill that compelled individuals to purchase health insurance for old age but allowed a choice of competing private plans. Sen-ator Jacob Javitts of New York introduced a version of the idea in 1962 (6).

It was the election of 1964, thirty years after Roosevelt's aides first pitched the notion, that created Medicare's window of opportunity. Barry Goldwater and the Republicans got creamed. Armed with a huge electorate vote and large majorities in Congress, President Lyndon Johnson embarked on his Great Society agenda, of which Medicare was a linchpin. Three decades of steady advocacy and Social Security expansion had also paved the way. A January 1965 Gallup poll by found that 63 percent of responding Americans favored a "compulsory medical insurance program covering hospital and nursing home care for the elderly . . . financed out of increased Social Security taxes" (7).

Even this reservoir of public sentiment and Johnson's legislative majori-ties did not guarantee passage. A sizable contingent in Congress, including Republicans and centrist Democrats, resisted the core notion of a federal monopoly on retiree health insurance. Part of the problem was indeed the continued political power of the American Medical Association, still warning about the dangers of Washington dictating the terms of the health-care marketplace. However, it is simplistic to view the opposition as nothing more than a manifestation of a special interest group. Many lawmakers were convinced that the nation's doctors were right, that lodging too much power in a federal insurance program would lead first to exploding costs, then to federal rules to contain costs that would have a ripple effect throughout the market. In 1964, Dr. Norman Welch, new chairman of the American Medical Association, testified that "it is axiomatic . . . that control follows money when the government steps in." Representative Thomas Curtis, a Republican from Missouri, echoed Welch's insight, complaining that the 1965 bill creating Medicare would put Washington "into the business of making final determinations as to whether these charges are reasonable and whether these services are the kinds that are to be covered" (10).

The opposition coalesced around two legislative alternatives to the reintroduced King-Anderson bill, which a reporter had dubbed "Medicare." Representative John W. Byrnes of Wisconsin, the senior Republican on the Ways and Means Committee chaired by Mills, introduced a bill that became known as "Better-care." It set up a voluntary health insurance system for seniors, covering both hospital and physician charges and funded by a combination of premiums and general tax revenues. Another bill focused attention once again on the problem of the elderly poor. Missouri's Curtis, along with Democratic Representative Albert Herlong of Florida and the American Medical Association, fashioned "Elder-care" to strengthen the Kerr-Mills program that helped states with medical expenses and long-term care for poor retirees. Elder-care attracted attention because of its supporters' shrewd observation that Medicare, for all the rhetoric about poor seniors being "bankrupted" by lengthy hospitalizations and chronic illnesses, actually did nothing about the problem, since it was limited to short-term hospital stays. An exchange during a Senate Finance Committee hearing between Health, Education, and Welfare Secretary Anthony Celebrezze and Chairman Russell Long of Louisiana made the point well. Asked why Medicare ignored catastrophic illnesses, Celebrezze replied that it was "not intended for those that are going to stay in institutions year-in and year-out." Long was incredulous. "Well, in arguing for your plan," he said, "you say let's not strip poor old grandma of the last dress she has and of her home and what little resources she has and you bring us a plan that does exactly that unless she gets well in 60 days" (7).

Despite three decades of spadework by both government insiders (Social Security administrators) and outsiders, Medicare remained vulnerable. Its proponents realized that, so the bill was carefully designed to minimize risk, obscure the program's finances and benefits, and take full advantage of the Social Security connection. First, the 1965 version of the bill was introduced not as a stand-alone measure but as part of the "Social Security Amendments of 1965." The package included an across-the-board 7 percent increase in Social Security benefits and loosened eligibility rules for disability benefits. In fact, Congress had declined to sweeten Social Security benefits the previous year, as originally planned. "The amendments to the old-age, survivors, and disability insurance sections of this bill could have been passed last fall," observed Representative Byrnes in 1965, "if the word had not come down, and the insistence made that, 'Oh, no, you have to tie all of these together because of the fear that the medical part of this program could not stand on its own merits'" (13).

Medicare supporters also used the same technique that Social Security creators had used to suggest to Americans that the program was not a welfare system but a method of prepaying for benefits. It was to be funded by a payroll tax, split between employer and employee like Social Security. The tax rate was set low, with additional tax hikes to be phased in over several years—not by visible rate increases but by nearly invisible increases in the taxable wage base. As Charlotte Twight, a political scientist and author of an excellent article on Medicare's history in *The Cato Journal,* observed, "people were told that during their working years they would be paying for 'insurance' to defray the costs of illnesses in their old age," and indeed were assured that the new payroll taxes were an "opportunity" to make "contributions" to their own retiree health care. When pressed in congressional testimony, Johnson administration officials admitted that the program was set up as a "pay-as-you-go" system, not as a prepaid insurance model. One official granted that "the use of the term 'paid-up insurance' by the proponents tends to be misleading and creates false impressions that individual equity is present." Still, the official line, parroted by Celebrezze, was that with Medicare, "people can contribute during their productive years toward the hospital insurance that they will need in later years" (12).

THE "THREE-LAYER CAKE"

The House Ways and Means Committee, headed by Wilbur Mills, was the stage on which the Medicare and Medicaid dramas were to play out. After the 1964 elections, Democratic leaders reorganized the committee to ensure two Democrats for every one Republican, thus weakening support for the Better-care and Elder-care alternatives. Mills, nursing his deep skepticism about Medicare but seeking to steer the process rather than simply to obstruct it, decided to hold much of the committee's 1965 deliberations in closed, executive session and limited the testimony of experts to mostly technical issues rather than to broad policy issues. Finally, Mills decided to invite executives from the Blue Cross associations in an attempt to impose a private, nonprofit firewall between federal funding of retiree health and control of the nation's hospitals, physician practices, and the medical marketplace. Lobbyists for hospitals favored having Blue Cross handle hospital payments and cost reimbursements for Medicare. Others viewed some kind of private component of Medicare to be essential to keep the system from devolving into full-fledged national health care. Asked about this issue by the Ways and Means Committee, official Wilbur Cohen of Health, Education, and Welfare invented a metaphor that later became policy:

> [It] seems to me that [Medicare expansion] could be avoided by so designing a system of what some people have either called a three-legged stool or a three-layer cake of basic protection through Social Security, through Kerr-Mills, and private insurance. (15)

Cohen himself almost certainly did not view such a system as erecting a wall against subsequent expansion. Remember that it was Cohen who had helped refashion the drive for national health insurance in the early 1950s along gradualist lines. Cohen's later reflections about his strategy are worth repeating:

> The men and women I worked with, while they were Populists, while they were Progressives, while they were strong believers in social legislation, they were also strongly of the belief of the inevitableness of gradualism. In other words, they felt it was more important to take one step at a time. Or perhaps

I ought to put it this way—to digest one meal at a time rather than eating breakfast, lunch, and dinner all at once and getting indigestion. This was their philosophy. I think it's the right social philosophy.[20]

Whatever Cohen's motivation for broaching the idea, Mills ran with it. Meeting in closed session, his committee fashioned a compromise package of Social Security amendments that created three new federal entitlements:

1. Medicare Part A hospital insurance, compulsory and funded by payroll taxes;

2. Medicare Part B insurance for outpatient physician charges, voluntary and funded by subscriber premiums and general revenues along the lines of Better-care; and

3. Medicaid, a joint federal-state program for the poor, elderly or not, that built on the previous Kerr-Mills program and the Elder-care proposal.

Johnson signed the amendments into law on July 30, 1995. Appearing before a crowd of three thousand at the Harry Truman Library in Independence, Missouri, Johnson recognized his predecessor for helping laying the foundation for Medicare and promised: "No longer will older Americans be denied the healing miracle of modern medicine. No long will illness crush and destroy the savings they have so carefully put away over a lifetime."[21]

From a legislative standpoint, it was a clever compromise. Along the way, however, any aspects of Better-care and Elder-care that might have ensured a strong private-sector role in retiree health insurance, and confined public subsidies to the truly poor, were stripped out. The cost-reimbursement policies of the Blue Cross plans were adopted for Medicare Part A, but administration of hospital payments was given to the federal government, not to Blue Cross or to any other private contractor. Furthermore, Medicare Part B, while retaining the voluntary and funding aspects of Better-care, did not provide for a choice of private insurers but merely offered a federally run plan so heavily subsidized with federal tax dollars (50 percent of average cost at first, later upped to 75 percent) that private insurers wishing to compete for the same business never had a chance. In this way, the "voluntary" nature of Part B turned out to be an illusion. It was Medicare coverage for doctor bills, or nothing. Finally, as discussed later, the Medicaid section of the package was drafted in a careless, haphazard manner, resulting in far greater coverage than originally intended. Lawyers and benefits consultants did not take long to figure out how middle-income seniors could juggle or hide their assets and have Medicaid pay their nursing-home bills without having to sell their homes or otherwise reduce the value of assets they hoped to pass on to their children.

Mills had the right instincts but failed to fashion legislation that reflected them. Far from keeping Medicare promises affordable and the federal role in health care limited, the 1965 legislation resulted in a revolutionary change in American medicine. Federal administration of Medicare proved to be particularly disastrous. Even as lawmakers were adopting the traditional "cost-plus" reimbursement policies of the Blues, the private insurance marketplace was in the process of discarding them as costly and ineffective. Employer-based plans began to experiment with utilization review, capitation, preferred providers, and other ways to rein in the tendency for cost-plus finance to encourage patients to consume medical services without regard to price or cost-effectiveness. As Robert Helms of the American Enterprise Institute points out, "the Medicare legislation locked the government program into a historical straightjacket."[22]

Medicare, created in the heyday of federal government growth and the myth of Social Security's financial success, fueled a massive increase in health care infrastructure and services. Hospitals expanded capacity. Equipment manufacturers made expensive new devices to diagnose and treat disease. The training of new physicians itself became dependent on Medicare funding of major teaching hospitals. But the program grew far more rapidly than its creators intended or that its funding stream could finance. In 1964, the Johnson administration projected that Medicare would cost $12 billion by 1990 (after adjusting for inflation). The real number was $110 billion.[23] Just four years into the program, a Senate Finance Committee probe found that some physicians were charging Medicare four times what they billed private insurers. But limited cost controls enacted in 1972 failed to control Medicare's growth. One reason was that the same legislation expanded coverage to include the disabled, just as Social Security had been expanded to include disability insurance in 1957.[24]

By the early 1980s, it was clear that Medicare could not survive as originally constituted. In 1983, the Health Care Financing Administration (HCFA), which ran the Medicare and Medicaid programs, instituted a new system to contain costs in Part A. It allotted fixed reimbursements for about five hundred diagnosis-related groups (DRGs), updated and carefully controlled by later Congresses and administrations.[25] Likewise, in 1989 Congress instituted a series of cost and practice regulations for Part B physician coverage. It was based on a Relative Value System (RVS) that attempted to rationalize fees for some seven thousand different services, in part by using a "comparable worth" approach that second-guessed the market by hiking reimbursements for primary care doctors and slicing them for specialists.[26]

The 1980s reforms were nearly incomprehensible attempts to define the value of labor not by market-generated prices but by bureaucratic dictate. They shifted costs for Medicare services from the federal government to patients with private health insurance. These costs never show up on the federal ledgers, but they are real nonetheless. As providers responded to price controls by "gaming the system"—by scheduling more visits to maximize per-patient revenue, or using sophisticated software to classify ailments at the highest possible reimbursement—HCFA introduced so-called "expenditure controls" to dictate proper medical practice. This is precisely what the American Medical Association and Congressional critics of the original Medicare bill predicted.[27] By 1990, the American Medical Association itself stated that "physicians today are overwhelmed by government paperwork. In the last 10 years, under the guise of cost-containment, the government has shackled the medical profession with rules and regulations."[28]

THE 1990S AND "MEDISCARE"

The 1990s were a period of tremendous political turmoil for Medicare. Attempts at price controls on hospitals and doctors failed to resolve the program's financial woes, although they did slow the rate of spending growth a bit.[29] A few lonely voices began to call for radical reform. One of these was Representative Leon Panetta, a Democrat from California who later became chief of staff in the Clinton White House. In 1991, he proposed sharp reductions in Medicare spending. Panetta warned that, without controlling costs and redesigning the program, it would continue to grow rapidly, crowding out deficit reduction and programs for younger, less affluent Americans and necessitating stiff tax hikes. "We really want to provide some straight talk here," Panetta said. "We cannot just pretend that things can be passed off to the future."[30] Gun-shy Republicans in the Bush administration as well as his own Democratic colleagues in Congress ignored his plan.

By 1993, the Medicare Part A payroll tax rate was a combined 2.9 percent of income, split evenly between employee and employer and applied, like Social Security, to only a portion of wages. Recognizing that Medicare's shaky finances would continue to imperil the federal budget, newly elected President Bill Clinton proposed that the wage base of the payroll tax, then capped at $135,000.00 per person, be delimited. The idea was included in Clinton's 1993 tax-hike package, narrowly passed by Congress. As with Social Security tax hikes, the change did nothing more than worsen the deal, forcing middle- and upper-income workers to pay more for the same Medicare benefits.[31]

The next episode in the drama came in 1994. President Clinton had proposed a sprawling, complicated, and poorly crafted health-care reform plan the previous year that broke every rule of liberal entitlement advocacy. It tried to address dozens of issues at once. It was spelled out in great detail, published in book form for average Americans to read, and, it must be said, was intellectually honest. Instead of sticking to the gradualism that had served activists so well in the past, the president—or perhaps more accurately, his wife—overreached. The consequences were significant. Interest groups picked the plan apart and savaged it with television ads. Republicans in Congress were energized. The debacle played a critical role in the GOP's stunning electoral gains in 1994. Republicans seized Congress for the first time since the 1950s and toppled numerous state and local Democratic officeholders as well.

Emboldened by the victory, Congressional Republicans turned their attention to Medicare reform in 1995. Throughout the spring and summer, GOP leaders discussed such ideas as converting Medicare subsidies into vouchers, expanding choice among private plans, and allowing seniors to use medical savings accounts (MSAs) to pay for routine expenses. MSAs have long been a popular idea among conservative think tankers and reformers. Like traditional IRAs, MSA deposits and earnings would be tax-deductible. But so would withdrawals. Only in this way would paying for medical services with savings instead of insurance enjoy the same tax benefits. Not surprisingly, health maintenance organizations (HMOs) and other private insurers whose business is built on third-party payment of medical bills do not like the idea of MSAs. Since they dominate the health-care field, experiments with MSAs have been limited—companies with much to lose if MSAs became widespread are unlikely to invest a lot of time and money developing salable MSA products. Furthermore, federal law makes MSAs excessively complicated in an attempt to prevent tax-free withdrawals for nonmedical purposes. Still, MSAs combined with a high-deductible, catastrophic health insurance plan form an attractive alternative to traditional private insurance or Medicare, because they offer the prospect of empowering consumers in the marketplace to shop for better deals. It is not surprising that Republicans have gravitated towards the idea, even if they do not fully understand its implications.

In June 1995, Republican National Committee Chairman Haley Barbour sent a memo to Republican members summarizing recent polls on the issue. "Voters will not support the reforms needed to protect and preserve Medicare unless they realize the system is in trouble," Barbour observed. Republicans enjoyed a honeymoon period with the American public, who trusted them over President Clinton on Medicare reform by a 52 to 33 percent margin. But there was significant risk, Barbour warned: "Do not let the Democrats or the media get away with saying Medicare will be cut."[32]

Following Barbour's advice, GOP leaders organized a campaign of interviews and appearances to make the case for reform along market lines. *The Washington Post* followed the efforts of Representative Mark Neumann (R-Indiana) to sell the reform message. After an appearance by Neumann in Janesville, Indiana, a *Post* reporter asked attendee Helen Extrom, 81, what she thought. "I'm not really understanding all I'm hearing," she admitted. "That's what I'm not understanding—which [option] would be better for me. You get one answer and you turn it around, you get three or four answers."[33] This was a sign of things to come. Clinton, Democrats, and their allies counterpunched with a massive advertising blitz to convince Americans that Republicans were, in fact, cutting Medicare, not reforming it. "More people will die," said one hysterical ad from the AFL-CIO. "It is only for the sake of tax cuts for the rich," said another.[34]

The Republican plan, announced in September, drew withering attacks. Despite a desperate attempt to break through with their message, GOP leaders found themselves outmaneuvered. Clinton vetoed the budget bill late in the year, citing the Medicare plan as a key reason. He went on to win reelection in 1996, and his party regained some of its lost ground in Congress. Most observers credited the Democrats' "Mediscare" campaign of

1995 and 1996 as playing a major role. In 1997, the chastened Republicans tried again. Their 1995 rhetoric about intransigent Democrats being "totally morally bankrupt" gave way to assurances that the 1997 plan was designed to avoid "a clear conflict line with the White House."[35] The plan lowered reimbursement rates for immediate savings, shifted some Part A expenses (primarily home health care, a rapidly growing expense) to Part B in order to shore up the health insurance trust fund, gave incentives to choose private plans, offered a limited number of MSA options, and created a special bipartisan commission to resolve Medicare's long-run financial problems. Clinton, having used Medicare as a wedge issue in the 1996 elections, now wanted a deal. The 1997 Balanced Budget Act included most of the Republicans' ideas, and cut spending growth in exactly the ways Clinton had criticized before the election. The legislation even included tax cuts benefiting "the wealthy."[36]

It is too early to tell what the long-term impact of the 1997 reforms will be. At best, they delayed Medicare's fiscal crisis a bit and offered some elders private-sector options previously unavailable. Perhaps the most promising element of the bill—the creation of the National Bipartisan Commission on the Future of Medicare—did not bear immediate fruit. Chaired by centrist Democratic Senator John Breaux of Louisiana and Republican Representative Bill Thomas of California, the panel came up with an innovative plan, called "premium supports." Medicare recipients would be given a wide choice of private plans, each covering a basic package of benefits, and federal subsidies would be adjusted for income and medical need. In 1999, the plan received majority support on the committee, but not the supermajority formally needed for approval. Furthermore, Clinton declined to support the idea, preferring instead to push expanding Medicare to cover prescription drugs and uninsured over the age of fifty-five.[37]

Political demagoguery can change the course of elections, but it cannot change reality. Sometime during the first two decades of the twenty-first century, Medicare as we know it today will collapse. By 2016—the same year as projected for Social Security—Medicare Part A expenses will begin to exceed revenues, meaning that either general revenues or tax hikes will be needed to make up the difference.[38] According to the program's trustees, it will require $6 trillion more by 2075 to pay promised benefits than current revenue sources will provide. The Part A tax rate would have to rise to nearly 10 percent of wages by 2020 and to almost 14 percent by 2040 just to pay current benefits.[39]

With the advent of federal budget surpluses, some thought that the Medicare crisis had been alleviated. But projected surpluses in the Medicare trust fund are largely ephemeral. Over half of the $393 billion surplus for the years 2002 through 2011 projected by Medicare trustees in early 2001 is simply "interest" expected from current securities—interest to be paid by taxpayers through general revenues. The remainder of the surplus reflects prior shifting of expenses from Part A to Part B. In reality, as even *The Washington Post* admitted in an editorial, the Medicare surplus "is an illusion."[40]

The problem is a structural one. Because of its origins as a ramshackle contraption of dissimilar ideas, Medicare was not designed to solve a clearly identified problem. Instead, it extended expensive, nearly first-dollar coverage for hospitalization—a dominant mode of treatment in 1965 but merely a last resort by 1995. At its birth, Medicare included cost-sharing provisions that, lacking proper adjustment for medical inflation, have been seriously eroded over three decades. It provided no reimbursement for prescription drugs, which in 1965 were rarely included in health plans because of the lack of a significant number of useful treatments for ailments commonly afflicting the elderly, but today are a basic part of the daily regimen of millions of longer-lived seniors. In 1965, proponents of Medicare warned that without federal insurance, poor elders would spent their last dime at the doctor's office and then become a permanent ward either of the state or of their own children. Today, after decades of significant asset accumulation and government-sanctioned transfers of wealth, Americans over the age of 65 are a larger and far wealthier group than lawmakers in 1965 could have imagined.

As health-care economist Mark Pauly points out, if Medicare was originally intended to help seniors of modest incomes buy more health insurance than they could afford on their own, "the current system is both inefficient and inequitable since it encourages excessive use and ends up redistributing income from the poor to the rich."[41] Poor Americans, for example, including minorities, generally have shorter life expectancies. Yet, they pay huge sums in payroll taxes during their working years to a Medicare system that many will not have an opportunity to use much if at all. Furthermore, while the program is considered to be part of a social safety net, it helps to sustain the active, prosperous lifestyle of millions of American retirees while their cash-strapped children (supposedly freed from the responsibility of elder care, according to Medicare's founders) shoulder a payroll tax burden that would have been unthinkable a generation before. What is worse, workers whose parents die young still must pay the same as their luckier coworkers, who can continue to enjoy their parents' company and see their medical bills subsidized. Overall, according to a 1997 National Bureau of Economic Research study, the wealthiest 10 percent of Medicare recipients will receive significantly more in benefits than the poorest 10 percent, with the difference reaching 40 percent for recipients over 85.[42]

The Medicare crisis is real, but it can and will be addressed. Changes in life expectancy, technology, social relationships, and financial markets are pointing the way to a better system for helping American workers plan for their health care needs at retirement as well as providing a true safety net for those who, through debilitating illness or disability, have effectively become wards of the state. These two functions—financial planning for retirement and public assistance for the chronically ill or disabled—are distinct. They merit different policy approaches, as discussed below. Nor can they be properly separated and addressed without considering the other two legs of the federal medical triad, Medicaid and federal tax breaks for employer-provided insurance.

THE OTHER MEDI-PROGRAM

For all the political attention paid to Medicare in recent years, its sister program Medicaid faces serious problems of its own. Like Medicare, it was also supposed to remain a relatively low-cost program when lawmakers fashioned it out of the Kerr-Mills program in 1965. It was not to be. In its first year, the program cost $1.3 billion—$600 million from federal coffers and $700 million from the states. By 1970, the federal government had begun to pay a majority of the bill, although states continued to administer the program, and the total cost topped $5.3 billion.[43] Over the next thirty years, Medicaid expenditures grew exponentially, reaching $202 billion in fiscal year 2000. The federal government paid about $115 billion of that price tag, with the remaining $87 billion coming from state (and some county) budgets.[44]

The percentage of age groups enrolled in Medicaid follows an inverted bell-shaped curve. Medicaid covers about 37 percent of children up to five years of age, and another 24 percent of children between six and fourteen. In the middle of the age distribution—adults forty-five to sixty-four—only 6 percent are Medicaid recipients. By age eighty-five and over, the percentage goes back up to 31 percent.[45] What this really means is that a substantial number of American families are receiving medical assistance from their state governments to which at least one member of the family is entitled by federal law. For most of these families, however, the recipient is either a young child or an elderly parent or grandparent.

There are two main routes to Medicaid eligibility. The first—and the most important in terms of enrollment—is being "categorically needy." This simply means that the recipient becomes eligible for Medicaid by meeting income tests associated with other welfare programs, such as Supplemental Security Income (SSI). Other examples of "categorically needy" groups automatically eligible for Medicaid under federal law include recipients of adoption assistance and foster care, recipients who are transitioning from welfare to work, and Medicare recipients whose income and status qualify them for Medicaid, which is used to pay the premiums and cost-sharing expenses for Medicare services.[46]

In addition to these categories of eligibility, states can also elect to serve what are termed "medically needy." These recipients have too much income to qualify for cash welfare benefits or Medicaid by category, but who face significant expenses for medical or custodial care. In effect, this option allows them to "spend down" to Medicaid eligibility by incurring medical and/or custodial care expenses to offset their excess income, reducing it to the maximum allowed by their state's Medicaid program. States may also allow families to establish eligibility as medically needy by paying monthly premiums to the state representing the difference between family income and the income eligibility standard. The medically needy option, now in place in forty states, is mainly used by families of disabled or elderly individuals to qualify for medical assistance regardless of previous economic status. Combined with widely used techniques for shifting assets to children or others, it makes Medicaid a true middle-class entitlement for millions of recipients.[47]

States are allowed to charge nominal deductibles or copayments for Medicaid coverage, but in practice, this is rare. For one thing, federal law disallows cost sharing for emergency services or family planning. Many Medicaid recipients are also exempt by federal law, including pregnant women, children under eighteen, hospital or nursing home patients who are expected to contribute most of their income to institutional care, and all categorically needy recipients enrolled in managed care programs. These exemptions cover most Medicaid recipients.

If one carefully examines the wide variety of ways in which individuals can qualify for Medicaid, as well as the kinds of services they can receive, it becomes quickly obvious that talking about "Medicaid" as if it were a discrete program with clear goals or objectives is nonsensical. A helpful model for studying Medicaid might be to think of it in terms of four separate programs:

1. HEALTH INSURANCE FOR THE NON-ELDERLY POOR. This was a core purpose of Medicaid and remains its image among many policymakers, reporters, and the general public. This image is not unjustified. Most Medicaid recipients are children and nondisabled adults who receive coverage because of income. But expenditures on their behalf are a surprisingly small share of the total (about a quarter in 1998).[48] The key fact to recognize about this largest segment of the Medicaid population is that it represents people who may have health needs, but whose more fundamental problem is dependency on public assistance. They need help getting back on their feet, learning new skills or self-discipline, getting off drugs, and becoming more responsible. Because virtually all cash welfare recipients are on Medicaid, and more than 80 percent receive Food Stamps, it is instructive to think about these three programs as the "standard package" of public assistance benefits available to the able-bodied poor. In the median state, Medicaid accounts for more than 40 percent of the total value.[49]

2. HEALTH INSURANCE FOR NONPOOR PREGNANT WOMEN AND CHILDREN. A series of federal and state actions throughout the 1980s and early 1990s progressively expanded Medicaid to cover more pregnant women and children whose family incomes were above the poverty line. Some of these expansions had their origins in efforts to reduce infant mor-

tality, for which a government guarantee of prenatal and postnatal care was deemed essential.[50] Another factor was a 1990 United States Supreme Court decision that loosened SSI eligibility for children, increasing the number of "disabled" children from nonpoor families who qualified for SSI cash payments and thus for Medicaid. At about the same time, the Social Security Administration changed its regulations regarding childhood mental impairment, accounting for another surge in childhood SSI and Medicaid caseloads.[51] The effects of these decisions can be seen in the fact that about one out of every four children in the nation is currently enrolled in Medicaid. About one-third of all births in the United States are paid for by Medicaid, and the percentage is closer to one-half in some states.[52]

3. LONG-TERM MEDICAL AND CUSTODIAL CARE FOR THE DISABLED. This population of Medicaid recipients is perhaps the least familiar to the general public, but it is the most costly. About one-third of all Medicaid expenditures are for the non-elderly blind or disabled who represent only 16 percent of total recipients. Essentially, the disabled portion of the Medicaid population is a catchall category that includes individuals who have become "wards of the state" with serious and incurable diseases or disabilities, as well as those with temporary injuries or conditions, those with substance abuse or mental health conditions, and children with conditions ranging from severe physical and mental deformities to relatively mild behavioral problems. Through vendor payments to disabled persons, the Medicaid system has become a significant and sometimes dominant funder of public hospitals, mental hospitals, intermediate care facilities, and nursing homes.

4. LONG-TERM MEDICAL AND CUSTODIAL CARE FOR THE ELDERLY. About a third of Medicaid expenditures are for long-term care expenses, with the share approaching 50 percent in some states. The program has become the largest single funder of long-term care expenses in the United States, including those for middle-class Americans. Medicaid pays over 50 percent of all nursing home costs in the United States and pays at least part of the bill for 68 percent of all nursing home residents.[53] In one sense, of course, the "elderly" do not consume long-term care: a subset of seniors with a serious medical condition or disability do. One might even consider elderly and disabled Medicaid recipients as one group, in that they are often consuming similar services and have become eligible in similar ways. How-

ever, there is an important difference. The percentage of children or adults under sixty-five who are born with or develop serious medical conditions or disabilities is not very high. The kind of disability that makes one a permanent "ward of the state" for all practical purposes is rare.

But as an individual ages, the probability of developing conditions serious enough to warrant long-term care of some kind increases. More than 40 percent of those who turn sixty-five will spend some time in a nursing home. Of those who enter a nursing home, 55 percent will stay at least a year, and 21 percent—or nearly a tenth of all seniors—will remain longer than five years.[54] For someone approaching retirement, in other words, the chances are almost fifty-fifty of facing some nursing home bills, and even higher, that he or she will incur long-term care expenses of some kind. That surely places the elderly in a different situation than a child born with a congenital mental defect or an adult paralyzed in a traffic accident.

The elderly Medicaid population is made up of millions of Americans who have been in the middle class for most of their lives. Very few of the elderly actually "spend down" most of their assets before going on Medicaid—only 10 percent of those in nursing homes according to a Congressional Budget Office study.[55] The remaining caseload of elderly nursing home residents on Medicaid are receiving a middle-class entitlement by shielding their assets in some fashion or passing them on to heirs before rather than after death. There is an entire industry of lawyers, consultants, and publishers telling retirees how to do this. Taking advantage of the opportunity to preserve the value of family assets no doubt seems like a reasonable course to many. However, passing the costs of long-term care for middle-class seniors onto the general population, including unrelated young workers of modest means, poses serious problems of fairness and equity.

A second point to remember is that in the 1960s, when Medicaid was enacted, the life expectancy of older adults was far lower than it is now. The increased need for long-term care is in part the happy result of economic improvements and medical advances. Instead of dying at fifty of a stroke or heart attack, a person might live to be eighty-five or ninety, albeit perhaps spending the last couple of years of life in a nursing home. As in the Medicare case, demographics have great implications for the sustainability of Medicaid in its current form. Between 1960 and 1994, the general population of the United States grew by 45 percent. But the population aged six-ty-five and older doubled, and the over-eighty-five population grew by 274 percent, to 3 million. This "oldest of the old" population now makes up a tenth of the elderly population, but will be a third by the middle of the next century. While only 1 percent of those aged sixty-five to seventy-four are in nursing homes, 25 percent of those eighty-five and older are. More general-ly, while only about 10 percent of those aged sixty-five to seventy-four need assistance with everyday activities such as bathing or eating, fully half of those aged eighty-five and older do.[56]

As both the elderly population in general—and the core eighty-five-and-over population most needing medical and custodial services—continues to grow relative to the number of workers, open-ended entitlements to long-term care will simply become unaffordable. This is true even if, as pro-jected, the average health of the eighty-five-and-older population improves markedly over the next few years. The rate of institutionalization will prob-ably fall for the eighty-five-and-older cohort, but its growth will more than offset these trends. If, for example, more of the oldest of the old stay out of institutions through the increased use of home health care, the result will still be an expense far beyond the ability of the current funding stream to cover.[57] Overall, according to Stanford's Victor Fuchs, the percentage of gross domestic product devoted to retiree health care will likely double to 10 percent by 2020—with annual spending per senior rising from $9,200.00 in 1995 to almost $25,000.00 in 2020. "One way or another," he concluded in a 1998 study, "America will have to tame this health-care gorilla."[58]

Other fiscal problems face the younger portion of the Medicaid case-load. The design of the program encourages unnecessary, expensive med-ical consumption. Because Medicaid recipients pay little or nothing out-of-pocket, they tend to be frequent users of the system—and often choose convenient but costly care at hospital emergency rooms rather than less im-mediate care at doctors' offices. Studies show that Medicaid recipients use health-care services more often than do patients with private health insur-ance (who face out-of-pocket costs or other incentives to consume medical care more efficiently).[59] Another inflationary factor is that Medicaid usually covers chiropractors, optometrists, podiatrists, and dentists, even though the health insurance many American families buy individually or through their employers does not include such coverage. Such third-party payment of services usually funded with cash leads to overconsumption and higher prices.

There are other problems with the program besides cost. One is a mismatch of means and ends. For some recipients of cash welfare, free health insurance is not the most efficient way of helping them get back on their feet. After all, recipients can benefit from Medicaid only by consuming health care. If they choose not to obtain a particular service, or choose a lower-cost provider of the service, they do not get to keep the savings to purchase something they need or value more. And unlike those who buy private health insurance, Medicaid recipients cannot enroll in health insurance plans covering fewer services or procedures than Medicaid and then use the premium savings for something else. This "use it or lose it" aspect of Medicaid not only increases health-care consumption and the total cost of the program—as argued above—but also expends scarce public assistance dollars in ways that do not serve the overall needs of recipients in the long run. Since Medicaid makes up the largest component of the standard package of welfare benefits, its inflexible design prevents recipients from using a significant part of the public assistance spending they are eligible to receive to develop the occupational skills, literacy, savings, or assets they require to become self-sufficient.

Finally, there is also a place for moral argument concerning the Medicaid explosion. If the concept of limited government is to retain any meaning at all, then we must expect citizens to take responsibility for their actions and to make reasonable arrangements for their future needs. For adults, the prospect of incurring significant health costs as they age, including long-term care costs in their old age, should be no surprise. Many have seen friends or their own parents go through disability or debilitating illness.

It is true that until recently, private long-term care insurance was neither widely available nor tax-deductible. Our tax code has also punished those who save for future medical needs rather than spend income today. Setting aside for the moment tax changes to treat medical savings and long-term care insurance more fairly, the most likely reason why people don't plan ahead for future medical needs is that they know those needs, if serious enough, will be picked up by the government through the Medicaid system. This promise of free or subsidized long-term care not only discourages personal responsibility but also leads to an immoral transfer of money from current taxpayers, many young and of extremely modest means, to older Medicaid recipients who are, in many cases, solidly middle-class in background and family assets. Even if this practice were sustainable—and because of changing ratios of retirees to workers, it is not—it would be wrong.

HEALTH CARE AND HUMAN CAPITAL

As argued earlier, health care is both consumption and investment. It is a consumption good in that it alleviates immediate pain and suffering, increasing the quality and enjoyment of life. It is an investment good, as well, if it protects and enhances your ability to produce goods and services in the future. Consider preventive care. An inoculation has little immediate value. Neither does getting a physical, taking a vitamin, or exercising a sore neck. But in the long run, these activities reduce the risk of debilitating illness or injury, thus increasing the value of future consumption or production. Sick employees are less productive ones. Death at an early age, in addition to being tragic, also represents a loss of human capital. The income stream lost is a cost to one's family, employer, and consumers of the goods or services one would have made. It may seem a bit crass to treat human beings as capital assets. That is not all they are, of course, but it is part of what they are. Just as investment and preventive maintenance are necessary to make physical assets such as plants and equipment productive, so too early investments in health and well-being are important components in human capital formation.

That health care can be a form of investment is an idea with a long pedigree. When economists Theodore W. Schultz and Gary Becker were developing modern theories of human capital in the 1950s, they included health care as one of the investments that pays off in future wages. Schultz stated the matter concisely in a 1962 essay entitled "Reflections on Investment in Man":

> The economic capabilities of man are predominantly a produced means of production and that, except for some pure rent (in earnings) for differences in inherited abilities, most of the differences in earnings are a consequence of differences in the amounts that have been invested in people. Here, then, the hypothesis is that the structure of wages and salaries is primarily determined by investment in schooling, health, on-the-job training, searching for information about job opportunities, and by investment in migration.[60]

The idea is far older than that, however. In 1842, for example, Edwin Chadwick, while serving as secretary to Britain's Poor Law Commission, observed, "[T]he economist for the advancement of his science may well treat the human being simply as an investment of capital," and went on to estimate the nature of that investment with such costs as child rearing, health care, and premature death. In 1853, statistician William Farr computed the economic value of a human life by discounting the value of future earnings taking account of life expectancies and "maintenance costs," such as health care in youth, working age, and old age. After the turn of the century, noted American economist Irving Fisher updated and expanded Farr's work, estimating the economic cost of disease and the investment value of eliminating preventable deaths.[61]

Of course, distinguishing between the consumption and investment components of health care is extremely difficult, as is also true with education. Furthermore, some expenditures intended as health-care investments do not, in retrospect, add value. This is no different from a company that buys a new machine with an expectation that it will increase production, only to discover that it is outmoded or inefficient. In general, however, we can state with confidence that the extent to which health care is investment rather than consumption declines with age. Children do not consume a lot of medical services, on average, but most health-care spending on their behalf is preventive or developmental. Most working adults continue receiving preventive services but also make greater use of medicine to alleviate pain and improve quality of life. The severely disabled and elderly, on the other hand, engage in little health-care investment. By definition, they are largely out of the workforce and are unlikely to reenter. Their (relatively high) medical expenditures mostly involve treatment of acute or chronic illness.

From a tax policy perspective, investment expenditures should be excluded from any income taxed. The reasoning is straightforward. Investments that generate future taxable income (in the form of wages, dividends, or capital gains) should not themselves be taxed. Otherwise, the stream of future income is reduced by the same amount, resulting in double taxation.[62] While many understand and embrace this concept for financial assets such as stocks, bonds, and mutual funds, it applies equally well to human capital formation. Although it is impossible fully to disentangle the consumption and investment components of health care, providing no tax exclusion is tantamount to punishing the development of human capital.

The current tax exclusions for employer-provided health insurance, as well as smaller breaks for the self-employed and for families with catastrophic medical expenses, are not based on the concept that health care is an investment in human capital. They are special breaks for particular kinds of health care arrangements rather than exclusions aimed at creating neutrality between present and future consumption. An alternative would be to convert the current breaks (estimated at $136 billion in foregone federal and state revenues in 2000) into a set of income tax deductions for health-care expenditures or savings. The deductions would be capped at specific amounts based on age. This is the only feasible way of attempting to confine deductibility to health-care investment rather than consumption. For example, the health-care deduction might be set at a high amount for children (say, 75 percent of the average health-care spending on children, or about $1,200 per child in the late 1990s), a moderate amount for working adults (50 percent of average spending, or $2,000 per worker), and a small amount, say $500 a year, for retirees and the severely disabled, since they are unlikely to be accumulating human capital for the purpose of earning future income.

Families could take the deduction for spending their own money directly for medical services or health insurance. They could deduct deposits into MSAs, from which future medical expenses could be paid. And if they still preferred to receive health benefits from their employers—despite the removal of the artificial tax incentive for doing so, many will want to stick with it because of familiarity, bulk-buying advantages, or expertise—they could deduct the premiums paid on their behalf by employers, which would have to be reported annually to employees. Whatever the type of expense deducted, however, the total value of the deduction would remain capped. This reflects the reasoning behind the deduction, which is designed not as a "safety net" feature but as a means of achieving tax neutrality.

A salutary side effect is that capping the deduction would reduce the current exclusion's inflationary and regressive features. After all, excluding the value of employer health benefits, regardless of their cost, encourages employers and employees to maximize the value of health insurance over other forms of compensation and provides disproportionate benefits to the wealthy and employees of large companies. The larger, more comprehensive, and more expensive the health plan, the more tax savings you receive.[63] A 1999 study by the Lewin Group, a consulting firm, found that 69 percent of today's tax breaks for health insurance go to families making $50,000.00 or more—only 36 percent of the population.[64] Of course, my approach would be a deduction, not a credit, and would be of little benefit to those at poverty-level incomes. But the groups that would derive the least benefit from the new deduction—retirees, the disabled, and the poor—are the very ones to which huge government spending programs are already directed. Indeed, more sweeping proposals from conservatives to offer large tax credits to families to pay for health-care services or insurance would probably have a much larger impact on the ranks of the uninsured.[65] However, this would come at the cost of imbedding yet another subsidy program in the tax code where it does not belong.

The idea of replacing the current tax exclusion for employee benefits with health-care deductions for individuals will not be an easy sell. Some conservative analysts will object that deductions for health insurance and MSA deposits are inconsistent with fundamental tax reform as embodied in the flat tax or national sales tax. This is a mistaken view, for the reasons explained above, as well as an irrelevancy, since the prospects for enacting either idea in pristine form have been and shall remain remote. On the other hand, liberal activists and advocates for further expansion of the welfare state will complain that deductions do not provide additional help for low-income families who cannot afford health-care services or coverage. Interestingly, free-market organizations and analysts, including members of the optimistically named "Consensus Group" advocating a tax-credit solution to problems of health-care access, make the same argument. They note that most taxpayers don't itemize, thus precluding use of a deduction, and that tax subsidies will have to be large enough—50 percent of cost or more, according to some estimates—to induce the uninsured to buy insurance.[66]

But both sets of tax-credit advocates are really discussing welfare policy, not health-care or tax policy. Government subsidies for those unable to purchase the medical care they need should be on budget and carefully crafted, not hidden in the tax code. That is not to say that a tax-credit system would not be superior to expanding Medicaid or some other single-payer government program. Indeed, I helped to design a state tax credit in

North Carolina as an alternative to Medicaid expansion in 1998. More preferable, however, would be tax deductions for health-care investment by all coupled with a privatized, voucher-based medical safety net for the poor and disabled as outlined below.

Some may question the practicality of requiring employers to report to employees the health insurance premiums paid on their behalf, which would be required for the neutrality and fiscal control of individual deductions. Providing employees this information, perhaps in the form of an additional line on the W-2 form, does represent an administrative burden. It is a price well worth paying. One of the drawbacks of the current system (and of "tax simplification" proposals that try to minimize compliance costs for employees) is that individuals lack the information necessary to make sound decisions on their own behalf. Without an accounting of health premiums paid by their employers, for example, most workers do not know a basic piece of information about themselves—how much they are paid for their work.

Just as withholding and payroll tax collections keep American workers from fully recognizing the true cost of government programs, the current employer-based insurance system obscures a significant share of employee compensation. Workers who do not value health coverage as much as other forms of investment or consumption never learn the opportunity cost they are forced to pay, and thus lack the information they need to bargain for a compensation package that better meets their families' needs. Again, it is quite possible that many Americans would continue to prefer that their employers assist them with finding appropriate health plans. Employers have the experience and expertise, and can sometimes strike better deals by buying health care in bulk, although the advantages offered by workplace-based risk pooling are frequently exaggerated.[67] But by eliminating the artificial incentives that the current tax exclusion creates, individual deductions would allow workers to bargain better on their own behalf, and to demand plans that ensure the maximum amount of portability should they choose to change jobs, which will usually include a large MSA component.

Speaking of MSAs, some critics will point to the apparent lack of interest on the part of most Americans to existing MSA alternatives as proof that tax breaks for individual control of health care are unlikely to succeed. But when Congress set up a demonstration project in 1996, it imposed a number of restrictions that limit MSA eligibility and thwart their proper use. Only the self-employed and employees of small business may set up MSAs, for example. But it is precisely those large employers excluded from the bill that have the expertise and market power necessary to test the idea on a large scale. One barrier is technology. Ideally, patients should be able to withdraw MSA funds with the swipe of a debit card. Only approved medical providers would have the necessary card readers, thus eliminating the lengthy and costly process of submitting and evaluating paper claims. Such a system would have significant up-front costs. Only the prospect of attracting significant use would motivate hospitals, doctors' offices, and pharmacies to install MSA card technology—and only the guaranteed participation of large blocks of employees can create such a prospect. Other flaws in the bill that limit MSA participation include time limits, insufficient deductions and funding options for deposits, cost-sharing caps, and state regulation.[68]

I have found in my own personal experience that even a motivated consumer—one more informed about MSAs than the average insurance agent—finds it extremely difficult to purchase an affordable MSA plan as a small group, given the availability of HMO or preferred provider organization (PPO) products through multiemployer alliances. The bulk-buying advantages of purchasing high-cost, low-deductible coverage as a member of a chamber of commerce alliance, in my case, outweigh the savings from choosing high-deductible insurance and depositing the savings in employee MSAs. The rules impose high barriers to MSA participation; the fact that hundreds of thousands of Americans are using them anyway is testament to the appeal of exercising personal control over health purchasing decisions.

Finally, some may challenge my approach as too arbitrary. Why set the deductions at 75 percent of average medical expenses per child and 50 percent per adult? The distinction between medical investment and medical consumption is fuzzy, at best. So is the precise border between Greece and Turkey! The two sides might quibble about the status of a small Aegean island or stretch of water, but nobody thinks that Athens lies in Turkey or Ankara in Greece. Similarly, the complexity of distinguishing between investment and consumption cannot excuse a failure to do so. Sometimes, the only answer is complex policy questions to draw some bright, albeit arbitrary, lines. As the Urban Institute's Eugene Steuerle has observed:

The bottom line is that government is in considerable trouble if it cannot begin to reform one of the largest open-ended tax subsidies or expenditures—especially one as unfair, regressive, and inefficient as the current exclusion for employer-provided benefits . . . When we clearly can do better, we should not allow improvement to be held hostage to some unattainable standard of perfection.[69]

CONCLUSION

Rethinking America's health-care entitlements requires first that we decide precisely what it is we are trying to accomplish. Those government officials and political activists who did the spadework for Medicare and Medicaid and furthered their expansion had a clearly defined goal: national health insurance. In the 1950s, they made a fateful decision to adopt gradualism and get a foothold with retirees. Later, they added the disabled and children to the mix. Now they seek to expand Medicare again, both in services (prescription drugs) and in coverage (fifty-year-olds), as well as Medicaid or "Medicaid-look-alikes" for children like the State Child Health Insurance Program (S-CHIP).

Thought of as a whole, the current health care entitlement system attempts to perform at least three tasks:

1. require Americans to save some of their earnings each year in order to fund medical and institutional care needs at retirement,

2. provide subsidies and bulk-buying advantages to poor or disabled Americans who cannot obtain health insurance or services on their own, and

3. exempt a portion of health care expenditures from taxation, regardless of income or medical status.

To accomplish these tasks, federal and state governments devote more than half a trillion dollars in on-budget spending and foregone revenue. However, the system functions poorly. It rewards extravagance, wealth, age, and luck. It provides fewer choices to patients, weakens family responsibility, and locks many workers into jobs they would otherwise leave except for the health benefits. All of this, and it promises more than taxpayers can reasonably be expected to pay.

Applying Investor Politics to health care means matching up means and ends properly and relying on productive investment to create the greatest possible benefits at an affordable price. The first task, saving money for retiree health care, is philosophically indistinguishable from the core task of the Social Security system. In both cases, it is assumed that Americans cannot make rational decisions by themselves about retirement needs and must have government help in managing their finances. The reasoning is unabashedly paternalistic. At least with Social Security, however, retirees are not told how they must spend their monthly checks. They choose how much food, clothing, shelter, and entertainment they wish to consume, and from whom. Medicare is far stricter. To receive any benefit, you must follow its rules.

It need not be so. As with Social Security, workers should be allowed to direct a portion of their Medicare payroll taxes into private investment accounts. One such proposal, by Andrew J. Rettenmaier and Thomas R. Saving for the National Center for Policy Analysis, would set up Personal Retirement Insurance for Medical Expenses (PRIME) accounts for each worker (and nonworking spouse) born since 1946. The required deposit would vary according to age. A twenty-five-year-old would need to deposit 2.4 percent of wages each year until retirement in order to purchase a plan at age sixty-five that would completely replace Medicare. Those aged thirty-eight to forty-two would be responsible for about the same amount they currently contribute through payroll and income taxes to fund both parts of Medicare—about 4.4 percent of income in 1996. Workers aged forty-three to fifty-one could actually deposit more than 100 percent of current taxes, while those over fifty-one would stay in the current system. Sometime before their sixty-fifth birthday, individuals would use their PRIME account funds to purchase postretirement health insurance including at least coverage of "catastrophic" health expenses. Leftover funds would rollover into an MSA for use in financing out-of-pocket expenses or long-term care.[70]

Again, mirroring Social Security reforms, there would be significant transition costs associated with such a system. If workers are transferring between half and 100 percent of their Medicare taxes into savings accounts, that is money not available to finance current Medicare benefits. But this is not a new cost. The current system already has an unfunded liability of nearly $6 trillion through 2075. In fact, according to calculations by Rettenmaier and Saving, pre-funding benefits through PRIME accounts would dramatically shrink the unfunded liability to between $1.5 trillion and $400 million, depending on the type of health plan purchased at retirement, because of increased economic growth and the power of compound interest. Another way of looking at it is that the current Medicare tax burden of 4.4 percent (again, including both payroll taxes for Part A and general taxes for Part B) would have to be hiked immediately to 7.8 percent to rectify Medicare's unfunded liability. With PRIME accounts, the liability could be erased with a total tax burden of between 4.6 and 5.2 percent of income— which assumes no other cost-cutting measures, either within Medicare or in the federal budget generally.[71]

I would adjust Rettenmaier and Saving's plan in some ways. For one thing, workers should be able to integrate private Social Security and PRIME accounts if they wish. Second, the catastrophic health insurance savers would be required to purchase at retirement should include a long-term care benefit, albeit one with a large deductible, so that most Americans would never need a government program like Medicaid to finance their stay in a nursing home. Finally, the PRIME approach would preserve Medicare for the disabled and as an option at retirement. But Medicare itself should be significantly changed, from a defined-benefit system run by the federal government to a defined-contribution system run by the states with federal financial assistance. Medicare and Medicaid should be merged into one program. Participants would receive subsidies, adjusted for income, age, and medical status, with which to purchase health coverage as a member of a state-assigned risk pool. Each state pool would invite bidders from certified insurers, following the Federal Employees Health Benefits Program model championed by the Heritage Foundation's Stuart Butler and Bob Moffit.[72] Like the PRIME approach, the only required benefits would be catastrophic medical and long-term care expenses. Participants would be able to deposit unspent funds in MSAs or IRAs for future use, thus encouraging frugality and holding down medical inflation. Butler, Moffit, and other Heritage analysts have sketched the outlines of such a program and answered most obvious criticisms.[73]

Together with the deductions outlined earlier for individual medical expenses and MSA deposits, these proposals would harness the power of private markets to promote efficiency, medical innovation, and consumer satisfaction with their health-care options, while building real economic assets to finance the expensive retiree health needs of the Baby Boomers in the next two decades. Most importantly, much of the agenda can be pursued gradually. The history of health care in the twentieth century shows that Americans will accept significant change only if it moves slowly and gives them time to adjust. Keep in mind that at the eve of the twenty-first century, one-eighth of Americans were enrolled in Medicare. A generation from now, it will be one-fourth.[74] Federal provision and control of health care is a huge ship that can only be turned slowly.

Policymakers can start with some simple changes. Current law allows employers to set up flexible spending accounts (FSAs) for their employees in which pretax dollars can be invested and spent on medical care. But unspent FSA funds revert to the employer, creating a use-it-or-lose-it dynamic and limiting the ability of workers to accumulate assets for future health needs. Eliminating the reversion requirement would give millions of Americans an easy way to establish MSAs. Also, current law will allow self-employed Americans to take large individual deductions for the purchase of health insurance by the early 2000s. Lawmakers should consider expanding eligibility for the deduction to all children, to those currently uninsured, and to employees of small businesses. Furthermore, the deductions can be phased in over time to reduce their immediate "cost" to the federal budget. Such expansions will be popular moves by themselves, while also setting the stage for folding the tax exclusion for employer benefits into a new system of individual deductions.

Medicare should be converted into a savings program, and Medicaid into a system of health-purchasing cooperatives for the poor and disabled. These changes won't happen unless reformers can gain the credibility Congressional Republicans sought but didn't earn in 1995 and 1996. Opinion polls reveal that Haley Barbour was correct: Entitlement reform will be impossible without a clear public understanding of the funding crisis faced by Social Security, Medicare, and other programs. Despite years of trying, reformers have not persuaded the people most likely to base their votes on entitlement issues—seniors—that reform is necessary. A 1999 survey by National Public Radio, the Kaiser Foundation, and Harvard University found that only 11 percent of seniors thought Social Security was in crisis, while 34 percent of those under sixty-five, and close to a majority of young voters, thought so. Similarly, almost two-thirds of working-age voters believe that major changes must be made in Medicare soon, while only 34 percent of seniors agree. Regarding what to do about it, nearly half of younger voters trust private insurance plans more than the current Medicare program, while only 14 percent of seniors do.[75] Will Baby Boomers retain their fear about Medicare along with their support for private insurance and savings options as they approach retirement age, thus creating a powerful constituency for reform? Can Medicare survive long enough for this generational change to happen? These issues lie at the core of the coming Investor Politics.

CHAPTER 7

HOUSES, HIGHWAYS,
AND PHYSICAL CAPITAL

OCIAL SECURITY, MEDICARE, AND MEDICAID
are the largest components of the American entitlement state. However, the next biggest program on the
list is also the oldest. The home mortgage interest deduction, val-
ued at $61 billion in fiscal year 2001, has a far larger impact on the
federal budget than do Food Stamps, Supplemental Security Income, public housing subsidies, Unemployment Insurance, or
cash welfare. Its benefits accrue mostly to upper-middle-income
households and the wealthy, because of their higher tax rates and
propensity to itemize. Its popularity—maintained by what former
presidential candidate John McCain might term an "iron triangle"
of real estate, labor union, and building lobbies—has proven to be
the single greatest impediment to the flattening and simplification
of the federal income tax. Yet, for all these notable characteristics,
the origins of the home mortgage interest deduction have remained largely obscure. There is no record of lengthy, passionate
debate about its merits on the floor of Congress. No interest group
lobbied for its creation. No prescient journalists or political observers predicted the size and scope the entitlement would assume.
Its introduction was, instead, an understandable solution to a

problem that still plagues the application of income taxes to physical (or human) capital: How to divide the cost of an asset between investment and consumption.

Why is this important? Because, as I state elsewhere in this book, investment is merely deferred consumption. If you tax the amount that someone invests today, you are really taxing the amount of consumption that the investment will allow tomorrow. A 10 percent tax in investment reduces future consumption by the same 10 percent. So far, so good. But if you then impose another tax on the same future consumption—by taxing earnings on the investment, for example, or on its inheritance by children—you violate the basic rule of good income tax policy: neutrality. Future consumption should not be taxed any more (or less) than current consumption. Therefore, it is important for any income tax code to identify what is an investment and to exclude it from the tax base, so that it can be taxed only once, in the future, as consumed income. Unfortunately, this is far easier said than done.

Plenty of glib "experts" on tax policy try to wish or define the problem away, but it stubbornly refuses to leave. A classic example of the problem is the so-called "three-martini lunch." On the face of it, allowing business owners or employees to deduct the cost of taking a client out to lunch is an unjustified, even outrageous tax break, only tenuously connected to investment. After all, the diners are literally "consuming." Whether they have business to do or not, most people eat lunch. The problem is that, *in the real world, many people do expend more at lunch when entertaining a business prospect than they ordinarily would by themselves.* I have experienced the practice myself many times, from both sides of the table. It is natural to attempt to ingratiate yourself with a potential client by generously offering to pay for a sumptuous meal at a fine restaurant.

More broadly, corporations spend many millions of dollars subsidizing a variety of activities—ranging from meals and entertainment to civic or fitness club memberships for their employees—on the grounds that they pay dividends in the future through more or better relationships with customers, vendors, investors, or coworkers. There is no easy way to distinguish between the "investment" component of a business lunch (the magnanimity or atmosphere) and the "consumption" component (the steak). Perhaps the only feasible solution is what we have, a partial deduction that allows for an arbitrary but consistent percentage of such expenses to be excluded from taxable income, in a manner similar to my proposal in the previous chapter about how to tax family investments in health care.

When Congress was designing America's first income tax during the Civil War, it faced an investment/consumption dilemma with respect to debt. For most potential taxpayers, the only significant assets and liabilities were found in and around their homes. But homes weren't just places to live. Until the late nineteenth century, a majority of Americans farmed. Their homes were also their places of business. Furthermore, many non-farmers operated small businesses housed in or adjacent to their living quarters, such as ground-floor retail shops in the cities or blacksmith shops in frontier towns. A mortgage loan did not only allow a family to buy and live in a nicer home than their meager savings could have bought outright, it was also the most common type of business loan—making it possible for farmers or shopkeepers to earn a (soon-to-be-taxable) income.

Even then, most advocates of income taxes understood the importance of allowing reasonable deductions for investment expenses. Nevertheless, they didn't relish the idea of gathering detailed information from each taxpayer and attempting to determine what portion of a home loan should be considered a tax-deductible business expense. Therefore, they took the easy way out. They exempted from the income tax base all money spent paying off debts. After the wartime tax was repealed, some states continued to experiment with income taxation, and most retained the deduction for debt. In 1913, when Congress, armed with the new Sixteenth Amendment, began to fashion the income tax provisions of its tariff bill, it emulated the previous federal and state codes and exempted all consumer debt service.[1] It was an understandable decision. Even today, with more experience and technology at our disposal, it is often quite hard to determine what portion of a house (and its financing and utility costs) should be considered deductible as a home office for such professionals as doctors, attorneys, accountants, and writers. Furthermore, in 1913 millions of Americans used costly items such as farm tools and sewing machines for both business and personal use. The administrative complexities of applying tax to these expenses were staggering. They remain challenging today with regard to personal computers, for example.

Few members of Congress in 1913 could have foreseen that the next three decades would bring two world wars and such a dramatic expansion of the federal income tax that by 1946 about two-thirds of workers would be paying it. Nor could lawmakers have foretold the postwar housing boom, inflationary bracket creep, and other factors that have made the home mortgage interest deduction so valuable to millions of middle-income taxpayers during the past four decades. With the benefit of hindsight, and of more sophisticated financial markets and technologies, we can see that the idea of making consumer debts tax-deductible was a bad solution to a bad problem. When coupled with the double taxation of income from investment in corporations (dividends and capital gains, unlike debt service, are taxable), it created a societal bias against saving and investment and in favor of debt and consumption. But tax reformers who seek to uproot the mortgage interest deduction will find it a difficult prospect, to say the least. What is needed is a larger agenda for reforming both taxes and spending programs that recognizes the unique nature of physical capital formation—and its importance for Investor Politics.

GOVERNMENTS AND PHYSICAL CAPITAL

Most physical capital formation has been and remains a private-sector activity. Farming, for example, has always required costly investments in land improvement, tools, storage facilities, pens, and livestock. Furthermore, governments did not create the earliest avenues of land transportation. They were paths trod and sometimes hacked through forbidding terrain by settlers looking for a new place to farm or traders seeking their fortunes over the next hill. But even the earliest governments financed public investment, primarily in physical capital. To aid their soldiers in battling internal and external enemies, for example, they purchased arms and materiel, built ships and docks, and laid "royal roads" so that their armies could move quickly to areas of rebellion or invasion. Governments also invested in immense irrigation projects to protect farms and cities from flooding and to facilitate agriculture and trade. They designed city water and sewer systems to promote sanitation and to attract people to their temples and markets. They built walls and fortifications, some massive in scale, to protect their citizens against predators.

It is, of course, possible for any society to waste a lot of effort building excessive or unproductive assets. Private enterprise, groping for the right balance of investments, often makes mistakes. A merchant spends his scarce resources forming and outfitting a caravan, although it would have been more efficient to rent capacity from an existing caravan and use the savings to produce additional trade goods. In modern times, firms are faced with a variety of complex decisions every day. Should it spend a dollar on computers, on production equipment, or on advertising? Managers make the best decisions they can, calling upon their own experience, available data about consumer preferences and market conditions, and the behavior of competitors. Usually, if markets are relatively unregulated and prices allowed to communicate such information efficiently, businesses tend to make the right decisions (or disappear, teaching others an important lesson). With regard to physical capital, those who choose unwisely end up with expensive factories or equipment they cannot put to productive use, as many businesses did in the late 1920s after the Federal Reserve's artificially low interest rates encouraged investment in low-yielding assets. The results can be disastrous for these companies—but in a competitive market economy, other firms learn from their mistakes and find more efficient ways to employ workers and satisfy customers.

With public assets, the critical feedback loops that keep private companies from misallocating their investments are largely missing. When a government builds a road that serves neither to facilitate national defense nor commerce, but simply benefits a special interest with political pull, a lack of consumer demand does not necessarily translate into a loss of revenue, particularly if the source of the revenue is widely diffused. Similarly, ancient societies squandered a massive amount of labor and resources on monuments, armaments, and the personal aggrandizement of their leaders. The great pyramids of Egypt, the coliseums and circuses of Rome, the sacrificial towers of Mesoamerica—all are archaeological marvels to behold; they are also gruesome reminders of government waste and tyranny. Lacking the price signals of competitive markets, even history's most well-intentioned leaders found it difficult to determine the proper extent and mix of public investment.

Trade, cultural exchange, and social progress have, throughout most of human history, centered on rivers and seacoasts. Transportation costs are the key. Until very recently, the cost of moving anything—freight, troops, ideas—has been far lower on water than on land. Economist Thomas Sowell has observed that ease of transportation helps to explain the historical importance of the Mediterranean, across which an unequalled number and variety of cultures could trade (or invade). On the other hand, territory blessed neither with good natural harbors nor navigable rivers, like sub-Saharan Africa, has tended to lag behind the rest of the world in economic and social advancement—a result often mistakenly blamed on a variety of other factors, race among them, that are quite beside the point.[2]

Rivers, lakes, and oceans are forms of transportation infrastructure that governments need not build and maintain. Of course, accessing them requires the active creation of physical capital, such as ships or port facilities. Governments have traditionally played a role in both, building or chartering ships for military or other state uses as well as imposing taxes on ports to generate revenue. These government contracts and port investments paid salutary dividends in stimulating private shipping. However, water transportation, particularly the smaller-scale variety along rivers and lakes, has been and remains predominantly a market institution.

Not so highways. Dirt paths are a logical consequence of voluntary trade, but paved roads have until recently lacked a practical means of recouping their costs from commercial users. Ancient civilizations like those of the Persians, Romans, Incas, or Han Chinese built extensive intercity road networks by taxes or forced labor for sound military reasons. Merchants used the routes, too, but the extent of long-range trade conducted by land remained a small fraction of sea-borne commerce. As the empires receded, so did the road networks, not to be revived and expanded for centuries. Without a military power to use them, highways simply did not add enough value to be worth the expense of maintaining them. Furthermore, as centuries of experience have shown, paying for the upkeep of highways by charging tolls is a challenge because of the ease of evasion. Port facilities, on the other hand, can be funded relatively easily by user fees.

Within cities, governments have also always dominated the construction of streets and other infrastructure. Until recently, at least, it was difficult if not impossible to price their use. Furthermore, both market and nonmarket institutions require a basic street grid and at least a modicum of urban planning. Those who strain to argue that city streets can be created and maintained solely within markets must rely on tendentious readings of history as well as futuristic and, at present, unworkable pricing schemes. The fact that so many advocates of big government have abused the concept of public goods does not mean that they do not exist. Unlimited-access city streets are clearly public in a way that seaports, airports, and railroads—limited-access infrastructure whose users can be easily identified and charged—are not.[3]

INFRASTRUCTURE IN EARLY AMERICA

Early America reflected all of these age-old characteristics of public infrastructure. Throughout the Colonial era until the advent of railroads, most commerce and communication was by sea. It was easier and quicker to travel from Charleston to Boston than to travel a fraction of the same distance into South Carolina's interior. Commerce thrived along rivers but rarely extended far beyond them to the frontier, where settlers engaged predominantly in subsistence farming. Animal paths and Indian trails constituted the bulk of overland routes. Gradually, as the population of the interior grew, settlers made some improvements. They chopped down trees to widen the trails. They removed stumps and roads. They marked them as "one-chop," "two-chop," and "three-chop" roads, based on their width and smoothness. In swamps, the settlers created at least a temporarily solid surface by laying logs side to side, prompting the name *corduroy roads*. Across brooks and streams, they built crude bridges. These early, private infrastructure improvements, such as Daniel Boone's "Wilderness Road" built from North Carolina to Kentucky during the 1770s, gave pioneers a way of moving west. Still, these roads were bumpy, winding, narrow, and often impassable during seasons of rain or snow. They were sufficient for would-be subsistence farmers, but they were ill suited for the needs of trade and commerce.[4]

In the early nineteenth century, farmers and merchants began in earnest to seek solutions to the problem of interior transportation. Two emerged: *turnpikes* and *canals*. As discussed in chapter 3, states chartered private corporations to construct roads using private as well as public funds. Turnpikes, named for the pike-studded pole used to block travelers at tollgates, were more carefully designed than the modified Indian trails of the Colonial era, employing surveyors to straighten the route and engineers to construct a more permanent surface using a new technique invented by Scottish engineer John L. McAdam. A *macadam* was a wide road of crushed limestone and gravel that stood up pretty well to rain and snow. Turnpikes proliferated throughout New England and the mid-Atlantic states. In more rural environments in the South and West, private corporations built *plank roads* primarily to carry farmers' produce to market. Like it sounds, a plank road consisted of a raised platform of planks perpendicular to the road's direction. If maintained, they were excellent surfaces for wagons or coaches. Both turnpikes and plank roads benefited from state assistance, though in the latter case it was relatively minor. The federal government financed its first major highway in 1806, when the Jefferson administration began the National Road running from just outside Baltimore through Pennsylvania, Ohio, Indiana, and Illinois to connect to the Mississippi River at St. Louis. The project, justified even by Jeffersonian Republicans on military grounds, would take thirty-four years. Its completion in 1840 signaled not the beginning but the end of significant public or private investment in highways for the rest of the century.[5]

The problem was that the turnpikes and plank roads found it difficult to turn a profit for shareholders, be they private investors or state governments. They were not yet competitive in price and service with river-based transport. Furthermore, they deteriorated over time because of lack of maintenance funds. It was too easy to evade the toll booths, typically set up every seven miles or so. The most popular means of toll evasion was the use of "shunpikes"—short, dirt-path detours around the tollhouses. Economic historian Larry Schweikart reports that turnpike companies lost as much as 60 percent of their potential revenues from shunpikes alone.[6]

Because of their early struggles, many private companies operating turnpikes and plank roads turned to government for help. President James Madison sent a clear message that Washington's role would not extend much beyond the National Road by vetoing legislation that would have sent federal money to states for internal improvements—a policy maintained by future presidents from Monroe to Polk which helped to split Jefferson's Republican Party into the Democrats and Whigs by 1828.[7] Still, many state governments, especially those trending Whiggish in the late 1820s and 1830s, were eager to bail out the road companies either by buying their stock or by guaranteeing their bonds. The result was additional growth in road mileage but also substantial financial risk to states. Also, state aid actually worsened the problem of adequate revenue collection for maintenance because legislators often made subsidies conditional on artificially low tolls.[8] In sum, highways as a practical means of American transportation would have to wait for effective means of charging users and competing with waterways.

Water transportation became even more of a threat to the struggling highway companies from 1820 to 1840, the golden age of canal building. Again, private entrepreneurs obtained corporate charters from states to construct most of the canals. Again, state (but not federal) money and regulations were heavily involved. One study estimates that between 1817 and 1844, public and private investors spent some $200 million building more than four thousand miles of canals linking America's major rivers and Great Lakes. The Erie Canal, completed largely with state funds in 1825, connected New York's Hudson River to Lake Erie. It cut transportation costs between the two points from $100.00 to $5.00 a ton and travel time from twenty days to eight. It even earned a net rate of return of 8 percent and helped cement New York City's role as the country's major commercial center.[9] Other canals were no less daring but far less remunerative for their public and private investors. Indeed, during the financial panic of 1837, state-backed canal bonds collapsed, bankrupting the states of Indiana and Pennsylvania as well as a number of private banks. Southern states found that their poor credit, decimated by bond guarantees or direct investments in canals, stayed with them until the Civil War, precluding significant foreign assistance for the war effort.[10]

Canal building was far more capital intensive than road building. Because the nation's private capital markets were still young and small, states had decided to "help things along." About 75 percent of canal building was financed either by state purchases of stock or by state-guaranteed bonds.[11] Politicians defended the practice by arguing that, even if canals did not recoup the investment directly in the form of fares, surrounding communities would benefit to such a degree that public expenditure was justified. Indeed, canals could lose money from inception, they said, and still be successful. Whigs, in particular, made this case forcefully in the early 1830s and soon applied it to the subsidy of railroads. It is fundamentally flawed, however. The possibility of a benefit to third parties from an investment, what economists call a "positive externality," is insufficient to justify government involvement. Canals were not public goods because they facilitated economic development. The only way they could be considered public goods—worthy of public investment—would have been because private operators were unable to exclude nonpaying users. But this problem was far less pronounced on the water than on land.

One of the reasons that railroads supplanted canals and turnpikes as a means of American transportation was precisely because their users could be charged an accurate price, providing a stable means for maintaining tracks and yielding a return to investors. Still, many railroads followed the course laid by canals in seeking state aid for their immense up-front costs. Some railroads were financed by states using a federal budget surplus distributed to the states by the Van Buren administration in 1937. Others received state land or tax abatements. From 1830—when the *Best Friend of Charleston* took the first steam locomotive trip in American history along the South Carolina Railroad—until 1840, railroad companies laid nearly three thousand miles of track.[12] Quite a few also went bankrupt, letting their exuberance about the new technology get in the way of good judgment.

States losing money on these deals backed away from future investment in transportation. Indeed, popular revulsion against state loans and loan guarantees to transportation companies led to statutory and constitutional prohibitions in most northeastern and midwestern states that had previously funded canals and early rail lines. "The state shall not be a party to, or interested in, any work of internal improvement, nor engaged in carrying out such work," stated the Michigan state constitution of 1851. The Ohio constitution of the same year forbade counties or municipalities from owning stock in or lending money to private ventures. Ten years earlier, the governor of New York proclaimed, "taxation for purposes of internal improvement deservedly finds no advocate among the people."[13]

So during the 1840s and 1850s, as rail mileage grew by a factor of ten and railroads truly became a national transportation network, most of the needed capital came from private investors. While three-quarters of the investment in canals had come from governments, only one-quarter of pre-Civil War railroad investment was public. As discussed in chapter 3, the railroad corporations dominated antebellum securities markets, creating a new industry of financiers, bankers, brokers, and bond analysts. They also represented the lion's share of demand for the emerging iron industry.

Largely following the railroads' trunk lines, private companies such as Wells-Fargo and Western Union turned Samuel Morse's invention of the telegraph into a national communications network from the late 1840s until the Civil War—a development that had further impact on American finance by contributing to the ascendancy of the New York Stock Exchange and the Chicago Board of Trade over smaller, regional financial centers.[14]

During and after the Civil War, railroads became far more dependent on and entwined with government. Part of the reason was that, having established a dense network of lines east of the Mississippi, rail lines began to look west towards the Pacific. Sparse populations and markets made westward expansion far less cost-effective than the rail network built in the 1840s and 1850s. Railroads would need huge quantities of financial capital to make a go of it. Unlikely to attract private or foreign investors to the questionable venture, they turned to Washington. The federal government began to provide land grants to railroad companies throughout the Midwest and West. In exchange for agreeing to transport federal freight and mail at reduced rates, the railroads could then sell most of the acreage to raise funds, lay track on the remaining land, and provide service to the settlers, ranchers, and miners who had bought the land from them. Federal land grants gave railroads about $500 million with which to lay track to the Pacific.[15] Other subsidies and tax breaks from states and localities helped the process along. A generation had passed since the Panic of 1837 and widespread failure of state-backed transportation ventures, reducing popular opposition to the idea.

American commerce clearly expanded during the latter half of the nineteenth century, much of it conducted along rail lines or engaged in the production of steel, timber, stone, engines, and other related industries. But was government subsidy necessary? The Great Northern Railway, built by James J. Hill during the last quarter of the century, proved that private entrepreneurs could build transcontinental rail lines. Yes, the Great Northern grew more slowly than its subsidized competitors did—because Hill had to justify his investment on the basis of commerce rather than politics. He paid settlers to move in the intended path of the line and build farming or ranching enterprises that he could then serve. His company funded agricultural research and education on crop rotation and other techniques. His line was planned carefully to minimize cost and to permit effective maintenance. All the way, he had to battle not only federal subsidies to his rivals, but also active interference by federal regulators. Still, by the early 1890s, there were five transcontinental lines, of which the Great Northern from St. Paul to Seattle was the only truly private one. During the financial crisis of 1893, three of his subsidized rivals—the Northern Pacific, the Union Pacific, and the Santa Fe—went bankrupt. Before and after their reorganization, Hill's private railroad consistently delivered better service at lower prices.[16]

The old argument, begun with the issue of canals, that "externalities" associated with transportation infrastructure justified government subsidy, had proven incorrect. If those not directly shipping products via railroads benefited from their existence, the benefits were largely captured by the prices these "third parties" paid for the goods and services they consumed. There was no economic reason for subsidy, which had adverse political consequences for railroads as well as other businesses, as explained in chapter 2. A slow and steady growth in private rail investment would have created far more economic value than the spectacle of subsidized lines hurtling towards each other in a race for federal goodies. As Schweikart put it:

> In retrospect, the subsidies themselves accounted for much of the mismanagement of the roads, in that subsidies were given based on miles completed, not the quality of the miles completed or the effectiveness of the road. The incentives of subsidies encouraged overbuilding and constructing circuitous routes aimed at laying as many miles of track as possible. With no concern for terrain, the subsidized roads ran up steep gradients that increased fuel costs or along weak shoulders that contributed to accidents. . . . Everywhere, the subsidies encouraged higher repairs and operating costs, while at the same time fostering a contemptuous attitude toward settlers; after all, the farmers needed the roads, not vice versa.[17]

THE PHYSICAL CAPITAL OF CITIES

At the same time that transcontinental railroads were expanding westward at such a rapid clip, transportation within America's cities was undergoing a marked transformation of its own. Steam-driven trains, a technology well suited for freight and intercity passenger traffic, was too costly, noisy, and smoky for intracity travel. Until the mid-nineteenth century, people had gotten around in cities primarily on foot. Horse-drawn carriages (in some places evolving into horse-drawn trains) played a minor role, but served mostly the elite. As a result, cities were compact. The most valuable land was at the city center, where pedestrians had the easiest access to work and home, and least valuable on the outskirts. It was the introduction of electricity in the 1880s that facilitated mass transit and the first urban sprawl.[18]

Streetcars, powered by overhanging electric lines, proved a flexible and economical means of moving many people around cities. They expanded easily after the initial investment in a central power station, because the addition of lines to the system was relatively cheap. The larger the streetcar system, the lower the operating costs per mile. They made urban leaders feel like their communities were "progressive"—and to the extent that they reduced the amount of horse manure in the city streets, they were right. Streetcar lines led to urban growth by linking central cities to popular destinations on the outskirts of towns, such as carnivals or cemeteries. Homebuilders, industrialists, and merchants then built along the streetcar lines.

It was the Golden Age of mass transit. But it was not to last. In most cities, streetcar companies received exclusive franchises. In exchange, they had to follow city rate regulations. Typically, they charged a flat rate for all travelers—usually a nickel—with free transfers between routes. Streetcar systems practiced what was called "cross-subsidization," in which riders taking short trips (that cost less than five cents to provide) helped to pay the higher costs of others taking longer trips. As long as the short-run riders had no other option but walking, streetcars could maintain the flat-rate system. But when a technology came along that offered competition for those riders, the cross-subsidy system was doomed to collapse.[19]

The streetcar was not the only factor in the changing landscape of American cities. Massive waves of immigration, both from foreign lands and from unprofitable domestic farms, swelled the nation's urban population. From 1880 to 1920, the percentage of Americans living in urban areas rose from one-quarter to one-half. Just in the last two decades of the nineteenth century, New York City grew from less than 2 million residents to 3.5 million. Chicago's population tripled to 1.7 million. Looked at another away, rural areas—at least those east of the Mississippi—stopped growing. Indeed, 60 percent of the rural townships of the Northeast lost population during the period.[20] The nature of American housing and infrastructure changed accordingly. Most families owned their own homes before 1880. That rate declined steadily until the 1920s, after which it moderated briefly before plunging again in the 1930s.[21] Families who once occupied small farmhouses or modest homes on the outskirts of small towns now rented apartments in the massive tenement complexes that arose to house workers in factories, meatpacking plants, textile mills, and other industries.

Still, the vast majority of housing was privately built, financed, and owned. Cities increasingly began to regulate the construction of residential and commercial structures, but few viewed the provision of a home as a government entitlement. City officials justified regulation on health and safety grounds. It was reasonable, for example, to make sure that a new structure going up in a city did not pose a risk to neighboring buildings through fire or collapse. Increasing concerns about public health also led to the development of water and sewer systems. Even ancient cities had often featured water systems, with some Roman aqueducts and sewers still in use today. But until the early twentieth century, most Americans lived and worked on self-sufficient farms. They owned and operated their own infrastructure—wells, drainage systems, outhouses, and fireplaces. When they (or their immigrant cousins) moved to the cities, they exchanged ownership of such capital assets for "renting" them from public or private utilities, just as they had swapped self-employment and homeownership for factory jobs and apartments.

The result was a boom in municipal utility finance and construction. Earlier in the century, growing cities had begun using older, storm-water drainage systems to transport human and other wastes to nearby rivers, lakes, and tidal estuaries. As American city dwellers discovered in the 1880s and 1890s, this was not a real solution. Germs spread easily from water sources back to the cities, leading to epidemics of cholera, typhoid fever, and other diseases. By 1900, ten cities had developed filtration systems to help separate wastes for safe disposal. The effectiveness of water treatment grew dramatically in 1908 when chlorine disinfection was introduced. Cities began to refurbish, expand, and improve their water and sewer systems, financed by investors eager to purchase tax-free municipal bonds after the 1913 passage of the federal income tax. By 1930, waterborne diseases had largely disappeared from the nation.[22]

Power generation followed a different path. Most new city dwellers, it is true, stopped generating power for their own household needs (using wood or coal) and became customers of new utilities. However, starting with Thomas Edison's own generation and distribution system for New York City in 1882, electric utilities were largely private rather than public. At first, they focused either on powering streetcar systems or on wiring dense commercial and residential areas. Major cities had a host of competing electric companies supplying different neighborhoods or industries. Some were in direct head-to-head competition. In 1905, Chicago awarded twenty-one franchises, three of them citywide, to supply electricity. As late as 1922, there were 3,774 privately owned electric utilities in the United States, and some customers could literally choose which overhead lines they wished to be connected to. During the 1920s, the industry matured and expanded. Marginal companies folded or merged with larger ones. About sixteen hundred electric companies disappeared.[23] Taking advantage of new technologies and economies of scale, the remaining utilities saw dramatic increases in customers. In 1914, only one in five American homes had electricity. By 1929, 70 percent did. Similarly, only 30 percent of factories were electrically powered in 1914, compared to 70 percent in 1929.[24]

Why were most electric utilities private while water and sewer utilities were public? The problem should sound familiar: the ability to price. From the beginning, electric systems could charge virtually all customers accurate prices based on the amount of power they used. The first workable electric meter came along in 1888, and by 1895 inventor Oliver B. Shallenberger had patented the induction watt-hour meter that became the industry standard. By contrast, measuring a household's water and sewer usage would remain a challenge for decades to come. Early water utilities could charge a hookup fee to homes or businesses and attempt to price on the assumption that larger and more valuable property equated with higher water and sewer use. However, the benefits of better sanitation weren't necessarily captured by such crude pricing schemes. Only later were cities able to install water meters to measure monthly use, and they still estimate rather than directly measure sewer use. By the time technology allowed better pricing of water and sewer service, governments had established themselves as the presumed provider. Even so, the introduction of water meters led most cities to pull their water and sewer utilities out of their general budgets and set them up under enterprise funds. Customer charges, not general revenues, fund the operations of these utilities and serve to finance their revenue bonds. One of the hottest trends of the past three decades has been contracting out the management (and in some cases selling the assets) of water and wastewater treatment to private companies in municipalities across the United States. In this way, physical capital that remains controlled and usually owned by governments has nevertheless been subjected to prices and competitive pressures that resemble those in private markets. The result has been a better rate of return on investment in such capital as well as improved service and cost for customers.[25]

THE AUTOMOBILITY ERA

Present-day advocates of dense, transit-friendly development patterns view the 1880–1920 period as a high point of urban planning. In retrospect, however, it was a brief and fleeting turn towards urbanization and regimentation that never "took" with most Americans. Dense urban living bred social disorder and crime, or at least the perception of it. Transit restricted residents' personal freedom by dictating where and when they could travel. Coupled with the fact that so many urban dwellers had traded self-employment on the farm (whether in upstate New York or in rural Italy, Poland, or Russia) for hourly employment in the city, they felt less autonomous, less in control of their own lives. As soon as circumstances and technology allowed, they sought a less compact, more independent lifestyle reminiscent of their largely rural roots. They found it in the suburbs that automobiles and other factors made possible. Suburbs allowed them to realize all the benefits of city life—and there were and are many, including employment, shopping, recreation, culture, sanitation, and access to health care—without having to feel so dependent on impersonal landlords, employers, and transit operators.

Tinkerers, foreign and domestic, had introduced the automobile during the 1890s as a curiosity. It did not stay that way for long. During the next decade, entrepreneurs such as Henry Ford, William Durant, and Henry Leland created not just a new, more individualized form of mass transportation but also the beginnings of the modern mass-production system. There were 4,100 cars sold in America in 1900. By 1910, there were 450,000 registered in the United States. By 1920, there were 9 million. At first, the automobile affected cities not in the form of mass ownership but as competition for streetcars. Recall that urban transit relied on a cross-subsidy of long-distance travelers by those riding for only a few city blocks. By the 1910s, there were thousands of car owners looking for ways to defray some of the cost of their significant investment in automobility. Some saw an opportunity by offering to pick up and drop off passengers for the same nickel the streetcars charged, but with greater comfort and convenience. After all, autos could pick you up quickly and carry you directly to your destination. With streetcars, you might have to wait for a while, then get on a crowded car and wait through several stops. Within a few years, there were an estimated 60,000 cars picking up American passengers in this manner.[26]

The proto-taxis, called "jitneys" for a slang word meaning nickel, posed significant competition to streetcars. The transit companies retaliated by pressing local governments to ban jitneys or at least heavily regulate them through high operating bonds and licensing fees. It only delayed the inevitable. Jitneys eventually gave way to buses, which offered more routes and greater flexibility for passengers. Furthermore, as mass production geared up in the 1920s, more and more Americans bought their own cars. Streetcar systems, losing their precious short-trip riders, were forced to jack up their fares, chasing more customers away. Streetcars and their rail-transit successors, subways and elevated lines, peaked in 1926 at 15.3 billion rides and shrank steadily thereafter.[27]

As far as freight and intercity passenger traffic was concerned, the impact of the automobile was more gradual. Since the rise of the railroads in the 1840s, most states had neglected the few good roads that connected the major cities. At late as 1902, states spent a collective $4 million on highways, or a scant 2 percent of their budgets. As automobiles became ubiquitous in the first two decades of the century, however, an increasingly vocal share of the population began to protest about the poor quality of the mostly dirt roads they were traversing. The nascent trucking industry also began to complain. Trucks began hauling cargo across the country as early as 1912. By 1918, United States companies were turning out 230,000 trucks a year, though some of these were for the war effort.[28] If trucks were to provide effective competition to rail, they would need better routes to ply than the twisting, muddy roads typical at the turn of the century.

Here is where things get a little sticky. As states and the federal government began to answer these calls for dramatic increases in public investment, did they engage in a massive intervention into the free market? It would certainly appear so. From 1902 to 1927, state spending on highways skyrocketed from $4 million to $514 million, or 25 percent of the average state budget.[29] The Federal Aid Highway Program of 1921 prodded states to upgrade and connect rural roads, creating what would become the interstate highway system. During the 1920s, Washington spent about $75 million in federal revenues to construct and improve roads. Between 1921 and 1929, paved road mileage in the United States nearly doubled. The ripple effects of this massive public investment reached virtually every corner of the economy. New companies supplying rubber, steel, glass, cloth, and other materials to automakers flourished. By 1930, one out of nine American workers had a job related to automobile manufacturing.[30] Even more worked in the roadside shops and restaurants, the tourism industry, housing construction, or others nurtured by automobility.

Cars remade cities, too. Although city spending on streets did not rise much during the same period as a percentage of total local budgets, far more avenues and side streets were paved by 1930.[31] Cities invested in signage, traffic lights, police, and other services related to car travel. More importantly, the advent of buses and later, personal autos, made possible the first true suburbs. Workers could live far enough away from factories, shops, or offices to be able to afford larger homes, whether bought or rented. The population of Shaker Heights, a suburb of Cleveland, grew tenfold during the 1920s. New York City's Scarsdale tripled in size.[32] Cars also contributed to the growth of supermarkets and other retail during the decade, as drivers could carry more items away in their cars than transit riders could.

Apologists for mass transit, environmental extremists, and even a few cranky conservatives have described the transformation of American life by the automobile as an intrusive act of government. But this is a superficial conclusion. The real reason for the success of the auto is that, for the first time, there was a feasible means of charging those who used roads and streets: the gas tax. It was not a direct fee for service, like the electric meter allowed. Nor did it resemble the roundabout way—property taxes—that households and businesses paid for early water and sewer service. Motor fuel taxes fell somewhere in the middle. They created a link, albeit an imperfect one, between use and cost. The more someone drove, the more they paid to maintain and expand the road network.

Unfortunately, there was no way of collecting gas charges voluntarily. Coercion was needed to prevent people from becoming (literal) free riders. Still, the ability to collect a rough user fee solved the pricing problem that had plagued older turnpikes, plank roads, and city streets. Far from being the beneficiaries of unwarranted government intervention in free enterprise, automobiles were a market-friendly development that made roads a far more valuable asset for public or private investment. There was no need for government to manufacture an insatiable public appetite for automobiles. It came naturally. Cars empowered individuals instead of bureaucracies and central planners. They added a significant amount of new land to the real estate market that, being too far from streetcar lines or railroad stops, had previously been poorly used, much of it as marginal and unproductive farms. One result was that homeownership, which had been declining for decades, would rebound and (after an interruption for depression and war) soar to unprecedented heights.

HOUSING BECOMES AN ENTITLEMENT

The next big change in public policy towards physical capital began in the 1930s. As discussed in chapter 4, the Roosevelt administration sought to prop up employment through a variety of federally funded public works projects. Some of the projects, including roads, utility improvements, and other infrastructure, may well have added significant value to local economies. Others were nothing more than pork barrel projects. In addition to direct expenditures, which worsened the budget deficit (against which Roosevelt had railed in the 1932 election), the administration decided to use federal credit to leverage private economic activity and increase employment in the (unionized) construction trades. The Federal Home Loan Bank system created a series of district banks that purchased loans from private lenders in order to encourage mortgage loans and new housing construction. The Home Owners Loan Corporation helped families refinance their mortgages rather than face foreclosure, offering long-term government-backed loans in exchange for short-term private loans. Between 1933 and 1935, it issued $8 billion in loans to a million American families. In 1934, Congress passed a Housing Act that created federal mortgage insurance for small homes. The new Federal Housing Administration (FHA) would pay off lenders in the event of a default. The act also created the Federal Savings and Loan Insurance Corporation to bail out savings and loan companies overextended in their core mortgage business. In 1937, another Housing Act expanded federal loan guarantees further and established ongoing federal support for states and municipalities to build and operate public housing projects for the poor. Finally, in a 1938 amendment, Congress created the Federal National Mortgage Association (FNMA, or "Fannie Mae") to buy and sell mortgage loans on the secondary market.[33]

This alphabet soup of new agencies, spending federal "credit" rather than actual dollars at first to minimize their impact on the budget deficit, had dramatic long-term consequences. By 1940, FHA mortgage insurance covered 40 percent of housing starts. Private lenders emulated the FHA's twenty- to thirty-year loan terms, even for more affluent homebuyers ineligible for FHA insurance. Previously, private lenders had typically required a 40 to 50 percent down payment and offered mortgage loans for three to ten years. With FHA insurance, lenders cut the down payment amount to 20 percent, and later to 10 percent.[34] It particularly made sense to lengthen terms and minimize down payments because of the impact of the mortgage insurance deduction discussed earlier. World War II brought the first widespread income tax and gave average Americans a strong incentive to prefer debt over equity in buying a home. It might cost a family more in the long run to pay little down and borrow over thirty years, but much of the additional debt service evaporated in lower taxes.

The Roosevelt administration's original political constituency for these initiatives was organized labor, as its more candid leaders acknowledged. But later, private-sector interests that initially opposed a federal role in housing—such as associations of realtors, lumber dealers, homebuilders, and savings and loan companies—came to champion their protection and expansion. No wonder. From a historical trough of 44 percent in 1940, the homeownership rate shot up to 63 percent by 1965.[35] Millions of Americans took out long-term mortgage loans, deducted the interest, and headed to suburbia on new state and federal highways to buy more spacious and comfortable homes than had ever been seen, thanks to standardization and new homebuilding materials and technologies. Bankers, mortgage lenders, realtors, and property insurers made a killing. And unlike the prewar trends, these really were due in large measure to government intervention in the market. By providing generous tax breaks and manipulating credit markets to favor residential construction, Washington had engineered a societal result unlikely to have come from a market process.

Nor has the result been an unqualified plus from the standpoint of Investor Politics. Yes, personal ownership of capital assets—homes—did rise markedly. But so did personal debt. Furthermore, until legislation in the late 1970s and early 1980s shielded IRAs and 401(k)s from tax, the mortgage interest deduction and other breaks led many Americans to treat homes as their sole form of retirement savings. During the 1970s, in particular, as families poured their savings into their homes as a hedge against both inflation and taxes, markets for other personal investment tanked. The average corporate stock lost 23 percent of its value during the 1970s, while the average house appreciated 155 percent.[36] One memorable innovation during the period was the condominium, which was little more than a way of giving apartment dwellers the same tax and credit advantages that single-family homeowners already enjoyed. Author Philip Longman is particularly caustic about the economic consequences of the federal government favoring housing over other forms of investment:

> In the short run, all the subsidies pouring into the housing sector did help to stimulate economic growth and forestall recession—providing yet another reason why cutting the subsidies became politically impossible, no matter what damage they might be doing to America's future standard of living . . . [But] capital that could have gone for retooling American industry at a time of mounting foreign competition went instead for financing the sale and resale of houses and condominiums at ever higher prices.[37]

The alphabet soup of housing-credit agencies that Roosevelt created still exists to a large degree, conferring unjustified windfalls to some industries at the expense of others and attracting scarce financial capital into increasingly marginal investments. Fannie Mae and Freddie Mac, for example, have used their special governmental privileges—which include access to federal credit as well as exemption from federal regulations and state income taxes—to grow in size and influence far beyond what even New Dealers might have dreamed. As late as 1980, commercial banks and savings and loan companies retained up to three-quarters of residential mortgages in their portfolios. But over the past two decades, Fannie Mae and Freddie Mac have significantly increased their participation in the market, now purchasing more than half of all newly originated home mortgages.[38] Many of these are then pooled as mortgage-backed securities and sold in the secondary market to institutional investors. Still, according to an analysis of Fannie Mae and Freddie Mac by the American Enterprise Institute, the two government-subsidized companies will have assumed risk for nearly half of all residential mortgages in the United States by 2003. The financial exposure to taxpayers should the housing market suffer a downturn could be staggering.[39]

On the other hand, at a local level the dynamics of Investor Politics did begin to assert themselves noticeably in the late 1960s and 1970s. For the first time in the twentieth century, homeowners made up an overwhelming majority of voters, with the heaviest concentration in the fast-growing states of the Sunbelt. For this newly re-created capitalist class, the prospect of escalating taxes on the one major asset they owned—their homes—turned out to be anathema. Of course, even renters "pay" property taxes in the sense that most of the *ad valorem* tax levied on landlords is passed along in the form of higher rents. But renters never get a bill. They have little information with which to evaluate whether the amount and quality of local services they receive is worth the price they are paying. Homeowners, however, see the bill. A high property tax bill does represent another federal tax deduction—and a justifiable one, I might add, since households ought not to be forced to pay tax on income they do not consume. But for those who view homes as investments, the property tax feels like an onerous burden, indeed. It reduces the real return on the investment, and is owed, albeit at a lower level, even if the asset is declining in value and thus delivering no investment return at all.

It is no accident that the American tax revolt of the late twentieth century began at the local level, with homeowners battling property revaluations and rate hikes. In a few short years after homeownership reached critical mass in the mid-1960s, California's Proposition 13 and similar measures, championed by new taxpayer associations in a number of states, began to rein in government's ability to tax real property. At the end of World War II, about half the revenues collected by states and localities derived from property taxes. In 1965, the percentage had dipped only slightly to 45 percent, but by 1980 it had fallen to 30 percent, where it remains. In terms of the share of personal income taken in property taxes, the burden rose by 29 percent from 1950 to 1965, then fell by nearly the same amount during the next fifteen years of tax revolt. Since 1980, it has risen at a far more modest rate.[40]

CURRENT CONTROVERSIES: TAX REFORM

Public policy towards physical capital formation intersects with several pressing political issues at the turn of the twenty-first century. Two merit discussion here: tax reform and urban planning. I remember the moment I first realized the ferocity of the mortgage interest lobby. I was sitting in on a 1996 board meeting of a state chapter of the National Association of Realtors. Later on the agenda, I would seek funding for a study of housing regulations. First, however, the board discussed the association's recent lobbying activities against the flat tax, which had leapt off the pages of think tank papers and into the headlines with the surprising presidential candidacy of Steve Forbes. The board reviewed a recent massive campaign of mailings, faxes, and phone calls by their members. A lobbyist from the national office related reassuring meetings with congressional leaders (Republicans, no less) who promised not to advance reform legislation that would affect tax breaks favoring homeownership. Above all, the realtors in the room seem to snarl every time they hear the term "flat tax." It was not a question of theory. It was an integral part of their livelihood and they knew it.

The mortgage interest deduction did not only boost the number of Americans who could afford homes. Indeed, most of that gain occurred before 1965. More important in recent years has been the increase in the size and amenities of homes, financed by larger, tax-deductible mortgage loans. Consider how the average house has changed just in the past quarter-century. In 1995, 80 percent of all new single-family homes had central air-conditioning. In 1971, only 36 percent did. The average 1995 home was also three times as likely to have more than two bathrooms and twice as likely to have fireplaces as their 1971 counterparts. Homeowners are buying a larger and more valuable product. However, they are paying more for the privilege. During roughly the same period, the median price of a new home more than tripled to $137,000.00 (including the land), representing an average 5.8 percent annual price increase. That rate outpaced general inflation and wage growth.[41] Therefore, while those itemizing their tax returns are paying for nicer homes and writing off the interest, the home ownership rate itself has not risen much at all since the postwar boom. These changes in average housing surely represent progress, and I for one am particularly glad about the air-conditioning. But it does not change the fact that, because of bad tax policy, some of the nation's capital was devoted to more and larger housing rather than to other productive assets, thus shrinking the economic pie in the long run. Would higher productivity and personal income growth have boosted homeownership by a similar rate, anyway? We will never know.

Meanwhile, on the tax ledger side, the mortgage interest deduction contributes to the use of other tax breaks. Usually the largest deduction available to average taxpayers, it makes it worthwhile for many to itemize rather than to take the standard deduction. Introduced in 1944, the standard deduction was a clever if arbitrary solution to the problem of excluding investment expenses from the income tax base. Instead of tallying them up, taxpayers were invited to take a shortcut, trading precision for simplicity. But after the war, lawmakers neglected to adjust the value of the deduction for inflation. Taxpayers found itemizing increasingly attractive, particularly during the housing boom of the next two decades. By the early 1960s, the share of taxpayers choosing to itemize had grown from 20 percent to nearly half and the number of itemized returns from 8 million to 25 million. In 1963, the Kennedy administration tried to trim deductions and make the tax system flatter and broader. It succeeded in cutting marginal rates. The top rate fell from 91 percent to 70 percent, helping boost work effort, investment, and growth. But the administration failed in an attempt to allow tax deductions for only those itemized expenses (including mortgage interest) that exceeded 5 percent of income. The real estate and building lobbies combined with the American Medical Association, college and nonprofit executives, and state and local governments to defend the most popular tax deductions against the proposed limit. It never had a chance.[42]

Amazingly, the reformers did not give up. Their leader in the Kennedy and Johnson administrations was Stanley Surrey, a former Harvard law professor. During the 1950s, he and other advocates of tax reform inside and outside of government convinced powerful House Ways and Means Committee Chairman Wilbur Mills to commission a series of academic studies on tax reform and base-broadening ideas in 1959. Then, as assistant treasury secretary, he helped draft Kennedy's 1963 tax reform package, in-

cluding the ill-fated income limit on deductions. After the president was assassinated, Surrey found a less sympathetic ear in Johnson, whose interests
lay on the spending side of the budget and who saw reform of tax exclusions as a threat to Texas oil interests. Still, Surrey pressed on. He coined the
somewhat unfortunate phrase "tax expenditure" to describe government
subsidies like the mortgage interest deduction that were embedded in the
tax code. In 1969, thanks to his efforts, the Treasury Department published
the first tax expenditure budget, which helped expose the extent to which
tax deductions tended to bestow benefits on upper-income households
with higher tax brackets and homeownership rates.[43]

Surrey's work helped pave the way for the next, and more successful, assault on the mortgage interest deduction. By 1981, the deduction had enjoyed massive growth, as the surging inflation of the 1970s pushed up home
values and interest rates while eroding the value of the standard deduction
and inducing bracket creep. Economists and policy experts with the incom-
ing Reagan administration understood the problem, but shied away from
the frontal assault on tax preferences Kennedy had attempted. Instead, they
began with an indirect approach. Reagan's 1981 tax bill cut marginal rates
across the board, with the top rate falling from 70 percent to 50 percent. A
low marginal rate made all deductions less valuable. In 1986, after an
abortive attempt at direct limitation, Congress and the administration further reduced the real value of the mortgage interest deduction in the Tax
Reform Act by cutting rates again (the top rate fell to 33 percent) and increasing the value of the personal exemption and standard deduction, adjusting both for inflation for the first time. The number of taxpayers claim-
ing the standard deduction grew, making up about 70 percent by 1997.[44]
Finally, changes in the tax code in 1987 and 1990 placed caps on deductions
for wealthy Americans.[45]

Still, these successes only slowed the growth of the program. They did
not come close to ending it. Particularly after President Clinton jacked up
the top rate to nearly 40 percent in 1993, most upper-middle-income and
affluent taxpayers still had strong incentives to find ways to reduce their
taxable income. The 1986 tax reform bill actually created a powerful new incentive by ending the long-standing deductibility of consumer debt, such
as interest on credit cards. Lenders were quick to seize upon the mortgage
interest deduction as a loophole in the law. They promoted home-equity

loans, with which homeowners could finance not just home improvements but cars, boats, college tuitions, and consumer goods. From 1980 to 1995, the total mortgage interest deduction claimed by taxpayers rose by an inflation-adjusted 5.7 percent a year—slower than in the 1960s and 1970s but still a rate faster than the overall economy or federal budget growth.[46]

At the turn of the twenty-first century, the mortgage interest deduction remained a troubling bias in the tax code favoring debt over equity and housing over other forms of physical capital formation. Not all tax breaks related to housing are unjustified. As already mentioned, excluding income devoted to paying property taxes (as well as other state and local levies) from the federal income tax is proper because the money is not being consumed by the earner. By itself, the property tax exclusion was worth $23 billion in 2001.[47] In addition, like the mortgage interest deduction, it favors the relatively well-to-do, since those lacking the equity or income to own homes pay property taxes indirectly, in the form of higher rents, which are not deductible. And it makes states and localities a bit more likely to hike taxes, knowing that their citizens will get some of the taxes back from Washington. Another important tax break concerns selling a home. In 1964, Congress excluded capital gains from a home for persons fifty-five or over. It later widened the exclusion to capital gains up to $500,000.00. Finally, in 1997, Congress and President Clinton enacted a tax-cut bill that included penalty-free withdrawals from IRAs to make a down payment on a first home.

These last two tax policies are aimed in the right direction, but they are flawed. For one thing, eligibility for both is limited, directly or indirectly, by household income. If the policies advance economic efficiency and tax neutrality, they do so for all households, not just those middle-income taxpayers who are undecided in presidential elections. Second, what is needed is a clear, coherent policy that reflects the unique nature of buying a house. Like the purchase of other durable assets, such as cars or furniture, buying a house is a mixture of consumption and investment. A homeowner consumes the amenities of having a house every day he lives in it. But he also builds equity in an asset he hopes to sell or leave to heirs. It is impossible to clearly define the difference between the two. If you could, you would be able to identify what portion of the equity and debt service required to buy the house is an investment and then treat it like a traditional IRA deposit—

make it deductible up front while taxing the return at sale. But there is no way to do that.

The alternative is to treat investment in housing like a back-ended Roth IRA. In reality, the tax code already applies this rule to other physical assets such as cars. You cannot deduct the cost of buying a car from your income tax (unless, of course, you use a home-equity loan to finance it). On the other hand, you need not report the money you receive when selling your car. Because the principal of the investment in the car was taxed, the return has already been reduced by the same rate. No need to tax it again. Furthermore, because driving the car depreciates its value at resale, no amount of the tax exclusion finances consumption. The same policy should apply to homes. Regardless of how long the home is owned, the age and income of the homeowner, and whether it is a primary residence or an investment property, all capital gains from the sale of the home should be free from tax. Correspondingly, all costs associated with buying the home—both the down payment and the cost of servicing the mortgage loan—should be fully taxable. The home mortgage interest deduction, by contrast, is a blunt instrument at best. It provides tax relief not for the investment component of buying a house but simply for maximizing debt and minimizing equity.

The political lobbies that protect the mortgage interest deduction know what they want and are willing to spend considerable resources to protect it. It is essentially pointless to argue, as some flat taxers have, that elimination of the deduction in the context of fundamental tax reform would not have much of an effect on housing prices because interest rates would fall.[48] The impact of tax reform on interest rates is a speculative and controversial issue. There is no question that, all other things being equal, the mortgage interest deduction draws personal financial capital away from other forms of investment. If the special tax treatment of homes disappears, it is unreasonable to expect the housing market not to be negatively impacted, at least to some degree.[49] Politicians might seek to ameliorate the impact by lifting regulations that impose additional costs on homeowners. Unfortunately, while the interest deduction is federal, the regulatory burden is a state and local problem. Perhaps the best short-run policy to pursue is to offer a tradeoff—eliminate the income caps and regulations on deducting capital gains from the sale of a home in exchange for imposing a meaningful income cap on deducting mortgage interest. Over time, as Americans gain more experience with tax-deductible IRAs, Social Security and Medicare accounts, and other investment vehicles, they will not value the mortgage interest deduction as much. They are likely to accept fewer deductions for home buying if they can get even higher caps on deductible deposits into their personal savings accounts.

As far as IRA withdrawals for home purchases are concerned, the problem is that the law does not go far enough. It is limited to first-time homebuyers and subject to income capping. In reality, all withdrawals from tax-deferred savings accounts should be penalty-free for everyone. Getting a tax deduction for savings account deposits is not a special favor. It is the proper way to treat current consumption and future consumption equally. As long as withdrawals—whether for retirement, buying a home, or taking a trip—are fully taxable, the system is neutral. Only one complication remains. If the taxpayer makes his deposit in the prime of his working years, when his marginal rate is high, and then withdraws it when his rate falls, such as after retirement, the result is a tax subsidy. The solution is obvious: Move towards a single-rate tax system, which would have many other advantages.[50]

CURRENT CONTROVERSIES: URBAN PLANNING AND INFRASTRUCTURE

During the last two decades of the twentieth century, one of the most vexing problems facing states and localities has been dealing with population growth and, correspondingly, a demand for public services. Part of their dilemma is self-inflicted. Politicians constantly talk about and pass legislation to promote economic development. However, when their efforts succeed—to the extent they do, which is debatable—the result is often immigration. People follow jobs. Particularly in the low-unemployment environment typical in many fast-growing jurisdictions, corporate relocations often involve bringing their employees with them, rather than increased employment of natives. At the same time, many economic development policies have compromised the ability of state and local governments to keep up with their infrastructure and other public service needs. Politicians have made their tax codes as porous as Swiss cheese by offering abatements, tax credits, and other goodies to companies locating or expanding within their jurisdictions. Since the developments do impose costs on the public sector, such as increased traffic or higher school enrollment, many communities are now told that they must pay higher average taxes to fund the government services needed to accommodate growth—begging the question of why, if growth actually costs long-time residents money, they should want it.

Politicians have also taken advantage of a well-established federal tax break to promote economic development. Virtually since their inception, income tax codes have excluded interest earned from state and municipal bonds. Because investors are willing to settle for a lower interest rate on the bonds in exchange for the tax exclusion, it has the effect of reducing borrowing costs for these governments. Many states allow local governments to use various devices to allow private companies to get the same break on borrowing costs. In my own state of North Carolina, for example, a state constitutional amendment allows localities to extend their tax-exempt bonding authority to private industry or quasi-public ventures such as sports stadiums. In this way, federal taxpayers who live far from the affected community help to subsidize economic growth. When growth translates into increased need for local services, however, the local taxpayer must often foot the bill.

In short, many a politician talks out of both sides of his mouth on growth. Even without extra incentives from confused elected officials, however, growth will occur. Furthermore, it has many salutary effects. More people means more potential customers or employees—along with amenities such as recreation, health care, and shopping that smaller communities cannot sustain. As the late Julian Simon wrote in his book *The Ultimate Resource,* an increase in population increases the potential wealth of the community, as the number of potential entrepreneurs, scientists, or inventors grows proportionally.

For public policy, the challenge is making sure that growth pays for itself. As with tax policy, urban planning policies must minimize distortions in the marketplace. To the extent possible, an influx of new businesses or residents to a community should yield sufficient revenues with which to pay for the public services they require. Advocates of "Smart Growth"—the latest name for that mix of environmentalism, communitarianism, and snobbery popular in university towns and editorial board meetings—argue that the kind of development encouraged by government housing and transportation policies makes growth unmanageable and unaffordable. "Urban sprawl," as they call development based around highways and single-family homeownership, disrupts communities, promotes air and water pollution, and makes it costly to provide water and sewer, streets, and other public services. There is a modicum of truth to the critique—just enough to muddy the waters a bit. Unquestionably, the mortgage interest deduction encourages many families to spend more on their homes, in terms of square footage, acreage, or amenities, than they might otherwise choose to do. All other things being equal, an extra $10,000.00 invested in housing is worth more after taxes than a similar investment in a boat, an art collection, a trip around the world, or some other means of enhancing one's quality of life. And the presence of highways, particularly those permitting relatively easy commutes to business centers from faraway bedroom communities, will tend to lower the density of development patterns in a region, making mass transit infeasible and making Smart Growth-ers mad.

However, it is fanciful to suggest that the low-density, auto-friendly communities so typical of American suburbs and "edge cities" today are simply the product of market-distorting subsidies. These policies were not created against the popular will. They do not conflict with natural inclinations on the part of the average commuter or homeowner. They reflect the deeply felt preferences of millions of consumers.

Even before the mortgage interest deduction and other housing credit subsidies played a significant role in home buying, city residents were moving away from central cities to suburban neighborhoods. At first, the "sprawl" followed the streetcar lines. Later, as consumers bought cars and began to demand better road surfaces upon which to drive them, a growing network of streets and highways—largely paid for by the drivers themselves in gas taxes and later by charges to homeowners through developer impact fees—vastly multiplied the potential locations of homes, businesses, shopping centers, and other development. Without subsidy, homeownership rates would likely have risen rapidly since the 1940s, as higher incomes and changes in the technology of homebuilding put better-quality homes within reach of more and more families. Most would have chosen detached dwellings with garages and grass to mow, not because of government incentives but because they value the freedom of automobility and the comforts of a spacious home and lawn. There will always be those, such as young singles and older retirees, who do not like driving or gardening and will sustain a market for condos, townhouses, and true urban living. But to suggest that many or most American families are champing at the bit for dense, neo-urban development is to defy logic, history, and the operation of real estate markets across the country.

In a way, the Smart Growth-ers are correct. Government housing and transportation policies are causing severe growth-related problems such as traffic congestion. However, regulating development more strictly and spending less money on highways, as they advocate, are precisely the opposite policies to pursue. With regard to development patterns, the problem is not excessive, low-density growth. It is the rigid separation of residential, commercial, and industrial uses of land. Zoning, yet another Progressive-era policy with complex origins, forces many workers to live far from where they work or shop, thus requiring more daily travel on overburdened highways. I am not arguing against building codes and local rules protecting property owners from true nuisances such as noise, smoke, odor, or environmental degradation. Nor do I think that the probable impact of a new development on nearby traffic patterns should be ignored (though impact fees and infrastructure mandates on developers are a more market-friendly tool than prohibition). But current land-use rules go far beyond these legitimate concerns. Zoning codes should be completely redesigned to facilitate, rather than to block, the natural mix of residential, commercial, and industrial developments that once typified cities and that choices by real people in the marketplace would likely generate.

Even with restrictive land-use policies eased, however, there would still be significant demand for roadways. The automobile will not be supplanted by other transportation options, be they mass transit or walking. "The value of automobility is strongly complementary to other core values of our culture," writes philosopher Loren Lomasky, "values such as the freedom of association, pursuit of knowledge, economic advancement, privacy, even the expression of religious values and affectional preference."[51] The challenge is to design public policies that make sure driving pays its own way and that investment in highways pays a high rate of return in mobility, freedom, and productivity.

The current system is inadequate to the task. First, the involvement of the federal government in financing and administering significant portions of the nation's highway system actually reduces the extent and productivity of highway investment. Any benefit that poorer states receive from the redistribution of gas tax revenues inherent in federal financing is more than offset by administrative costs, costly set-aside programs, and the higher, union-scale wages that states and localities must pay on federally funded projects, compliments of another Depression-era miscue called the Davis-Bacon Act. These federal strings translate into a 25 percent to 30 percent increase in the cost of constructing highways and other public infrastructure. Federal funding of transportation also invites some of the most outrageous pork barrel spending in which Congress engages, further squandering scarce resources that could better be spent locally fixing real needs.[52]

Finally, lobbies for transit and other Smart Growth policies are more powerful in Washington than in most state capitals. As a result, dollars collected from highway users via gasoline taxes have been wastefully diverted since the early 1970s into generous subsidies for mass transit systems. Local officials are not dumb. They respond to these incentives by expanding their transit systems. Between 1980 and the early 1990s alone, seventeen major cities built new rail transit systems or extended existing ones, including Atlanta, Baltimore, Boston, Chicago, Los Angeles, Miami, St. Louis, and Portland. Most of the work was financed largely by federal transit grants. The St. Louis project, for example, was 98 percent funded from Washington. Portland's was 82 percent federally funded.[53] Unfortunately, since ridership remains so low—in the single digits in share of daily commutes in most communities—the result is increased traffic congestion and inadequate maintenance of parts of the existing highway system.

Another major problem with the current system is that increases in fuel efficiency, while providing welcome economic and environmental benefits, are compromising the ability of gasoline taxes to serve as user fees for highways. Even as the combined per gallon federal and state tax on gasoline has been rising, actual revenues paid per driver have risen little if at all in real dollars, while revenues per mile traveled have fallen substantially since mid-century. From 1960 to 1970, total gas tax collections per mile traveled declined slightly, from 3.4 cents per mile to 3.2 cents. During the next decade, however, revenue collections collapsed as surging gas prices and federal regulations prodded drivers to purchase smaller, more fuel-efficient cars. By 1980, gas tax collections per mile totaled only 1.7 cents. The deteriorating condition of the nation's highways and bridges then sparked talk of an "infrastructure crisis" during much of the 1980s. States and the federal government raised tax rates on gasoline and other auto-related commodities and imposed more weight-based charges on trucks in an attempt to recoup lost revenue and increase investment in highway assets. The trend against gas-guzzlers moderated a bit as well, with oil prices dropping and families gravitating towards minivans and sport utility vehicles as updated versions of the old, staid station wagon. From 1980 to 1995, real gas tax collections per mile rose 35 percent to 2.3 cents, but remained far below the 1960 rate.[54]

No one should assume, of course, that there is a direct correlation between infrastructure spending and infrastructure quality or sufficiency. As stated earlier, federal gas tax collections and disbursements actually reduce real highway investment because of the higher labor costs and wasteful pork barrel projects (including transit) it brings. Furthermore, as University of North Carolina-Charlotte economist David Hartgen has demonstrated in his pathbreaking research, states vary widely in the cost-effectiveness of their highway spending. In a 1998 report, Hartgen used expenditure and performance data to rate Wyoming, South Carolina, North Dakota, Idaho, and Nebraska highest among the states in the cost-effectiveness of their highway systems, while Colorado, New York, Hawaii, Massachusetts, New Jersey, and Rhode Island ranked lowest. Nine states in Hartgen's study spent more than 10 percent of their highway budgets on administration, with Louisiana, California, Connecticut, and Massachusetts actually spending about as much on administration as on highway maintenance.[55]

Still, the long-term patterns in highway revenues and expenditures have been reflected in the quality of the public capital they generate. During the revenue slide of the 1970s, the quality of pavement, the structural soundness of bridges and overpasses, and traffic congestion all deteriorated. Since the mid-1980s, as politicians began to react to the infrastructure crisis, conditions have improved somewhat, although changes in data collection may account for some of the apparent improvement.[56] During the 1990s, particularly, states did devote more of their increasing revenue to maintenance needs. According to the United States Department of Transportation, for example, the percentage of major and minor roads considered "poor" or "mediocre" generally declined during the decade, while those considered "good" rose a bit, although the gains were more heavily concentrated in rural areas than in urban areas, where some categories of roads actually got worse. The percentage of structurally deficient bridges also declined.[57]

Gains in highway quality, however, came at the expense of insufficient highway quantity. Too many drivers attempted to access too few highway lanes, resulting in dramatic increases in congestion. During the 1990s, most states saw the number of hours lost to road delays rise by more than a third, with some communities seeing four-fold increases or more since the early 1980s. By the year 2000, the average annual delay per driver in the sixty-eight largest American cities was fifty hours, up from thirty-four hours in 1990. Similarly, a roadway congestion index developed by the Texas Transportation Institute found a median increase of about 30 percent from 1982 to 1996. Highway congestion imposed a "tax," in terms of lost time and business, of roughly $600.00 a driver in 1996, with drivers in highly congested cities such as Los Angeles and Washington, D.C., paying about twice that amount.[58]

One of the greatest myths of the Smart Growth movement is that highway spending does not alleviate congestion. "Roads fill up as soon as you build them," they are fond of saying. But the argument makes no logical sense. If new roads are quickly discovered and used by drivers, that is a clear sign that they are meeting customer needs. What should throw up a red flag is a new road that *does not* attract significant traffic, that lies largely unused (as do some rural highways built to please powerful legislators rather than traffic engineers). In fact, the only major cities that have reduced their traffic congestion in recent years have been precisely those such as Houston and Dallas that have invested heavily in expanding their highway mileage. On the other hand, America's most congested metropolitan area, Los Angeles, also has the fewest freeway miles per capita. Although most "urban sprawl" opponents point to traffic in Los Angeles as the natural consequence of suburban-style growth, the city's famous congestion is mostly being caused by too few roads, not too many.[59]

To the extent that Smart Growth is becoming a salient force in state and local politics, it is driven primarily by legitimate public concerns about traffic congestion and other strained public infrastructure, not the neo-Green ideology and communitarianism typical of Smart Growth activists. Public officials can address these concerns through public policies that reduce government's role in private market decisions while increasing the productivity of the public capital stock. Local officials, for example, should liberalize zoning and other land-use rules that force people to travel longer distances to work, shop, or recreate. They should also make more use of private contracting for public assets such as water and wastewater treatment, where their expertise and greater efficiency can help local communities accommodate the demands of growth without having to impose new taxes on residents.

At the federal level, the best policy would be to get out of the business of funding state and local infrastructure. As Angela Antonelli and Mark Wilson of the Heritage Foundation ask, "Why must citizens send their money through Washington only to have it cycle back out to states and local communities? Should not states determine how much to tax and spend in order to maintain their infrastructure?"[60] The federal government interferes with local capital formation not just through spending programs such as the Highway Trust Fund but also by making interest income on state and local bonds tax-deductible. If these subsidies cannot simply be ended outright (probably a correct assumption), policymakers could attempt to lift costly regulations on state and local building projects and dedicate all highway-related taxes to highway construction and maintenance, eliminating transfers to transit or general operations. As far as subsidizing the borrowing costs of states and localities goes, the current tax deduction does not work well. As former New York State Comptroller Edward Regan explains, federal rules essentially exclude corporations and many institutional investors from fully benefiting from the deduction, thus reducing the number of potential buyers and raising interest rates accordingly. Since states and localities seek more capital than wealthy individual investors can provide, their bonds tend to be priced according to the demands of those individual investors with low marginal rates, to whom the income deduction is less valuable. These investors demand higher interest rates on municipal bonds than do their affluent peers, in return reducing the interest savings to states and localities by as much as one third.[61]

If the federal government wants to fund the creation of more public capital, it should do so at the state and local level where 85 percent of non-defense public investment occurs. For example, Congress could change the rules regarding federal trust funds for Social Security, Medicare, and other programs to allow for investment in high-grade state and local bonds rather than confining the funds to federal treasury securities. This would increase demand for such bonds, thus reducing their interest rates and increasing the amount of money state and municipalities could put into highways or other productive assets. Similarly, Jay Levy and Walter Cadette of Bard College's Jerome Levy Institute have proposed that the Federal Reserve be allowed to conduct its open-market operations in part with high-grade municipal bonds.[62] Both policies would likely result in less money available for federal spending. Congress could either do nothing and spend (or retire federal debt) less than it otherwise would, or impose partial or full income tax on municipal bonds to make up some of the difference—a policy justified on the grounds of tax neutrality anyway.

States have options, too. Like the federal government, they should also dedicate 100 percent of auto-related taxes to the construction and maintenance of highways. Beyond that, however, states will find it exceeding difficult to collect more revenue. Although real state highway-use taxes are lower than they used to be, when adjusted for miles traveled, drivers are unlikely to countenance further tax hikes, even if all the proceeds are dedicated to providing services to them. Therefore, the states (aided by federal deregulation) should pursue other means of financing and maintaining new highway projects.

The most promising alternative at present is to "return to the past" by building most new limited-access highways as tollways, using private companies to build and operate them and new electronic technologies to collect tolls automatically so that congestion-causing toll booths are largely relegated to side lanes for out-of-state travelers or, through multistate coordination, simply eliminated entirely. More than twenty countries in the world, and several American states, already use electronic toll collection.[63] And as Reason Foundation President Robert Poole has written, many of these projects include significant private-sector involvement because public officials realize that private firms can often better identify demand for new corridors, tap new sources of capital such as equity financing, expand the property tax base, build projects more quickly, and provide better customer service.[64] Finally, tollways using the new technologies can charge more accurate prices for highway use, adjusting tolls for the time of day, for the type and weight of vehicles imposing wear and tear on the pavement, and, in conjunction with remote-sensing devices to measure tailpipe emissions, for the amount of air pollution imposed on the surrounding community. Like the automobile and gas taxes before them, automated and adjustable tolls and public-private tollways represent market-friendly innovations that allow users to shoulder the cost of building and maintaining roads. They are devices to increase the productivity of physical assets that have traditionally been owned and operated by government.

CONCLUSION

There is such a thing as public investment. Practitioners of the new Investor Politics would be wise to embrace policies that ensure an adequate level of investment in roads, bridges, water and sewer utilities, and other physical assets. At the same time, however, they should find ways to make public capital more productive by charging accurate prices to users, exploring privatization, and walling off decisions as much as possible from traditional pork barrel considerations. They should also resist efforts to treat housing as yet another subset of public investment, deserving of subsidy either through direct appropriation or through the mortgage interest deduction. Housing is not a public asset. Its use is easily priced and its construction easily financed in private capital markets. If policymakers want to subsidize poor families, they should do so directly through cash welfare and voucher programs rather than by devoting expenditures or tax subsidies to public housing projects that may not represent what poor families truly want or need to become self-sufficient.

The growth of homeownership during the middle part of the twentieth century was the result of both market forces and government intervention. To the extent that those lacking significant asset ownership suddenly found themselves to be investors in physical capital, there were important political consequences. After the homeownership rate reached its plateau of about two-thirds of American households in the mid-1960s, it became far harder for local politicians to hike property tax rates. The rise in homeownership predated by about three decades a similarly meteoric rise in corporate stock ownership, offering us tantalizing hints about the probable effects of the latter on political, economic, and social attitudes. This topic will be discussed in the concluding chapter. First, it is important to apply the principles of Investor Politics developed in earlier discussions of financial and physical capital to that human capital—the likely source of most growth in productivity and incomes over the next few decades.

CHAPTER 8

EDUCATION, TRAINING, AND HUMAN CAPITAL

MONG THE MANY CONTRIBUTIONS OF THE "CHICAGO School of Economics"—that pantheon of thinkers that includes the likes of Frank Knight, Milton Friedman, George Stigler, and Gary Becker—has been the modern theory of human capital. As discussed briefly in chapter 6, the consideration of human beings as capital assets is an old, even ancient concept. But in the late 1950s and early 1960s, Becker, then at Columbia University, and Chicago's Theodore W. Schultz—along with a variety of economists, historians, and other scholars—began to formalize a new way of looking at the issue. Perhaps more so than any other concept in this book, their notion of human capital helps clearly to distinguish the ideologies underlying welfare politics and investor politics. In an aforementioned essay by Schultz introducing a series of papers presented at a seminal 1962 conference on human capital at the Carnegie Endowment in New York City, he explained the fundamentals and implications of the theory:

> [Human capital theory] rests on the proposition that people enhance their capabilities as producers and as consumers by investing in themselves. It implies that not all of the economic capabilities of

217

a people are given at birth, or at age fourteen when some of them enter upon work, or at some later age when some complete their schooling; but that many of these capabilities are developed through activities that have the attributes of an investment. These investments in people turn out not to be trivial; on the contrary, they are of a magnitude to alter radically the usual measure of the amount of savings and capital formation. They also alter the structure of wages and salaries and the amount of earnings relative to income from property.

These alterations are clues to long-standing puzzles about economic growth, structure of relative earnings, and the distribution of personal income . . . One of the implications of this formulation is that modifications in income transfers [welfare], in progressive taxation, and in the distribution of privately owned wealth are relatively weak factors in altering the distribution of personal income.[1]

Much of the modern American welfare state is based on the premise Schultz directly challenges: that economic inequality is a product of previous inequality, of inadequate taxation, or of a lack of physical or mental inheritance. To understand why, you need only consider timing. The ideological foundations of the welfare state, as noted in chapter 2, were laid during the late nineteenth and early twentieth centuries. Both public perceptions and scholarly understanding of the nature and causes of economic growth were sorely lacking at this time. Wealth seemed to derive largely from managing large institutions, from manipulating the public sector to your benefit, or from inheriting fortunes in the old-fashioned medieval and European manner. The American economy seemed driven largely by investment in large, sprawling physical assets—in railroads, in steel mills, in electrical plants and telephone lines and, later, in fleets of manufactured autos, ships, and airplanes. Meanwhile, ordinary people who had once managed their own businesses (primarily farms), owned their own homes, and provided their own fuel and water were moving to cities, renting apartments, working in huge factories, and generally feeling like cogs in some giant wealth-generating machine. All they knew was that they did not own the machine. Whoever did was getting rich and calling the shots. That was all right as long as the workers saw their own standards of living rising, too. But when depression came, as it did in the 1890s and then again in the 1930s, these Americans looked to government to provide the security that appeared to lie beyond their grasp.

Scholars have since demonstrated that the nineteenth and early twentieth centuries were an atypical period in economic history during which investment in physical capital predominated. Moses Abramovitz of Standard University is one economist who has studied this issue in depth. "In the nineteenth century, technological progress was heavily biased in a physical capital-using direction," he writes. "It could be incorporated into production only by the agency of a large expansion in physical capital per worker." The increasing scale of industry leading to huge factories, the railroads, the rise of cities and a host of new physical assets from housing and streets to sewage plants—all were manifestations as well as causes of the physical capital explosion. "In the twentieth century, however, the physical capital-using bias weakened; it may have disappeared altogether," Abramovitz continues. "The bias shifted in an intangible, human and knowledge capital-using direction and produced the substantial contribution of education and of other intangible capital accumulation to this century's productivity growth."[2]

In the midst of the "New Economy" at the beginning of the twenty-first century, these words ring true. Many of the most valuable companies on world stock exchanges have few physical assets. Some have consistently lost money since their recent creation. Their value lies in ideas, which are intellectual capital, and in people, who are human capital. No less than physical capital, these forms of capital are costly to form and require constant maintenance and replenishment. The process of their formation is less visible, and from a public policy standpoint, poorly understood. You can see a bridge being built from one side of a river to another. You cannot see the bridge between two ideas that makes the physical bridge unnecessary. Unfortunately, politicians, lacking insight into these matters, continue to subsidize the former while thoughtlessly taxing and regulating the latter. Transforming public policy toward human and intellectual capital is perhaps the most important challenge facing practitioners of the new Investor Politics. Without this transformation, the economy will not grow fast enough over time to ease the transition from the entitlement state to self-sufficiency. The result will be crushing disappointment and painful adjustment, political upheaval, or worse.

THE EDUCATION AND TRAINING CRISIS

Few issues capture the public's attention today as frequently and as securely as education. Few are so fraught with mythology and misunderstanding, on all sides of the debate. Here are some of the most common falsehoods:

- Education and training are primarily provided by the government.
- Education would not exist to any significant degree without government subsidy.
- Education should be a wholly private affair, with no government involvement.
- The quality of education in the United States was once far better than it is now.
- The quality of education in the United States is far better than it used to be.
- The quality of education in the United States is inadequate only in inner cities.
- A college education is the only ticket to a good job and a prosperous economy.
- Having a degree significantly boosts the income of the typical college graduate.
- Tax credits or deductions for education expenses would violate flat tax principles.
- Vouchers would harm public schools and pierce the separation of church and state.

In each case, fierce advocates for their side cling passionately to "facts" that are demonstrably untrue or that answer an irrelevant question. Education has been a political issue for so long, and its history so influenced by mercenary or ideological interests, that separating truth from fiction is a great challenge. Still, policymakers must gain a firm understanding of the reality of education and training if they are to fashion public policies that expand and improve investment in human capital.

Understanding begins by realizing that education and training are different things. They overlap, yes, but they do not coincide. Education involves the accumulation of knowledge as well as the ability to reason and learn. Training is the imparting of specific skills useful in work, play, child rearing, worship, or citizenship. Often, we say that a child needs to be educated when what we mean is that she needs training in a particular skill. Similarly, we express disappointment that a certain graduate has not been trained well enough in high school to keep a job, when what we mean is that he did not gain the education he needed to be trainable by an employer. Too many critics of public education focus purely on low reading and math skills, which they properly warn will mean fewer job opportunities and lower productivity, while ignoring the extent to which a student might be unprepared for social responsibilities outside of work, such as participating in the political process or being a responsible parent and citizen.

Distinguishing between education and training helps to dispel some of the myths listed above. Most training, for example, occurs outside of school. It begins at birth. Parents teach infants to perform a variety of critical tasks, from toilet training and eating at the table to following directions and respecting the rights of others. Later, even as children are learning both academic and social skills at school, they have them reinforced and augmented at home. Upon graduation from high school or college, few students are actually trained to perform jobs, and must learn the requisite skills from their employers in formal or informal ways. According to *Training* magazine, America's employers spent $54 billion on formal training programs in 2000.[3] Using a well-established ratio of informal, on-the-job training to the formal kind, a good estimate of the total employer-provided training market in the United States that year would be about $324 billion, including the cost of supervision, publications and materials, and lost production time. Add that to the amount spent by private schools and colleges on both training and education, and you will find that private educational institutions or employers account for nearly half of all such expenditures in the United States—and these statistics do not include the contribution of parents, churches, and other nongovernmental institutions that regularly teach children, most notably in preschools.[4]

Education, as a separate category, does occur primarily in school, at least before adulthood. The American education market is heavily dominated today (92 percent at the K-12 level and two-thirds at the college level) by government institutions.[5] Education requires reading and study, not just for the accumulation of knowledge but also for expanding the mind's ability to make connections, to grasp difficult concepts, and to form opinions.

Many children (unfortunately) do most of their reading in or for school. Only about 23 percent of seventeen-year-olds say they spend any time reading in the average day other than for school. The percentage is a bit higher, 32 percent, for thirteen-year-olds.[6] While at home, their free time is devoted to other pursuits. As part of the 1998 reading exams conducted by the National Assessment of Educational Progress (NAEP), students were asked how many hours they spent watching television each day. Among fourth- and eighth-graders, the percentage watching TV for at least four hours a day was between 35 and 38 percent. Three-quarters of fourth-graders and 85 percent of eighth-graders watched TV for at least two hours.[7] Yes, there are some educational programs on television, more now that cable channels have proliferated. Still, most of this time is spent on entertainment, on immediate consumption. It is not being invested. And these numbers don't include time spent playing video games or chatting on the Internet.

The state of both education and training in the United States should concern everyone. NAEP tests in core subjects show desperately low levels of both knowledge and skills. About 38 percent of fourth-graders lack basic reading skills, while only 24 percent are proficient readers at grade level. By eighth grade, performance is still disappointing with 26 percent below a basic level and only 31 percent proficient.[8] For math, the numbers are about the same or worse: 36 percent lack basic math skills in the fourth grade, 38 percent in eighth, and only 21 percent of fourth-graders and 24 percent of eighth-graders are proficient. In subjects applicable more to a student role as citizen or parent than as worker, the picture is perhaps even bleaker. A shocking 57 percent of twelfth-graders lack even a rudimentary knowledge of United States history, with only 11 percent proficient in the subject. A third of high school seniors lack basic knowledge of geography, as well. Even in the arts, where precise measurement admittedly remains elusive, most students in a 1997 NAEP assessment lacked the ability to express themselves in visual or musical form, and many students could not adequately interpret theatrical or other performances.[9]

It is true that education achievement varies dramatically by the background of students. Nearly two-thirds of black and Hispanic students lack basic reading skills at fourth grade, and 40 percent or more still cannot read at grade level by the time they leave high school. The percentages of blacks and Hispanics proficient in math are often in the single digits. Similarly, students from inner cities and poor households score far worse than those from suburbs or middle-income families. That is not the end of the story. A reasonable goal on NAEP exams would be to have at least half of all students proficient and 90 percent able to demonstrate basic skills. By that measure, only children in the nation's private schools have reached or nearly reached that goal. Fewer than 40 percent of white fourth-graders are proficient readers, and 27 percent lack basic skills. Performance improves a bit at higher grade levels but remains almost 10 percentage points away from the goal.[10] In the crucial subject of history, only half of white twelfth-graders exhibit basic knowledge. Other "advantaged" groups fall short, too.[11] It is certainly justified to call the test scores of America's poor and minority students abysmal, and their educational plight a crisis. But even for public schools in largely white, middle-class suburbs, the general state is one of mediocrity, not of high achievement.

Other evidence of the nation's educational inadequacy abounds. Employers complain that many of their employees cannot fill out simple forms, follow directions, or communicate well with others. Many parents are deeply dissatisfied with the quality of education, and few are truly confident that their children know all that they need to know. Internationally, the few good studies that exist of academic performance suggest that, while American students match up pretty well to European and Asian nations when they are young, they fall to the bottom of the heap in math, science, and other subjects as they approach high school graduation.

The largest and most comprehensive study of global education ever conducted is the Third International Mathematics and Science Study (TIMSS), released in 1997. It found that while American students did well in fourth grade, our high school seniors ranked sixteenth in science and nineteenth in math out of twenty-one participating countries (which did not include most high-performing Asian nations). In other words, the longer our children are in school, the further they fall behind.[12] Other studies reveal similar results. Last year, in a study conducted by one of the nation's leading experts on international education evaluation, the Thomas B. Fordham Foundation reported that United States schools are the least productive in the world. The report found that our schools make the smallest year-to-year gains in academic achievement among comparable countries, ranking last in four of five comparisons of achievement progress. In reading, for example, United States students between the ages of nine and fourteen made the lowest gains of sixteen countries studied. On average, we make just 78 percent of the progress of our foreign counterparts.[13]

A BRIEF HISTORY OF AMERICAN EDUCATION

America's children are not learning what they need to learn to be productive workers or citizens. Were our schools at one time a lot more effective? Were American students far better educated a generation or two ago than they are today? To answer these questions, we must first review briefly the history of American education, how and why government institutions became involved, and the (sketchy) evidence that exists about long-term trends in student achievement.

Most parents in early America, as in virtually all cultures in history, made significant efforts to educate and train their children. From the colonial period until the mid-nineteenth century, private education existed alongside, and usually far exceeded, public education, with a range of schooling including parents and other in-home tutors, one-room schoolhouses, urban academies, church-run schools, and vocational training through apprenticeships and technical institutes. As former Microsoft engineer Andrew Coulson writes in his fascinating 1999 book *Market Education: The Unknown History,* school enrollment probably increased markedly during the first half of the nineteenth century as rising family incomes put education within the reach of more Americans and the demand for skilled laborers rose. For those unable to afford tuition, philanthropists and religious societies founded free schools in cities across the country.[14]

To characterize, as Massachusetts educator Horace Mann and other public education advocates did in the 1830s and 1840s, the state of private education as elitist and stultifying would be to do great injustice to the truth. Before public schools became ubiquitous in America, millions of people read newspapers, studied their Bibles, and ran their own farms through careful tallying of purchases and yields. Many children learned not just to read and write English but to master foreign languages, great works of literature, and high-level math. Even the poorest of families typically provided their children with some exposure to reading, writing, and mathematics. Education was a growing, lively, and relatively efficient market throughout the period.[15]

On the other hand, some advocates of purely private education and a strict separation between school and state go too far when they allege, lacking credible evidence, that American children were, on average, as well as or better educated before public education than afterward. For example, they cite nineteenth century records of voting, marriage registrations, or wills to prove that 80 percent or more of Americans were literate.[16] But the ability to sign one's name is hardly evidence of literacy in the modern sense of the term. Nor is the fact that, as Coulson reports, 90 percent of Americans identified themselves as literate in the 1850 census. "It is safe to say," he writes, "that between three-quarters and four-fifths of the population was already literate before public schooling as we know it had gotten off the ground."[17] By the definition of literacy that then existed, this is no doubt true. By the definition we use today—the ability not to write one's name or follow single instructions but the ability to read and comprehend extended passages of unfamiliar writing—it is highly unlikely to be true. Unfortunately, useful measurements of student performance and knowledge do not extend so far back in time, so this issue cannot be definitively settled.

Where Coulson and other private education advocates stand on firmer ground is with their account of the origins of public education. It is undeniably true that, at least in much of the North and Midwest, a primary motivation for the expansion of state financial support for local schools into a near-universal system of public education was anti-Catholic bigotry. An influx of non-Protestant immigrants—first from Catholic Ireland in the mid-nineteenth century and from Italy, Poland, and elsewhere later in the century—led many native-born Americans to wonder if the newcomers could be integrated into a largely English and Protestant society. For some, skepticism devolved into paranoia and bigotry towards Catholics, Jews, and other groups. Since most schools, public and private, included religious instruction as a core element of their curriculum, the fight over control of education became a bitter and contentious one. Layered on top of these trends was the elitism of Mann and others who viewed parents as incapable of making educational decisions for their children. Summarizing both the elitist and anti-Catholic sentiments behind public education is a strident 1851 article from *The Massachusetts Teacher*:

> The rising generation [of immigrants] must be taught as our own children are taught. We say must be, because in many cases this can only be accom-

plished by coercion. In too many instances the parents are unfit guardians of their own children. If left to their discretion the young will be brought up in idle, dissolute, vagrant habits, which will make them worse members of society than their parents are . . . Nothing can operate effectually here but stringent legislation, thoroughly carried out by an efficient police; the children must be gathered up and forced into school, and those who resist or impede this plan, whether parents or priests, must be held accountable and punished.[18]

Not all advocates of public education were motivated by such distasteful views, of course. Many leaders of industry viewed the American education system as too chaotic and diverse to generate large numbers of workers skilled enough to permit economic growth. Particularly after Bismarck took power in the 1860s, they pointed across the ocean to Germany as an example of the centralized, orderly, and state-controlled education system that an industrial society required. Furthermore, as farmers and unions began to organize into a political force to be reckoned with in the 1870s and 1880s, they made more spending on public education a key demand. For many of these citizens, public schools offered the prospect of progress and opportunity for their children, providing more and better instruction than they thought they could procure on their own.[19]

The public education movement, in other words, combined several strains of political and social agitation, some less attractive than others. Government involvement in education increased during the 1840s and 1850s, but really took off after the Civil War. In 1870, there were about 160 public high schools in the entire country. Most adults could read and write, but had an average of only about four years of formal instruction. Over the next three decades, state subsidies for public school construction, teacher salaries, and supplies skyrocketed. It was also a time of significant growth in higher education, aided by federal land grants and other taxpayer assistance. The new colleges trained teachers to staff the new public schools. By 1900, the concept of providing a tuition-free public education to all children was widely accepted, and there were six thousand public high schools.[20] In the same year, public schools enrolled 72 percent of all children aged five to seventeen, while private schools enrolled just over 7 percent. Private education's market share is actually larger today—about 11 percent—than it was at the turn of the century.[21] By 1930, there were about

262,000 public schools in the United States, enrolling almost 26 million children. I point to this year for several reasons. First, it was the first time that more than 80 percent of eligible students attended public schools, a number that would not reach 90 percent until 1990. It was the first year that more than 1 million Americans were enrolled in college. More on that later. In addition, 1930 ended the last decade in which local governments would play an overwhelming role in funding public schools—the Great Depression would change that in many jurisdictions—and the last decade when fewer than half of eighteen-year-olds graduated from high school. Finally, it is the first year for which comparable spending and inflation figures are available, allowing for comparisons over time in the productivity of American education.

THE PRODUCTIVITY PLUNGE

From 1930 on, public schools were to change markedly. Progressive education—a product of the musings of philosopher John Dewey and the fuzzy ideas and shoddy research of many a denizen of the nation's education schools—became the norm in most parts of the country. Members of the National Education Association, the Progressive Education Association, and other national groups devoted to the ideas of Dewey and to left-wing radicalism proliferated and took control of most educational institutions and school districts. The number of those schools and districts plummeted, by the way, as their leaders sought "economies of scale" in larger buildings and administrative units and, later, as desegregation ended separate systems for blacks and whites. The number of one-room schoolhouses fell from 150,000 in 1930 to 442 in 1994. The number of districts fell from about 130,000 to fewer than 15,000. Within the curriculum, the "look-say" method decisively displaced phonics-based reading instruction. As Coulson explains, popular textbooks were "lobotomized" after about 1930, with the old McGuffey Reader type of rigor giving way to books that publishers and educators termed more "readable."[22]

Some of these academic trends reversed themselves briefly during the period, but for every retreat, there inevitably came a new advance. Thus, "progressive education," under attack in the post-Sputnik period of the 1950s, gave way to the "open classroom" of the 1970s and "child-centered education" of the 1990s. Many of the ideas were the same. Indeed, Horace

Mann had attacked what he saw as many teachers' over-emphasis of the alphabet in reading instruction as early as 1843. Nor were these developments disastrous for every child. Some did, indeed, have special needs and benefited from an individualized learning plan. Some children do thrive in the chaotic classrooms and "group learning" of many of today's schools, as compared with the more traditional lectures and teaching methods of previous generations. However, many others are not receiving the structure and guidance they need to excel. They are not mastering grade-level material before being promoted; they are not reading challenging histories or literature; and they are not forming an accurate assessment of their own academic accomplishments.

Far more qualified writers than I have written lengthy books analyzing the problems of American education today. I will not attempt to review all their arguments here. Nor will I try to settle the case of whether public schools are significantly better or worse than they used to be. Few objective measures of performance predate 1970, and those that do show no huge changes, one way or the other. My concern, as befits the general thesis of this book, is the productivity of investment in human capital. Since 1930, taxpayers have invested huge quantities of money in public schools. Adjusted for inflation, public schools spent $1,048.00 per student in 1930, with an average of twenty-four students for each instructional employee. In 1998, the numbers were $7,801.00 per student and twelve students per instructional staffer (which includes not only classroom teachers but also teaching assistants, arts and physical education teachers, reading specialists, librarians, and others).[23] The level of public investment, in other words, grew by 644 percent in real terms. What was the return on this investment?

For most of the period, all we can go on is the quantitative output of the system. In the first four decades, from 1930 to 1970, the percentage of eighteen-year-olds receiving a high school diploma rose from 29 percent to 75 percent. Since then, the rate actually fell to 69 percent by 1998—lower than the 1960 rate.[24] Spending per pupil cannot be the culprit. It rose from $4,020.00 in 1970 to $7,801.00 in 1998. Overburdened personnel won't explain it, either. The number of students per instructor declined from eighteen to twelve.[25]

For qualitative outcomes, the Scholastic Assessment Test (SAT) provides the longest trend. From 1950 to 1970, scores fluctuated but, towards the end of the period, began to trend downward a bit in reading. From 1972 to 1981, the average verbal score dropped from 530 to 502. It then rebounded to 509 by 1986, and dropped again to 499 in 1994 before rising slowly to 505 in 1998. The overall trend is a drop of 25 points on a 600-point scale. Math scores dropped as well for the first part of the period before recovering their 1971 level.[26] Many apologists for the public schools hasten to point out that more minorities and poor whites began to take the test in preparation for college during the period. They also complain that the SAT, designed to predict freshman performance in college, is not necessarily reflective of overall educational achievement in high school. These are valid points, although careful analysis shows that they do not explain away the drop in verbal scores.

Furthermore, the point is irrelevant. Assume that *adjusted* SAT scores didn't drop at all from 1970 to 1996. I do not believe this is true, but it would fit the pattern of other, broader tests of American children. NAEP reading and math scores for seventeen-year-olds were essentially flat from the early 1970s to the late 1990s. The International Evaluation of Education Achievement found a drop in reading achievement for United States fourteen-year-olds from 1970 to 1990, while its math and science tests found, on average, another flat line from 1964 to the early 1980s.[27] While some quibble about these results, no one suggests that adjusting any of these tests for changes in the test-taking population would result in an *increase* in student achievement over the past quarter-century. Yet, taxpayers nearly doubled their investment in public schools in real, per-pupil terms. That is, by itself, a damning indictment of the productivity of American public education. In any other field of investment, from stocks and bonds to housing and public infrastructure, such a consistently paltry return would get you fired.

HIGHER EDUCATION: THE TICKET TO WEALTH?

Many Americans who recognize the mediocrity and low productivity of the current public school system simultaneously praise America's colleges and universities as the best in the world—as generators of economic growth, innovation, and upward mobility for millions. Of course, much of this is true. American higher education is the best in the world at many things, explaining why so many students from faraway lands clamor to study here. Researchers based at the nation's leading universities have contributed mightily to the explosion of knowledge and invention that has marked the last half of the twentieth century. Nor can it be denied that a rapid growth in enrollment, particularly after World War II, provided educational opportunities to many whose parents and grandparents never finished high school, much less college.

Unfortunately, higher education is plagued by some of the same productivity problems that elementary and secondary education faces. From 1930, when total enrollment in public and private colleges surpassed 1 million for the first time, until 1996, education spending by American higher education (not including hospitals and other ancillary enterprises) rose by 265 percent in constant dollars per enrolled student. Surely, you might say, this investment has paid off handsomely. But the evidence for that supposition is astonishingly lacking. Although massive growth in public subsidies after World War II helped colleges and universities expand their enrollments by 436 percent from 1950 to 1996, the percentage of those aged twenty-five to twenty-nine who had yet earned a bachelor's degree has reached only 28 percent—a number that, in my experience, surprises many who hear it, since college has supposedly become so routine for most high school graduates. As early as 1970, the rate had already reached 16 percent, and after hitting 23 percent in 1980 it scarcely budged at all for most of the next fifteen years, even though subsidies were pouring into the system.[28]

The problem was and remains a failure to move undergraduate students smoothly through four years of college. Only about half of college freshmen finish school within four years. Many take five or six years, or drop out before completing their degrees. Higher education analysts fault lower admissions standards for the pathetic completion rates, and for the fact that three-quarters of all colleges and universities offer remedial education for students who lack the basic high school competencies necessary for college-level work.[29] The average college puts 30 percent of its freshmen in such courses. By contrast, in 1939, before the advent of mass higher education, only 2 percent of colleges offered remediation. Huge increases in student admissions have also changed the nature of the degrees being earned. In 1939, about a quarter of all courses required for college graduation were mandatory. They formed a core curriculum of literature, history, science, and the classics that all students were expected to master. Today, the percentage is no higher than 7 percent.[30] Students can gain college degrees by fulfilling requirements with the most trivial and airy of courses, calling into question what a degree actually signifies.

Another problem is that increased levels of federal subsidy have largely benefited the faculty and administrators of colleges and universities rather than the students and their families. Starting with the GI Bill and later expanding to include guaranteed student loans, Pell Grants, work-study programs, and federal tax credits, total federal student assistance has grown rapidly in the past half-century. Unfortunately, so has the average price of college. From 1970 to 1996 alone, total federal aid grew by about 50 percent in constant dollars. Public college tuition and fees grew by precisely the same rate of 50 percent, while private tuition and fees nearly doubled.[31] Instead of making college relatively more affordable, the additional federal assistance—totaling in fiscal year 2001 approximately $22 billion in grants, tax credits, and foregone interest as well as $42 billion in loan guarantees[32]—simply allowed colleges and universities to jack up their prices to capture the additional revenue. Not surprisingly, colleges went on a spending spree during the period, roughly doubling their employment, hiking faculty pay, and entering a variety of ancillary but prestige-building activities such as research centers, industrial parks, and athletic and recreational amenities.

Finally, and most importantly, the much-vaunted economic benefits of a college education are much less than meets the eye. The United States economy grew as rapidly, if not more so, before the advent of mass higher education in the 1960s than afterward. Furthermore, despite what you have seen in breathless media reports, the fastest-growing occupations in the United States in the next decade will be those not requiring a college degree; they include cashier, truck driver, nursing and home health aide, and clerk. People in these jobs get most of their required education in high school and most of their required training on the job.[33]

Also, the conventional wisdom about the financial payoff from getting a college education is wrong. Studies estimating the salary boost from getting a diploma rely on national averages that obscure more than they elucidate. Highly paid professionals such as doctors, lawyers, and college professors require a four-year degree in order to pursue graduate education and enter the workforce. Those for whom a bachelor's degree is terminal are actually paid far less of a wage premium for their education. It is true that, in 1997, college graduates on average earned 69 percent more than did nongraduates. This simple calculation "ignores the fact that college graduates tend to come from higher socioeconomic levels, are more highly motivated, and probably have higher IQs than non-graduates," explains the Hudson Institute's Ed Rubenstein. He points to studies that adjust for these factors and yield a far smaller, 15 percent or so, wage premium for college. Even this overstates the gain for most students. "If you don't go on to graduate school or are not among the top graduates at one of the nation's elite colleges, chances are your sky-high tuition is buying you no economic advantage whatsoever."[34]

What actually matters is not the sheepskin but whether it represents knowledge and skills useful to employers. Economists Frederic Pryor and David Schaffer examined the "functional literacy" of college graduates to see if it affects their economic futures. In their 1999 book *Who's Not Working and Why*, Pryor and Schaffer report that college graduates whose ability to read, write, and compute is the same as their peers who did not go college have not seen increases in wages or employment since 1970. Those with high functional literacy after college, especially in professional fields, have seen a 20 percent real gain in hourly wages since 1970 and earn substantially more—67 percent—than do other college graduates. "In sum," they write, "skill-biased technical change has resulted in a faster increase in demand for workers with high cognitive skills than the increase in supply. It is these university graduates who are experiencing an increase in real wages. For the other university graduates, by way of contrast, the supply is greater than the demand. As a result, their wages are stagnating."[35]

Another way to express their findings is that, for most workers, what affects their productivity and thus their real earnings is training, not education. Although both high school and college can impart some of these skills, much of them are job specific, most likely to be acquired after employment. Is a lack of skills a significant impediment to employment? Many policymakers have thought so. Since the 1970s, the federal government and the states have attempted to provide job-training programs for poor or displaced workers. In fiscal year 2001, job-training programs funded by the Department of Labor alone cost nearly $8 billion.[36] Unfortunately, most government job-training programs have had lackluster results at best. In some cases, participants actually earned less money than similar workers who did not participate.[37]

Most useful job training occurs on the job, which is rarely subsidized by government at any level. One way to gauge the value of workplace training to employees is to look at survey data about how many workers needed training to qualify for the jobs they currently hold. A United States Bureau of Labor Statistics (BLS) study in the early 1990s found that 57 percent of workers said they needed training to qualify for their current jobs. About half of those workers received the training they needed through informal, on-the-job training. Another 21 percent received their training from formal company programs. Much smaller percentages said they got necessary training from high schools or colleges. Similarly, when BLS asked workers where they had received training to improve their skills (not necessarily to qualify for employment in the first place), formal and informal company programs again accounted for about three-quarters of the training provided. One interesting finding of the study was that many workers with college degrees earned less than workers with less formal education who nevertheless had obtained specific training, often through formal or informal company programs, for their jobs. In terms of the cost-effectiveness of various public or private means of delivering training, BLS economist Alan Eck wrote that company-provided training programs "have more of an impact on increasing those workers' earnings than does any other source of training."[38]

INCREASING THE PRODUCTIVITY OF EDUCATION

Few politicians, regardless of the office they seek, can afford not to make education a centerpiece of their agenda. Fortunately, the principles of Investor Politics suggest a reform agenda that is different from both the tax-and-spend mentality of the past three decades or so—which have squandered billions of dollars in taxpayer money without providing significant academic gains—and the well-meaning but futile position of some conservatives and libertarians that education should be a purely local, or even purely private, affair. It is entirely consistent for advocates of limited government to support a governmental role in education. Thomas Jefferson made the best case himself in a variety of letters and essays. Widespread education, aided by taxpayers, Jefferson argued in his *Notes on Virginia*, is justified as a necessary element of a self-governing republic:

In every government on earth is some trace of human weakness, some germ of corruption and degeneracy, which cunning will discover and wickedness insensibly open, cultivate, and improve. Every government degenerates when trusted to the rulers of the people alone. The people themselves are its only safe depositories. And to render even them safe, their minds must be improved to a certain degree ... An amendment of our [state] constitution must here come in aid of *the public education*. The influence over government must be shared among all the people. If every individual ... participates in the ultimate authority, the government will be safe.[39]

Notice that Jefferson used the term "the public education" (emphasis added). He neither argued for a government monopoly in teaching children nor in coercing families to send their children to government schools. His view was that states and localities should aid teachers, parents, and community leaders to build and operate independent schools. His concern was simply that all families, including those of little means, have access to educational opportunities. Jefferson's vision for public education later yielded to the early twentieth-century model of uniform, state-controlled schools reflecting Progressivism and the German envy of some industry leaders. The rediscovery of Jefferson's vision can be seen in the modern charter school movement, in which the government's role is primarily financial and parents exercise accountability through choice.

There are good reasons not to view public education, at least in the Jeffersonian sense, as one suitable only for local government involvement. Some conservatives allege that local control and finance through property taxes is the only legitimate model for public education and yields superior results. Their theory is that school districts have strong incentives to excel if they are funded by property taxes, since parents choose where to live based partly on test scores. I am not convinced. First, they cite spurious correlations to prove their case. States like New Hampshire with a school system that is overwhelmingly local and funded by property taxes do tend to have higher test scores than states relying on sales or income taxes for the bulk of school funding. However, adjusting for family income and other factors shrinks the gap between local-funded and state-funded systems dramatically.

Furthermore, public schools are not public utilities. We should not presume that parents will or even should choose housing based on proximity to a neighborhood school. A truly competitive education marketplace, which is essential to increasing the productivity of school spending, will be far more chaotic than such a model would allow. Parents may well be choosing schools close to where they work, rather than where they live, and be presented with several school choices just among district-run public schools, not to mention charters, private, parochial, or home-based alternatives. Indeed, local control might well mean local monopoly. State involvement is important just to make sure that every parent has access to educational alternatives—to "bust the school trust" if necessary. I know from personal experience, for example, that few charter schools would exist if public education were truly local.

Finally, if Jefferson's argument is persuasive, then public education is really an entitlement, related to the right of citizenship, not a means of making a local community more attractive for development or boosting the vocational skills of the local work force. The property tax is a poor way to pay for entitlements. You do not benefit from public education according to how much real property you own in a given community. The benefits are more widely diffused. I think that imposing the cost of public education according to one's general "stake" in the society—measured through standard of living, that is, consumption—is more appropriate. Either a broad-based sales tax or a flat tax on consumed income will suffice, though as explained in the next chapter, I favor the latter.

Another argument for public education is prudence. The creation of the American welfare state, chronicled earlier in this book in detail, has likely made lasting changes in public sentiment about the role of government. I think that, through the growth of personal savings and investment as an alternative to transfer programs, the trend can be halted and ultimately reversed. For most Americans, the swap may well be complete—they will give up monthly checks from Washington in exchange for control of their own money. Even so, there will probably always remain a demand for a "safety net" for those making poor decisions, within the Social Security or Medicare programs for example. Education represents the safety net that I believe most Americans will demand in exchange for reducing such programs as cash welfare, Food Stamps, and public housing assistance. It will make sense to invest in the human capital of poor children so that they don't need public assistance programs in the future.

Of course, this argument only makes sense if investing in public education pays off. Right now, it does not, particularly for the very disadvantaged it purports to help the most. Therefore, practitioners of Investor Politics need to advocate a mix of policies to increase the productivity of such investment while allowing more families to exercise control over their children's education. Not surprisingly, it begins with Educational Savings Accounts. ESAs, an idea of which I claim some parentage, already exist at the federal level in limited form. Parents can save up to $500.00 a year in ESAs and pay no tax on investment earnings or withdrawals. Congressional Republicans have proposed expanding the ESA a bit, an idea taken up by George W. Bush during his 2000 presidential campaign.

Congress should expand the maximum annual contribution to $5,000.00, allow withdrawals at any time for any education or training expenditure—from preschool to medical school and with public, nonprofit, or for-profit providers—and make not only withdrawals but deposits tax-deductible. Withdrawals from ESAs for noneducation expenses (including retirement) would be subject to normal taxation but no penalty, so that families have incentives to shop around for economical education and pocket the savings. Finally, states could tack on their own ESA deductions as well as any tuition tax credits they might wish, and might decide to use ESAs as handy places to deposit scholarship for low-income students.

The logic for such a large tax deduction will sound familiar. Education and training are forms of investment that yield future, taxable income. Therefore, they should be at least partially deductible at the front end. Yes, some education expenditures mix investment and consumption. A college degree in engineering is largely an investment, while the same amount of time and money spent getting an art history degree will yield little in the job market but may well be an excellent form of intellectual consumption. As in other cases, policymakers have no alternative but to draw a somewhat arbitrary line between the two. An annual deduction of $5,000.00 represents enough money to pay for most private secondary schools and about $1,500.00 more than is needed for private elementary school, giving families extra "room" to save tax-free for college. It also would cover about half the price of the average college and more than a third of tuition and fees charged by the average private college in 1998.[40]

The goal of expanding ESAs is to make human capital formation more productive by introducing greater competition and consumer choice. Indeed, private human capital investment is one of the most punitively taxed activities in the United States. Consider the Smiths. They earn $60,000.00 a year and have two children in public schools. The Smiths would like to transfer their children to a nearby private school with an excellent college-preparatory curriculum. But the tuition would cost a total of $8,000.00. If the Smiths pay a combined state and federal marginal tax rate of 35 percent, then they must earn more than $12,300.00 a year—or 21 percent of their expected household income—in order to pay the tuition, with $4,300.00—going to the tax collector. It gets worse. By transferring their children, the Smiths are effectively giving up an annual government subsidy in their public school worth $7,800.00 per child. Of course, this looks only at the marginal tax on a tuition dollar spent. Because government programs such as Social Security in effect redistribute tax revenues in a downward direction, they impose another layer of punitive taxation. One study found that the more education a young worker acquires, the worse his return on Social Security "contributions."[41]

Not surprisingly, most folks in the Smiths' situation choose not to pay such a steep tax on private human capital investment. Instead, they settle for a passable, mediocre, or, in some cases, abysmal education in their local public school and use their money for consumption, tax-free retirement savings, or college (again, because of massive public subsidies, more often than not a public one). The overall quality of human capital formation in the economy remains lower than it could be, for both private and public institutions, because of the lack of competition and specialization that a broader market would bring. Productivity suffers as a result, hampering growth and the higher tax revenues it would bring from better-educated workers.

Under expanded ESAs, the Smiths face a different set of incentives. They can contribute a total of $10,000.00 a year into their children's accounts, from which $8,000.00 is withdrawn in the same year to pay tuition and the remaining $2,000.00 invested for their children's high school, college, or job-training needs. The deduction would save them $3,500.00 a year in taxes, a major incentive to exercise this option. Their savings would be even greater if they started making ESA deposits for their children at infancy, building a tax-free human capital nest egg from which they could withdraw when needed. The federal government's current mishmash of HOPE tax credits and other subsidies for higher education could be folded into the new ESAs, which would help to reduce the unfortunate tendency of such tax credits to jack up tuition more than truly helping families, as discussed above. Schools will not be able to game the system by raising tuition to capture the new tax relief. Unlike tax credits for college, ESA deposits are not a "use it or lose it" proposition. Unspent funds can be spent on other investments or consumption without penalty. That makes families more sensitive to price competition, something sorely needed in an education market where costs are soaring far faster than the value of a degree.

Within the existing public education system, policymakers should promote choice, competition, and accountability in a number of ways. They should allow open enrollment within and among school districts and allow private groups of parents, teachers, businesses, or community groups to obtain charters to operate their own independent public schools. Indeed, the very definition of a public school should be changed from one that is government owned and operated to any school that is open to the public, mostly funded by the public, and accountable to the public. As states like Texas and North Carolina have pioneered, legislators should impose strict accountability for academic outcomes in the form of rewards and punishments for public schools based on performance. They should also ditch centralized control of salaries, certification, budgets, textbook selection, and other critical educational decisions, allowing local officials and principals more flexibility to meet their students' needs in exchange for a willingness to submit themselves to accountability from above (test scores) and below (parental choice).

For low-income students trapped in ineffective government-run schools, the proper remedy is a voucher or scholarship financed by taxpayers. I am sympathetic to the argument that government vouchers might invite more government control over the private schools whose students use them. That is why a universal voucher program, as has long been the goal of many market-minded reformers, seems like a bad idea to me. Nevertheless, for the minority of students most injured by the status quo, the benefits far outweigh the risks. Promising studies of both government and private voucher programs created in the 1990s suggest that disadvantaged students can make significant strides in attitude, behavior, and test scores when compared with their peers who remain in public schools.[42] Furthermore, in my view at least partial funding of education is a proper government responsibility. If public schools do not provide the adequate education to which low-income children are entitled, I believe they have a right to take their money to a school that will educate and train them for the world of work, family, and citizenship they will ultimately enter.

UNEMPLOYMENT AND SAVINGS

In addition to education and training, government at all levels attempts to facilitate the formation and productive use of human capital through several other programs or tax subsidies. Let me briefly review each in turn and suggest policy alternatives consistent with the principles of Investor Politics.

The first is Unemployment Insurance. As discussed in chapter 2, the creation of federally funded job offices in many states during World War I helped pave the way for additional programs aimed at battling joblessness. Several states, including Governor Franklin Roosevelt's New York, had experimented with government unemployment compensation systems in the 1920s (muscling out emerging private systems) but none had taken root. After taking office in 1933, Roosevelt took the first step towards a national system with the creation of a federal Employment Service to fund local jobs offices for the unemployed. Two years later, emulating a European model that dated back to Bismarck's Germany, the Social Security Act authorized a payroll tax to fund state Unemployment Insurance pools (held, like Social Security funds, in federal "trust funds" denominated in nonnegotiable Treasuries) from which benefits would be paid to those who lost jobs through no fault or action of their own.[43]

Over the years, Unemployment Insurance was expanded in scope, as additional employers were required to participate, eligibility for benefits were liberalized, and state and local governments were forced into the system. Basically, the system forces workers (through the fiction of an employer-paid payroll tax) to pay a combination of about 1 percent of their income either to their state's trust fund or directly to the federal treasury. The money is used to fund job-placement offices, for low-cost loans to struggling states, and for weekly cash benefits paid to jobless workers who have not exceeded the time limit of twenty-six weeks. In 2000, about 8.3 million Americans received benefit checks worth an average of $210.00 a week at a total cost of $28 billion.[44]

Unlike other entitlements, Unemployment Insurance is not in danger of fiscal collapse. That does not make it a successful program, however. Most unemployed workers are ineligible to receive benefits, either because of how they lost their jobs or how long they worked before becoming jobless. That means they are forced to pay into a system that does not benefit them. Claims administration is cumbersome, costly, and rife with abuse (recall the varying schemes of George Constanza on "Seinfeld" to give Unemployment Insurance administrators the impression that he is searching for work). Nor is the job search component of the program an effective use of funds, with only 4 percent of recipients saying they found their subsequent jobs through state Employment Service offices.[45]

At the same time, the structure of the program—by offering essentially half one's wages during unemployment spells for up to twenty-six weeks—encourages recipients to stay out of work for longer periods than they otherwise would. Numerous studies have confirmed this effect. According to Martin Feldstein and Daniel Altman of the National Bureau of Economic Research (NBER), "the current system of [Unemployment Insurance] benefits not only increases the duration of unemployment of those who are unemployed but also increases the frequency of temporary layoffs."[46]

The problem with Unemployment Insurance, as with so many other entitlement programs, is that it was set up as a one-size-fits-all, income-redistribution scheme rather than as a system for encouraging and assisting workers to manage their risk of job loss through personal savings. In effect, American workers are forced to park a portion of their emergency funds in low-yielding Treasury securities and are allowed access to the money only according to bureaucratic mandate. A better system would be for workers to deposit a portion of their wages for each pay period into a personal account under their control, from which they could withdraw funds as needed. Both NBER and the organization I head, the John Locke Foundation, have proposed restructuring the Unemployment Insurance program along these lines. Here is the Locke Foundation version:[47]

• Devolve the current program to the states. This would include not only payroll tax collection and administration but also the financing and control of the Employment Service, which states might well consider a prime target for privatization.

• Allow states to set up Unemployment Savings Account (USA) systems in lieu of traditional social insurance programs. Each worker would set aside a minimum Unemployment Contribution Rate (UCR) of 1 percent on the first $12,600.00 of pre-tax income (with the tax base rising with inflation after that). Workers could deposit additional money into the system if they wished. The UCR would then fund:

1. a contribution to a personal USA, managed by a private bank, insurer, or other firm certified as a USA administrator by the state;

2. a contribution either to Employment Service or to a private job-placement company as a prepayment for job search assistance if needed; and

3. a contribution to an initial balance fund, controlled by the state, from which new workers would receive an initial grant of $1,000.00 and jobless workers exhausting their USA balances could receive loans.

Unlike the current system, workers would own their own USA accounts. It would be up to them (in negotiation with their plan administrators, who will be competing for their business) to decide the conditions and amounts of withdrawals. Instead of receiving small checks for twenty-six weeks, workers might elect to withdraw a larger sum immediately with which to go back to school, take a course from a community college or private training firm, or start a new business.

Those making few claims on the system, either because of job stability or frugality, could shelter a significant sum of retirement savings from taxation. Workers would have an incentive to stay informed about their own jobs and the availability of others, and to reduce their spells of unemployment, which would cost them money. On the other side of the ledger, private plan administrators would also have strong incentives to keep their customers employed at high wages, since that would maximize the funds they could invest for profit in the financial markets. Plan administrators would likely partner with job-placement and training firms to get claimants reemployed as quickly and successfully as possible. The current Unemployment Insurance system discourages rapid reemployment (as was originally intended in 1935, when jobs were scarce) and thus inhibits the human capital formation of workers, dragging down the entire economy.

Locke Foundation analysts estimate that, for the vast majority of workers, such a personalized system would afford significant benefits, including the possibility of building an additional nest egg for retirement of $60,000.00 or more in 1998 dollars.[48] Feldstein and Altman, studying a somewhat different proposal for Unemployment Insurance savings accounts, concluded that four-fifths of participants would have positive balances at the end of their working lives. In their system, negative balances would represent a cost to taxpayers, but the amount would be far less than the current cost to taxpayers for operating an Unemployment Insurance system that is heavy with administration, biased against reemployment, and poorly designed to meet the needs of most Americans.[49]

WELFARE REFORM AND HUMAN CAPITAL

In many ways, programs known by the popular name of "welfare"—Aid to Families with Dependent Children (AFDC), now called Temporary Assistance for Needy Families (TANF), and Food Stamps, primarily—are the least troubling elements of the American welfare state. Notice that I do not say they are least troubling because they have been well designed and effective. Quite the contrary. Not only have their drawbacks become widely known, particularly in the past fifteen years or so, but they are truly entitlements for the poor or near-poor and viewed as such. Even those Americans whose income tax bills are thousands of dollars lower due to special tax breaks, or whose mothers are in nursing homes on the taxpayers' dime, or whose children are attending a state college at a tuition that pays only a quarter of the actual cost, nevertheless view TANF and Food Stamps with great disdain. Polls and recent experience demonstrate that the public is willing to see strong limits placed on these programs, and often see their recipients as undeserving.

The American public does not oppose antipoverty programs. Politicians who sound like they do not care about the poor frequently find themselves on the short end of the rhetorical stick. What voters dislike is a perpetual dole, a welfare system they view as easily abused and ineffective in changing the behavior of the able-bodied poor so they can become self-sufficient members of society. With this observation, the public demonstrates more wisdom about human beings and a better understanding of history than many a welfare "expert" or talking head. Indeed, you can see the intersection of Investor Politics and fighting poverty as much in America's past as in its future.

American governments have always had an important role in assisting the poor. The federal government's entry into the field was relatively late, and had negative effects. During the colonial period, American states and localities emulated the English system from which most of their settlers had come. As the Cato Institute's Michael Tanner tells the story, England's Poor Law, passed in 1601, established four basic principles for government-run charity: first, care for the poor was a public responsibility; second, care for the poor was a local matter; third, public relief was denied to individuals who could be cared for by their families; and fourth, children of the poor could be removed from their parents' daily care and apprenticed to others to learn useful skills.[50]

Many justified public assistance as the logical extension of the government's duty to maintain order. If destitution led to homelessness, citizens would lose the unhampered use of city streets and public spaces. Furthermore, any government aid should include rules designed to reduce dependency and encourage self-reliance. The social consensus behind this argument was broad and deep. Consider the fact that John Locke, a patron saint of classical liberalism, complained as early as 1697 that England's public relief programs, then less than a century old, had strayed from their conservative roots, encouraging vagrancy and dependency. "The multiplying of the poor, and the increase of the tax for their maintenance, is so general an observation and complaint that it cannot be doubted," Locke wrote in a draft "welfare reform" plan for the London Board of Trade. He pointed out that relief rolls were rising even during times of plenty, so a lack of jobs was not causing the problem. "The growth of the poor must therefore have some other cause," he wrote, "and it can be nothing else but the relaxation of discipline, and corruption of manners, virtue, and industry being as constant companions on the one side as vice and idleness on the other." Locke advocated requiring work for relief and placing children in environments where they could learn job skills and sound moral values. He argued that the "true and proper relief of the poor . . . consists in finding work for them, and taking care they do not live like drones upon the labor of others" or live as "beggars swarming in the streets."[51]

In both England and early America, local officials established two main forms of public assistance. *Outdoor relief* provided the nonworking poor with small sums of cash, food, or fuel. Although most recipients were widows, children, or the disabled, shiftless men who lined up for outdoor relief gave it a bad name in most jurisdictions. Increasingly, governments created *poorhouses* where those living on the street were required to go for food and shelter. The able-bodied worked for their room and board, often in desperate conditions. To some extent, officials made poorhouses intentionally harsh to serve as a deterrent against going on the dole. After states began to require cities and counties to set up poorhouses in the 1830s, they became the dominant form of public assistance for much of the next century.[52]

Parallel to the poorhouses, and often greater in extent and impact, were private relief societies run primarily by religious organizations. Scholars such as Gertrude Himmelfarb and Marvin Olasky have chronicled the successes of Victorian-era private relief, which was based on reciprocity, temperance, and moral teaching. Like their modern-day counterparts, these programs were often more effective than government programs in assisting those whose poverty was behavioral—arising not from being widowed or disabled but from personal behaviors such as drinking or sexual promiscuity. Why does private relief work better for the behaviorally poor? Because it is not an entitlement. Charities set the rules, and can enforce them.

Behavioral poverty often reflects an inability or unwillingness to delay or resist gratification. A man gives in to his thirst for alcohol, ignoring what it will do to him in the future. A woman drops out of high school to take a job or have a child, oblivious to her inability to support herself or a family without first acquiring useful skills. To put the problem in terms that are, by now, familiar to the reader, the behaviorally poor think only about consumption and do not invest. They have not learned that reducing consumption in the short run—to build human and financial capital—allows for a higher standard of living in the future. Both public and private relief agencies once viewed their job as helping the poor, individual by individual, realize the importance of delayed gratification. The term welfare was not in use and would not have been accurate. "Unless the person were totally incapacitated," writes historian Clarence Carson, "more attention was given to reforming the poor, getting them to become productive and self-supporting, than helping them to fare well."[53]

However, as the Progressives began to take the reins of state power in the late nineteenth and early twentieth centuries, they fashioned a different model of poor relief. The American economy was undergoing rapid transformation as corporations merged to form trusts and holding companies and technological innovation introduced higher and higher levels of "churning" in the workforce. During the depressions of the 1890s, an unprecedented number of Americans lost their jobs, joining the ranks of the unemployed that already included displaced farmers and immigrants. Surely, poverty was no longer a condition for which individuals could be held responsible. It was, rather, the natural consequence of economic and social forces that politicians should learn to control—and that, in the meantime, government had a responsibility to ameliorate.

THE BIRTH AND REBIRTH OF AFDC

An early manifestation of the new Progressive thinking was an attack on the poorhouses. Children, in particular, became the subjects of immense attention. Reformers advocated removing children from the poorhouses in favor of foster care and orphanages that emphasized the education of dependent children over work. Later, reformers shifted their focus again to the idea of keeping families together rather than removing children from broken or abusive homes. Simultaneously, the late nineteenth century saw the creation of programs to assist widows of Civil War veterans. By the 1920s, many states had combined these two ideas—aiding children and widows in their homes—through programs collectively known as mothers' pensions. By 1935, almost every state had such pension programs, but their shaky finances led President Roosevelt to federalize them in the Aid to Dependent Children program, part of the Social Security Act of 1935.[54]

As chapter 4 lays out in some detail, the bill's old-age pensions garnered the lion's share of legislative and public attention. The ADC program was seen largely as a bailout of cash-strapped states more than as a major change in antipoverty policy. Spared the scrutiny it deserved, ADC caseloads grew rapidly, but the program remained a relatively small sliver of the federal budget. In 1950, Congress expanded ADC benefits to give mothers or other adult guardians a monthly allowance in addition to that of their children. In a pattern soon to become familiar, rising living standards and economic growth throughout the 1950s coincided with an increase, not a decrease, in ADC recipients and expenditures. By the time President

Kennedy took office in 1961, many analysts had correctly concluded that the mothers remained in poverty and on the dole not because of structural defects in the economy but instead because they lacked marketable skills. This conclusion harkened back to John Locke's observations about English welfare at the turn of the eighteenth century. Kennedy was more diplomatic and less specific than Locke. He promised to reform the system to give "a hand up, not a handout." Other than renaming the program Aid to Families with Dependent Children, Kennedy accomplished little before his assassination. But many of his aides remained to help Lyndon Johnson wage his "War on Poverty."

Following in the footsteps of the New Deal, Johnson's Great Society concocted a bewildering array of antipoverty programs: Head Start, the Job Corps, the Work Incentive Program, Community Actions grants, and so on. The new focus on job training and community development was meant to reduce dependency on AFDC. It did not, as Tanner relates:

> By 1965, the number of people receiving AFDC had risen to 4.3 million. By 1972, that number would more than double to nearly 10 million people. During the 1950s, welfare rolls had increased by 17 percent. During the 1960s, they increased by 107 percent, and three-quarters of that increase occurred between 1965 and 1968, at a time of relative economic prosperity and low unemployment.[55]

To give them their due, many Johnson administration officials had rightly agreed with Kennedy that simply handing out benefit checks was a mistake. It did little to discourage long-term dependency, and indeed might well reduce the natural economic disincentives that keep men and women from dropping out of school, having children out of wedlock, and opting out of the workforce—all sure routes to perpetual poverty. But their solutions were faulty. Some thought that government could reduce dependency by providing job training and other services. Others saw the solution in raising the minimum wage. To put it simply, if the poor lacked human capital with which to earn a living wage, the government would either fix the problem directly or compel employers to ignore it. These policies, coupled with federal court rulings that made AFDC into a legal entitlement, made things worse, not better. From 1965 to 1975, cash welfare expenditures tripled in real terms. Job training programs grew fifteen fold. Yet, the poverty rate actually improved more slowly from 1965 to 1975 than it had during the previous decade. By 1980, the poverty rate—13 percent of the population—was higher than in 1968.[56] The social and moral consequences of prolonged dependency were as serious as the persistence of chronic financial poverty. After these huge increases in AFDC caseloads, follow-up studies revealed a significant link between welfare dependency and a variety of social pathologies, especially among children. Even after adjusting for income, young women whose families received AFDC were almost twice as likely to drop out of high school and 50 percent more likely to have children out of wedlock themselves. Young men from AFDC households earned less money as adults and demonstrated more antisocial behaviors such as crime and delinquency than their poor but non-welfare-dependent peers. Finally, children who spent at least two months a year on AFDC scored 20 percent lower on tests of cognitive ability than similarly situated children without such a history.[57] To put it in Investor Politics terms, welfare dependency inhibited a family's ability to build the human capital of children—thus perpetuating the cycle when those children, poorly prepared for the world of work and parenthood as adults, turned to government for ongoing support.

Welfare was both a symptom and a cause of low rates of human capital formation. During the early and mid-1970s, Washington policymakers began to see the fallacy of attempting to spend or wish the problem away. The best way to get poor Americans out of poverty was to get them to work so they could gain useful skills and attitudes. President Richard Nixon proposed converting a variety of cash and in-kind welfare programs into a single program called the Family Assistance Plan (FAP). Eligible working families would receive the full monthly benefit check while nonworking families would get less. In effect, Nixon was proposing a kind of "negative income tax," an idea championed by economist Milton Friedman and other critics of the welfare bureaucracy. They had argued that if public assistance was going to be a federal role, it ought to be provided with as low an administrative cost as possible and without penalizing work. Nixon's plan passed the House but never made it through the Senate, where Finance Committee Chairman Russell Long (D-Louisiana) led the opposition. He thought it was too generous, as did many other conservative Southern Democrats and pro-business Republicans. His 1972 counterproposal was called "workfare." Only working families would receive benefits, albeit lower ones than Nixon recommended. Possibly in response to a proposal contained in Finance Committee testimony by then-California Governor Ronald Reagan, Long added a "work bonus" to, in effect, rebate income and payroll taxes paid by the poor. The Senate rejected even Long's version of the idea for several more years. North Carolina Senator Sam Irvin charged that it used "the Social Security system as an excuse for paying a guaranteed annual income out of the Treasury." Finally, in 1975, Long had it slipped into a tax bill with little fanfare. The Earned Income Tax Credit (EITC) was born.[58]

During the 1980s, lawmakers generally tried to encourage work over welfare through the twin reform paths of eligibility and benefits reforms on the one side and EITC expansion on the other. As president, Reagan was successful at slightly tightening eligibility for cash welfare. AFDC spending declined by 1 percent and Food Stamps by 4 percent during his administration. Unfortunately, these changes were more than offset by a doubling of the EITC and growth in other benefits. During his last year in office, Reagan worked with Senator Daniel Patrick Moynihan (D-New York) and other congressional leaders to fashion the Job Opportunities and Basic Skills (JOBS) program, which imposed employment goals and funded job-training activities for welfare recipients. "For fifty years the welfare system has been a maintenance program," Moynihan announced. "It has now become a jobs program."[59]

Right rhetoric, wrong policy. Welfare reformers had yet to realize that if the goal was getting the poor working, there was no substitute for work itself. The skills they needed the most could not be learned from job-training bureaucrats or community colleges. Nor could they be learned in public-sector "make-work jobs" that previous reforms had allowed. These skills had to be learned on the job, in a real job. Beginning in the mid 1980s, Wisconsin Governor Tommy Thompson implemented a series of real work requirements and other rules that dramatically reduced welfare rolls and increased private-sector employment of low-income recipients. From 1985 to 1990, Wisconsin's welfare caseload fell by 20 percent while the national trend was flat. From 1990 to 1994, including periods of both recession and recovery, it was Wisconsin's turn to have a flat trend while national AFDC caseloads soared by about 40 percent. It was obvious that Wisconsin, and a few other states following its lead in the early 1990s, had figured out how best to get recipients usefully employed. Indeed, the state's record remains enviable; from 1985 to 1998, Wisconsin's caseload declined by an astounding 90 percent.[60]

Bill Clinton was elected president in 1992 promising to "end welfare as we know it." After taking a detour for a few years, he and the Republican Congress finally fashioned a package in 1996. It authorized Wisconsin-like work programs across the country and ended the AFDC entitlement altogether in favor of TANF, a block-grant system that offered states incentives to get recipients reemployed and to rebuild broken families. At the time, left-wing critics savaged the bill as mean-spirited and predicted widespread homelessness and despair as a result. They were wildly off target. From its peak in 1994, AFDC/TANF caseloads dropped like a stone in most states, with the rate accelerating after 1996. The result was not an increase but a decrease in the child poverty rate, which in 1998 reached its lowest rate since 1980.

Robert Rector, a welfare analyst at the Heritage Foundation whose research during the 1980s and 1990s helped build the intellectual case for reform, cowrote a 1999 analysis of the TANF legislation with Sarah Youssef. He pointed out that, contrary to the predictions of alarmists, states with larger caseload reductions actually had faster drops in child poverty than states with more lenient policies. Nor, Rector and Youssef wrote, was a growing economy the main reason for dropping caseloads. Welfare dependency had risen during previous economic booms. This time, the policy mix appeared to be the critical variable. Just from 1997 to 1998, states that used the new TANF law to impose immediate work requirements and strict sanctions for noncompliance reduced caseloads by an average of 50 percent. States with lax requirements and sanctions saw caseloads drop by only 14 percent.[61]

At the same time that AFDC/TANF caseloads were dropping and benefit expenditures moderating, the Earned Income Tax Credit was growing by leaps and bounds. During the Reagan and Bush administrations, AFDC grew by an annual average increase of less than one percent. Food Stamp spending grew by 3.5 percent a year. During the same period, the EITC grew by an average of 11.4 percent.[62] No longer a small tax expenditure, but now a major antipoverty program that nearly equaled AFDC in 1992 expenditures, the EITC would take off again during the Clinton years. By fiscal year 2001, its budgetary impact ($31 billion) far exceeded both TANF ($16 billion) and Food Stamps ($22 billion).[63] The EITC had become the de facto linchpin of federal antipoverty policy.

In his book *The Hidden Welfare State,* tax policy analyst Christopher Howard explains that particularly after 1985, expanding the EITC became a favorite tactic of politicians of all stripes when faced with less-palatable legislation. Liberal Democrats, for example, viewed EITC expansion as a means of making the tax code more "progressive." Both Reagan's Tax Reform Act of 1986 and Clinton's tax hike package of 1993 included large EITC expansions. On the other hand, both moderate Republicans and so-called "New Democrats" saw the EITC as a better means of boosting the real wages of low-income workers than a minimum wage hike, which more liberal members and labor unions sought after the Republicans lost the Senate in 1986. A government-set minimum wage forces a wedge between those with low amounts of human capital and the job market. If your skills and work effort don't merit $6.00 an hour, but the government does not allow a lower wage, employers may choose automation or other alternatives to hiring you. Lawmakers intent on helping the poor without creating unemployment gravitated towards the EITC throughout the late 1980s. The result was a lower-than-proposed minimum wage boost and an EITC expansion in 1990.[64]

A PRO-INVESTMENT WELFARE POLICY

Applying the principles of Investor Politics to antipoverty programs would mean some significant changes in policy. First, state and federal policymakers should learn from the success of the 1996 welfare reform bill. Work requirements, time limits, and other reasonable conditions for receiving public assistance help welfare recipients build the human capital they need to become self-sufficient and productive members of society. Such capital includes "hard" skills required to perform certain jobs, "soft" skills such as punctuality and teamwork, and habits of responsible behavior such as avoiding single parenthood and getting off drugs. In addition, these rules deter some families from seeking cash benefits at all, either because they are unwilling to work or because they were contemplating fraud. "Serious work requirements make it difficult for individuals to receive AFDC benefits while simultaneously working at unreported jobs," Rector and Youssef point out.[65] Policymakers should apply work requirements, time limits, and similar rules to other antipoverty programs such as Food Stamps, housing assistance, and the women and children component of Medicaid.

Another promising reform in public assistance is the Individual Development Account (IDA). Currently the subject of experimentation by the nonprofit sector and a number of states, IDAs offer government matching funds for welfare recipients who save a portion of their income in the accounts.[66] In addition to their lack of human capital, one of the great barriers to upward mobility among the poor is their inexperience with savings and financial institutions. They have no financial assets to speak of, and most lack even something as basic as a bank account. IDAs offer the opportunity for these families to learn habits of frugality and the tools they need to manage their personal finances. President Clinton proposed what he called Universal Savings Accounts to provide a federal match for deposits similar to that available in private-sector 401(k) or SEP-IRA plans. His proposal, however, was too broad. It offered a new federal entitlement to millions of middle-class Americans. A more reasonable application of the idea would be simply to require all recipients of TANF, Food Stamps, or other welfare benefits to open at least an IDA bank account. States could use existing benefit dollars to match recipient deposits into the IDA, within which balances would accrue tax-free and from which they make tax-free withdrawals for education and medical expenses. They could also use their IDAs to buy homes, start businesses, or in retirement, but would have to pay taxes on withdrawals, similar to the treatment of IRAs.

Finally, policymakers should take a fresh look at the Earned Income Tax Credit. Its popularity is understandable. Unlike hiking the minimum wage, the EITC doesn't destroy jobs. Unlike traditional welfare programs, it does not teach idleness. In addition, it is relatively easy to administer. However, these advantages come with disadvantages. After all, administering welfare programs means determining who is eligible, imposing rules on recipients, and managing the caseload. The new TANF programs many states have created since 1996 do, in fact, have relatively high expenditures for administration (although the use of private contractors can and should be allowed to shave them a bit). The EITC may spare taxpayers much of these administrative costs, but the tradeoff is that it is overly broad, vulnerable to fraud, a perpetual entitlement. To reverse Kennedy's maxim, it is a handout, not a hand up.

One study estimated that a fourth of all EITC claims were fraudulent. Recipients claim fictitious income or children to goose their tax returns—a practice encouraged by electronic filing and the loans against projected refunds that many tax preparers now offer.[67] Even for those entitled to the EITC, that is the problem—they are entitled to it. Unlike TANF, they do not face time limits or other limits on their eligibility. Indeed, for some recipients the EITC becomes a disincentive to work and a reason to remain dependent. As family income rises, their maximum EITC amount shrinks. A study by researchers at the University of California at Berkeley found that two-parent families face as much as a 50 percent marginal tax rate (because of the EITC phase-out) if a second parent goes to work. Even for many single recipients, the phase-out adds several percentage points to their marginal rate.[68]

Fundamentally, the EITC writes into law a model for public assistance that is inconsistent with limited-government principles. Starting with the English poor laws of the seventeenth century, the idea was to provide long-term (and economical) assistance for the disabled but only short-term conditional assistance for the able bodied so that they did not, in Locke's words, "swarm the streets" or "live as drones upon the labor of others." The EITC's perpetuity encourages rather than discourages dependency. Of course, like the mortgage interest deduction, it has worked its way so deeply into the tax code that politicians seeking to get rid of it are unlikely to stay in office too long. Here are two more salable alternatives:

• Convert the EITC into additional funding for TANF, through increases in benefits or recipients or both. Although I can already hear the hackles, EITC is no less a welfare program than TANF is, but it lacks as much accountability. An expanded TANF program would subject more recipients to time limits and would help police fraud. This would also have the virtue of putting public assistance spending out on the table for all to see.

• Convert the EITC into a system of taxpayer matching funds for IDAs, MSAs, USAs, or ESAs. This would reduce the potential for fraud (since recipients would have to save for later rather than consume immediately) while dovetailing with broader goals of converting Social Security, Medicare, and other programs into savings accounts.

GOVERNMENT SUBSIDIES FOR
INTELLECTUAL CAPITAL

Politicians of all political stripes tend to view government subsidies for research and development as a profitable investment in intellectual capital. The National Science Foundation, the Department of Energy, and the Department of Agriculture, among others, operate multibillion-dollar programs to subsidize research, while private companies benefit from another $3.4 billion in federal research and development tax credits. Advocates for these policies employ a familiar argument: Research and development is a public good with positive externalities that are not fully captured by market participants. Less useful research will be conducted in the absence of government funding, resulting in lower rates of economic growth, less innovation, and fewer societal benefits.

To understand the issue of science funding more fully, you have to look below the surface. According to the National Science Foundation, total expenditures for United States research and development was about $264 billion in 2000. Federal expenditures accounted for about one-quarter of the total, while industry funded 68 percent and the remaining sectors—state governments, universities, and nonprofits—the remainder. It is true that science and technology used to be more dependent on Washington. Indeed, the federal government funded more than half of all American research and development from the end of World War II until 1978. Since then, its share of the total has continued to fall, and its current share—27 percent—is the smallest since comprehensive data began to be collected. Even after industry overtook government in the late 1970s as the primary funder of research and development, federal spending continued to grow. Its growth was particularly rapid from 1980 to 1985, as the Reagan administration beefed up the nation's defenses and civilian research and development in such areas as energy and health grew substantially. After 1985, however, federal research and development spending in inflation-adjusted dollars actually fell, by an average of 1.2 percent a year.[69]

Some might have predicted that this decline in government funding would result in technological backwardness, fewer discoveries, and fewer innovative products for consumers. Nothing could be further from the truth. Part of the story of science and technology in the past decade has been massive new investments in research by software companies, pharmaceutical manufacturers, and new industries such as biotechnology (which has alone spent more than $10 billion in the 1990s on research and development). Overall, the nonmanufacturing sector went from playing a minor role in research and development in 1984 ($3.2 billion) to investing $24 billion in 1994, or nearly 15 percent of all research and development spending that year. Microsoft Corporation alone spends about $2 billion a year, or more than 20 percent of its revenues. Even among traditional manufacturing sectors, the commitment is significant. The chemical industry spends twice as much on research and development than NASA. Electrical equipment firms spend twice as much as does the Department of Energy. Rubber and paper manufacturers, together, have a research budget larger than the National Science Foundation.[70] Government funding does, of course, continue to dominate research and development in such fields as aeronautics and aerospace, but for the perfectly understandable reason that government is the primary consumer for these industries (in the form of contracts for planes, weapons, and spacecraft) rather than just an investor.

Total research and development spending has grown consistently in real terms in recent years, as private spending has more than taken up the slack from government cutbacks. There is no reason to expect this pattern to change in the future. Indeed, when you look at how federal science money is spent, it becomes clear that Washington still spends a lot of money on research functions that might more properly be carried out by the private sector. Although there is some debate about this in academic circles, there is a consensus among policymakers of different political stripes that government should help fund basic or "pure" science—the kind of research in astronomy, for example, that has no apparent commercial value. However, most federal spending is not devoted to the basic science that many believe is in greater need of government investment. Only 32 percent of federal dollars go to basic science. Another 20 percent goes to applied research, and the remaining dollars fund product development. It is not only national defense that sops up lots of applied research and development spending. Less than half of all federal spending for civilian (non-defense, non-space) research and development is in basic science. From agricultural techniques to semiconductors, taxpayers are currently paying for research and development that should be the responsibility of firms, trade associations, and philanthropy. Meanwhile, 40 percent of all basic science is funded by private industry or nonprofits.[71]

While it is easy to demonstrate that private industry has been taken up where government science budgets have left off in recent years, it is not the whole story. Some critics argue that simply increasing research and development spending each year is not enough. The National Science Foundation warns ominously that even though research and development budgets have grown since 1990, the share of gross domestic product devoted to research and development has declined. Output, in other words, is growing even faster than science and technology spending. Does that mean there is really a crisis? Hardly. Rich people spend less of their incomes on food than do poor people, but eat better. There is no reason why the share of income devoted to science and technology should be any more meaningful than the share devoted to dining. The key issues are the size of the menu and the nutritional value of its offerings.

As we have seen, it is a mistake to judge investment simply in terms of dollars spent, anyway. One important problem is that the data are incomplete—lots of important informal research goes on at small companies but is not reported in a systematic way. Zoltan J. Acs, a professor at the University of Baltimore School of Business, has studied small-business innovation. He points out that small firms dominate technological progress in fields from steel to computers, and "have a virtual monopoly on innovations" in biotechnology.[72] In evaluating research expenditures, the name of the game should be results. Given the almost dizzying rate of technological innovation these days, there is little evidence to suggest that America's research and development engine is sputtering. Furthermore, as the private sector continues to increase its share of national research and development spending, we should expect better results from each dollar invested. Partly this reflects the natural tendency for companies in competitive markets to scrutinize every expenditure carefully to make sure it contributes to the bottom line, while government often squanders money on pork barrel projects and scientific dead ends.

It also reflects the historical fact that most new technological discoveries come not from cloistered academics or government research labs but from engineers and inventors in the private sector working directly on industrial machinery and processes.[73] As British biochemist Terence Kealey documents in his invaluable 1996 book *The Economic Laws of Scientific Research*, during the past two centuries the industrialized world ran a kind of practical experiment to test whether government spending on science and technology created more economic growth than a private sector-led effort. Countries such as France and Germany, and later the Soviet Union and China, invested lots of government money in science and technology. England and the United States, and later Switzerland and Japan, left most of the responsibility in the hands of industry, philanthropists, and so-called "hobby" scientists working on their own. It was the latter group of countries that hosted the most prolific and celebrated scientists, and the most dynamic and technologically advanced economies.[74]

Computers and the Internet have made many forms of research far less expensive than they once were, helping to soften whatever "blow" there has been from declining federal budgets.[75] Moreover, there is plenty of evidence to suggest that government research and development spending displaces private spending. The taxes required to fund government research and development remove money from the private sector, while creating the expectation among industry and philanthropists that the government will take care of the society's science needs. So there is much less to fret about than many politicians and doomsayers think—particularly if any federal budget cuts are targeted to those applied research and product development expenditures that lie clearly within the domain of the private sector. If the federal government retained its entire current civilian spending on basic science and cut only applied research and development, that would still save taxpayers nearly $12 billion—money better invested in private capital or in public capital formation at the state and local level.

One other quirk of current tax policy should be changed to encourage additional private investment in intellectual capital. Because corporate dividends are taxed while interest payments are not, business executives have a strong incentive to choose debt over equity in financing new investments. Since lenders have historically been far more willing to finance physical capital projects such as plants and machinery they can understand—or perhaps even repossess if necessary—than research projects or intellectual capital, businesses probably put more money in the former and less in the latter than they would if the tax bias did not exist. Indeed, some lobbyists have defended the current research and development tax credit on precisely these grounds. However, the relatively puny credit does little to rectify the situation. Congress should eliminate it and solve the debt-equity problem by making corporate dividends tax-deductible, which is, of course, the correct policy from the standpoint of tax neutrality, anyway.

CONCLUSION

The advent of personal computers and the Internet has, ironically, made physical capital less important to the economy at the beginning of the twenty-first century than ever before in modern times. Brainpower, not horsepower, will increasingly drive the economic engine of the future, which is even more reason for the country's leaders to take a fresh look at how human capital is really formed and what they can do to make investment in education, training, and other programs more productive.

There are many opportunities for reform. A monopoly system of public schools is poorly suited for the world of mass customization that modern technologies and organizational innovations have created. Colleges and universities receive hundreds of billions of dollars in public and private dollars but turn out many students who would have been far better off spending their time and money getting useful skills in the job market. Unemployment Insurance discourages workers from getting themselves rapidly retrained and reemployed filling emerging needs in the economy. Traditional welfare programs teach recipients all the wrong lessons about how to accumulate capital of all kinds so they can be self-sufficient and productive members of society. And government subsidies for research and development waste scarce resources on pork barrel projects and displace more productive private investment, while ignoring problems in the tax code that bias the investment decisions of corporate executives.

In each case, the general themes of Investor Politics emerge. Focus on helping Americans build and control their own assets, rather than substituting transfer programs and bureaucratic interference that encourage dependency and other social pathologies. Use the tools of personal investing and the magic of compound interest to give families opportunities to improve their lot. And make sure investment is as productive as it can be by subjecting it to the forces of choice and competition. If politicians can package and explain these policies in ways voters can grasp and take to heart, they will enjoy huge advantages in the elections of the coming decade—which will most likely be dominated by human capital issues such as education.

CHAPTER 9

THE SAVINGS
STRATEGY FOR SHRINKING
THE WELFARE STATE

OLITICIANS LIKE TO TALK THE LANGUAGE OF WARFARE.
Second only to sports, I would say, war provides candidates, activists, the news media, and other observers of the political process with the terminology they use to comprehend and explain politics. This should surprise no one. If, as Clausewitz wrote, war is the continuation of politics by other means, it is not much of a stretch to expect those who wage politics to think of their enterprise in military terms, even if they stop just short of fisticuffs and cutlasses.

Unfortunately, such analogies are frequently faulty. Those who compare politics to warfare are particularly prone to misapply military principles. For advocates of rolling back welfare state liberalism, the tendency has been to think about the conflict between freedom and government paternalism as a set-piece, open-field battle like Marathon or Waterloo. A conflict, in other words, in which it is immediately apparent who wins and who loses. After the Republican Revolution of 1994, a new Congress full of would-be budget cutters galloped on Washington and sought to force the issue. Many had grandiose plans for axing entire federal departments and lopping off huge chunks of entitlement programs such as Medicaid, Medicare, and Aid to Families with Dependent Children (AFDC). This gung ho mentality lasted a few months. As Congress and President Clinton faced off later in the year and the federal government shut down, Republican leaders appeared to be charging the enemy with reckless abandon, complete with partisan flags flying and a loud chorus of buglers such as conservative commentators, activists, and think tanks.

As we know, they did not win the day. President Bill Clinton prevailed in spin. Republicans saw their poll numbers tank and their prospects for the 1996 elections dim. However, it is important to recognize that the Republicans did not lose a political open-field battle. There was none. Clinton made no serious attempt to challenge Republican arguments or present an alternative way of reconciling the country's spending habits and revenue collections. Indeed, Clinton later made a budget deal that included budget savings not dissimilar from the Republican proposals on Medicare and other spending areas he had previously blasted in well-publicized public statements.

What the Republican Congress discovered during the government shutdown fiasco was that they were charging not an enemy army but a fortress. America's expensive and intrusive welfare state is best thought of not as a rival to be dueled but a castle to be taken. It is defended by an impressive array of moats, walls, salients, and garrisons. As we have seen, this elaborate fortification took decades to build, brick by brick. It will not fall quickly or easily. A frontal assault is impossible, as Newt Gingrich and surviving Republican leaders discovered to their dismay. Instead, advocates for smaller government, lower taxes, and personal responsibility must refine their tactics, lengthen their timetable, and expand their patience. They must, in other words, prepare not for a battle but for a siege.

THE ENTITLEMENT FORTRESS

So just how big and secure is the entitlement fortress? Let us review the intelligence reports detailed in earlier chapters. Almost 60 percent of the fiscal year 2001 federal budget was devoted to Social Security, Medicare, Medicaid, and other "mandatory" entitlement programs such as Unemployment Insurance, TANF (formerly AFDC), Food Stamps, and government retiree benefits. A scant 15 percent was devoted to national defense with 11 percent allocated to debt service and only 17 percent allocated to discretionary programs such as transportation, research, or community development.[1] At the state level, public education is the largest entitlement, making up 33 percent of the average state budget, with the state share of Medicaid consuming an additional 13 percent and aid to higher education (a constitutional entitlement in many states) an additional 12 percent.[2]

A rough, back-of-the-envelope calculation of how much we pay for entitlements can be developed by using the Tax Foundation's 1999 estimate of the "effective tax rate." This is simply the total collections of federal, state, and local taxes divided by personal income. The Tax Foundation pegs the effective tax rate at about 36 percent. The federal share is about 24 percent, the state share is about 7 percent, and the local share approaches 5 percent.[3] Applying the percentage of government at each level devoted to "social insurance," welfare programs, and other entitlements yields a share of personal income of about 19 percent. Add in the cash value of entitlements offered not in the federal budget but in the tax code (such as the Earned Income Tax Credit and the mortgage interest deduction), and the total cost of the welfare state exceeds one-fifth of personal income. Moreover, this represents only the short-run cost. Because of previous government borrowing to pay entitlement benefits and the unfunded liability of promised benefits in the future, the real cost of the entitlement state will surge in the first few decades of the twenty-first century to one-third of personal income, then to one-half of income, then beyond.

COGNITIVE DISSONANCE ON ENTITLEMENTS

To return to our fortress analogy, the walls of the modern entitlement state are defended by a series of middle-class programs we might call "bastions" (a bastion is a projection, heavily fortified, that allows defenders of a castle a wider firing range against attackers). These programs have been discussed in detail in previous chapters. They include Social Security, Unemployment Insurance, Medicare, the elderly and disabled portion of Medicaid, the mortgage interest deduction and other housing tax breaks, health-care tax breaks, and federal subsidies for education. Together, these programs totaled more than $1 trillion in fiscal year 2001.

If public opinion polls are any indication, most Americans have come to rely on these programs rather than their own work and savings to pay for the big-ticket items of life: losing a job, buying a house, educating children, retiring, or developing a serious illness. This is true despite the fact that most Americans also say they think government in general is too big, costs too much, gives too much away to "the poor," and usurps private initiative and responsibility. Indeed, the extent to which Americans say government is too big tracks closely with their increased reliance on it. As late as 1985, as many respondents in a CBS News/New York Times poll said they favored larger government with many services as said they favored smaller government with fewer services. But by the mid-1990s, as costs were exploding in programs such as Medicare and Medicaid, Americans were two-to-one in favor of a smaller government—even as they also told pollsters that they were suspicious of efforts to save money in Medicare and other entitlements.[4]

This cognitive dissonance goes a long way to explain why the entitlement fortress seems so impregnable. It does not rely on a fundamental, philosophical commitment to big, paternalistic government on the part of average Americans. Instead, it is based on the fact that, starting with Social Security and Unemployment Insurance in 1935 and continuing with the creation of Medicare and Medicaid in 1965, Americans have slowly but surely built their lives around government entitlements. The taxes needed to pay for the entitlements have risen so high that most families cannot afford to provide for their own needs. At the same time, politicians have promised them that they have no need to—that Social Security and Medicare will ensure their retirement security; Unemployment Insurance, their ability to weather a spell of joblessness; government grants and loans, the education of their children; special tax breaks, their ability to afford health care and homeownership; and Medicaid, the long-term care of an elderly parent or disabled family member.

Brick by brick, the entitlement state has established itself in American culture. Polls show overwhelmingly that while most Americans view "welfare" with disdain, they believe the federal government has taken on a crucial role in protecting them from life's biggest and most expensive challenges. The notion that families should save their own money to pay for these needs seems impossible (because of a lack of extra money to save) or unnecessary (because government will take care of it). A Business Week poll taken in November 1995—at the height of the conflict between the Republican Congress and a resurgent Clinton—illustrated the reservoir of public support for specific entitlements upon which the president could draw. Asked whether they agreed strongly or somewhat with a federal government "guarantee" in several areas, the 1,007 survey respondents said that they:

• Strongly (73 percent) or somewhat (19 percent) agreed on a "Social Security pension to help provide for retirement."

• Strongly (61 percent) or somewhat (25 percent) agreed on "some minimum level of health care."

• Strongly (53 percent) or somewhat (31 percent) agreed on "nursing-home care for the elderly."

• Strongly (42 percent) or somewhat (38 percent) agreed on "temporary unemployment insurance benefits."

• Strongly (32 percent) or somewhat (46 percent) agreed on "public assistance payments for those who cannot work."

Poll respondents were more skeptical of what might be termed "welfare" programs for the undeserving poor or for corporations. Still, 70 percent expressed support for the Earned Income Tax Credit. And while 63 percent said they agreed with the Congressional Republican's call for an "opportunity society" based on individual merit, an even larger number (79 percent) said they agreed with the proposition, tied to Clinton and Congressional Democrats, that "the federal government must protect the most vulnerable in society, especially the poor and elderly, by guaranteeing minimum living standards and providing social benefits."[5] The key word throughout the poll was "guarantee"—another word for entitlement. Obviously, critics of big government who seem as if their goal is simply to tear down the "guarantees" of the entitlement state have few friends among American voters.

THE ART OF SIEGECRAFT

America's entitlement state isn't just one huge monolith. It is an interlocked system of programs, dependencies, and public expectations that has been built up over decades of hard work by activists who believed passionately in a large, "helpful" government and were willing to accomplish their objective incrementally. The result of their efforts is a fortification that, as recent events have shown, resists frontal assault. Those political soldiers brave enough to venture out toward its walls are frequently enfiladed from the garrisons of Social Security, Medicare, or other bastions well-positioned to cover any line of attack.

The situation would have stumped all but the most skillful siege generals of history. Throughout the history of pre-gunpowder fortification, from the fabled walls of Jericho to the Crusades and the golden age of European feudalism, defenders enjoyed tremendous advantages. Indeed, there were few technological innovations in siegecraft after 397 B.C.E. Most of the methods of attack—battering rams, scaling ladders, siege towers, artillery, and so forth—were more picturesque than effective. Not even time was always on the side of the besieger. Frequently, attempts to starve a fortress into submission took so long that attacking forces succumbed to their own supply problems, the diseases rampant in their unhealthy encampments, or attack by a enemy column sent to relieve the fort.[6]

Another point to keep in mind from our siegecraft analogy is that fortifications, although defensive in design, were not solely defensive in purpose and effect. More often, a stronghold allowed a local lord or army to dominate the surrounding countryside by providing a base of operations from which to sally forth to forage or raid and to retreat to in the event of reprisal. We can see this clearly in the case of the modern entitlement state. Advocates of government expansion use each success as a "base of operations" from which to advance a broader agenda. The 1935 Social Security Act, for example, firmly established the notion of a significant federal role in relieving poverty and unemployment. Because of the peculiar nature of the program, which provided huge "returns" to retirees during its three decades before mass eligibility began to collapse the pyramid, Americans internalized the mistaken impression that the federal government was a safe and rewarding repository for their savings. Playing to these feelings, politicians amended the Social Security Act to add disability insurance (1956), then Medicare and Medicaid (1965). Medicaid, in turn, became a base from which advocates of government control of health care have argued (successfully) for subsidized benefits to nonpoor women and children in the 1980s and for a new Child Health Insurance Program (CHIP) in 1997. In each case, a hard-fought political struggle resulted in a new stronghold, from which entitlement advocates could pursue additional advances.

Fortunately, the art of siegecraft does offer the foe of big government some useful lessons about how best to attack a well-fortified stronghold.

Classic sieges such as the Roman capture of Jotapata during the Jewish revolt of 67 C.E., the First Crusade's capture of Jerusalem in 1099, and the Ottoman capture of Constantinople from the last remnants of the Byzantine Empire in 1453, all offer guidance about the importance of planning, deception, intrigue, and patience. Here are, in no particular order, some tactics used successfully in the past to invest well-guarded fortifications:[7]

• PROBING FOR WEAKNESS. There was no substitute for good intelligence. Generals who made careful surveys of the enemy fort often found vulnerabilities they could use to great effect. These might be weaknesses in the walls themselves, the existence of blind spots, or the deployment of defenders. At Jotapata, a Jewish deserter informed the Roman commander Vespasian (a future emperor) that just before dawn on every morning watch, Jewish sentries would nod off in their extreme fatigue. Vespasian used the information to time a stealthy assault on the wall guarded by the dozing soldiers. They succeeded, opening the doors to the main Roman army and ending an exhausting forty-day siege that might otherwise have gone badly for the empire.[8]

• UNDERMINING. The original derivation of this word comes from siegecraft. In brief, sappers would dig their way underneath a castle wall. They roofed their tunnel with planks supported by timbers. After completing the tunnel, they would light a fire so that the supports would collapse, along with the walls above. This would create a breach in the castle defenses on which attackers would be poised to capitalize. Most European castles that fell to siege (without treachery playing a hand) did so at least in part because of successful mining operations. Perhaps one of the most dramatic series of undermining efforts occurred during the fall of Constantinople in 1453, with Turkish miners and European counterminers fighting much of the battle underground with pickaxes, pikes, and shovels.[9]

• CONFUSING THE ENEMY. Defenders with sufficient supplies and manpower could outlast even the most ardent foe. Attackers had to rely on crafty methods to overcome this disadvantage. One was simply to harrass defenders with enough arrows, bolts, and stones thrown by catapults to keep them from recognizing what their miners and engineers were really up to (despite what you may have seen in the movies, most pre-gunpowder artillery didn't have a chance of toppling well-built walls because their trajectories limited their effective targets to the top of walls rather than to their bases).

• TURNING THE CASTLE'S DEFENSES AGAINST ITSELF. Sometimes, fortifications were made too well. A single bastion, once taken, might serve to give the attacking force a well-defended base from which to take the rest of the fort. In the case of the Crusader capture of Jerusalem in 1099, this defensive countermeasure became the tool of the attackers. The Crusaders had built massive siege towers (sometimes called a belfry) that they planned to wheel next to the city's walls and provide a base of attack. Unfortunately for them, the Egyptian defenders of the city had long managed to prevent this. They used volleys of flaming arrows, hot oil, and catapult loads of "Greek fire" (the napalm of the Middle Ages) to set towers ablaze and kill its waiting soldiers. Another countermeasure was to attach immense timbers to the walls to keep the towers from closing with them. But when a change of wind momentarily blinded the Egyptians, one such anti-tower timber became the city's downfall. Crusaders attached their tower to the timber, then scampered across the resulting bridge.[10]

• UTILIZING TURNCOATS. Even with all of these tools to use against castles, attackers still frequently failed. It is no exaggeration to say that, with few exceptions, the great sieges of history were won in whole or in part by inducing deserters, defenders, even defending generals to provide critical tactical information. This happened at the Ottoman siege of Constantinople, which despite massive Turkish superiority in manpower and tactics may have lasted much longer had not a former adversary, the Hungarian John Hunyadi, not provided the Turks with detailed instructions on how to breach the walls.[11]

UNDERMINING THE ENTITLEMENT STATE

Of all these tactics for taking a fortress, the one advocates of smaller government should make the mainstay of their assault on entitlements should be undermining. It has the greatest chance of success. Furthermore, recent debates about health-care, education, and Social Security reform have identified the key tool our sappers need with which to tunnel: personal savings accounts. For once, reformers who advance personal savings as an alternative to traditional government transfer programs have the public clearly on their side. A variety of opinion polls shows that Americans overwhelmingly favor some kind of personalization of Social Security accounts; that most would abandon the current system in favor of managing their own investments in stocks, bonds, or other financial assets; and that the savings account approach is far more popular than other proposed entitlement reforms such as raising eligibility ages or shaving benefit amounts.[12] Another body of research, discussed in detail in the following chapter, shows that those with at least $5,000 in stocks, bonds, or mutual funds exhibit decidedly free-market views on a host of political and economic issues. They view themselves as capitalists and believe that capitalism is worth defending.[13]

Personal saving will undermine the entitlement state in several ways. First, if done correctly, it will starve the government of revenue it would otherwise squander. Savings accounts should, as much as possible, be funded by diverting money now paid in payroll taxes to failed transfer programs such as Social Security, Medicare, and Unemployment Insurance. Make the diversion contingent on a reduction in eligibility for future government benefits. When that future is reached—when workers or retirees, having accumulated savings to pay for their family's needs, see entitlements merely as claims on their income—the underminer's tunnel will collapse. Americans who own their own education, health-care, and retirement assets will be more willing to accept means testing, other reductions in transfer payments, or outright elimination of programs from which they no longer receive any benefit.

Second, personal investment of these dollars in private markets will generate better long-term financial returns, boosting the economy while enticing more and more Americans to abandon public programs for savings alternatives that actually improve their standard of living. Some defenders of the current system go astray by attempting to argue that investment is investment—regardless of whether the federal government or private markets are in control. The core of the argument for privatization and savings accounts is that there is a big difference. "Investing" in the federal government does not pay well because the resulting "assets" aren't worth very much.

Consider the Ponzi scheme we call Medicare. If the federal government takes in just as much in payroll taxes as it needs to pay benefits, then obviously little investment is occurring. Today's dollars are simply funding today's consumption (except for the long-term benefits of some medical expenses funded indirectly by Medicare payments, such as the training of physicians or the discovery of new treatments). If, on the other hand, more dollars are collected than are spent within an entitlement program, the excess taxes finance other current federal spending, some of which may be thought of as investment. For example, federal dollars from trust fund surpluses help build interstate highways, fund research and development, or help defray the cost of accumulating human capital through higher education subsidies. All of these expenditures are commonly viewed as expanding the productive capacity of the economy, thus making possible higher future income growth and tax receipts.

But be careful not to forget opportunity cost. Dollars taken for federal spending necessarily trade off with state, local, or private spending. Federal highway projects are required to pay higher union wage scales than their state and local counterparts, thus reducing the real investment value of each highway dollar spent. Federal dollars also fund lots of useless research, harm rather than help public schools teach children basic skills, and entice college students into consuming higher education with little economic value (since they do not face the real cost of paying their loans back). If these dollars were not taken by the federal government in the first place, they would probably finance more productive investments in the private sector or at lower levels of government.

Back when Congress and the Johnson administration created Medicare in 1965, it probably never occurred to them to build in a lag between taxes or premiums paid and the onset of benefit payments. They were not creating a system of up-front savings and investment to create the real wealth necessary to promise all elderly Americans a medical safety net; they were simply devising new ways of redistributing income. As long as the ratio between workers and retirees remained unchanged, Medicare's creators figured their Ponzi scheme could be maintained indefinitely. Of course, the elderly failed to do their duty to keep dying early, while medical researchers unpatriotically kept devising new ways to cure disease and extend life. Medicare expenditures grew as per-recipient benefits rose (there was more useful medical care to buy) and the number of recipients ballooned (because this care kept more of them alive).

The last way that personal savings will undermine the entitlement state is that it will reconnect Americans to the free enterprise system. In recent decades, public support for the free enterprise system in general and corporations in specific has been eroding. In the midst of the Great Depression, polls showed that most Americans believed their interests and those of corporations were fundamentally the same. Today, despite a two-decades-long economic boom and a generally rosy public outlook for the future, most Americans say that corporations have fundamentally different interests, make too much profit, and in some cases are insufficiently taxed and regulated. By linking their own fortunes and dreams directly to the success of American business, rather than to the promises of politicians, personal savings accounts invested in private markets offer the hope of reversing this troubling trend.

A COMBINED-ARMS APPROACH

Undermining the entitlement state with personal savings will only work as part of a broader, combined-arms approach. The siege should be made up of the following elements:

• UNDERMINE THE BASTIONS. Expand ESAs to allow tax-deductible deposits and withdrawals for preschool, private schools, college, and retraining. Allow states to convert their Unemployment Insurance systems into personal savings accounts from which workers can withdraw to pay living expenses during jobless spells, open their own businesses, or go back to school to change careers. Allow all workers to deduct a portion of the money they spend on health-care services, insurance premiums, or MSAs, and allow unspent funds in company-funding flexible spending accounts to roll over without penalty. Get rid of restrictions on tax-free capital gains from the sale of a home, while simultaneously tightening eligibility for the mortgage interest deduction. Loosen income caps, deposit caps, and withdrawal penalties on IRAs to end multiple taxation of savings. Push for even just a toehold on Social Security and Medicare to allow a couple of percentage points of payroll taxes to be controlled and invested by workers.

In all cases, reformers shouldn't fall into the trap of back-ending the tax relief in savings accounts—as was done in 1997 with the creation of the Roth IRA—just because it costs the Treasury nothing today. There is a major advantage to allowing up-front tax deductions for personal savings despite their short-run fiscal implications. Up-front deductions give the tax relief to young people, working and busy raising children, while creating a tax liability for older retirees who have the time and knowledge needed to organize as a lobbying force against excessive taxation. It is no accident that the strongest taxpayer lobbies tend to organize locally around property tax increases, which hit seniors most visibly because they pay property taxes out-of-pocket rather than from escrow accounts. Anybody who has been to a local taxpayer association meeting knows which age group dominates the crowd.

One last note on this tactic: Remember that once a bastion is seized, it becomes a powerful place from which to launch other attacks. You do not have to take them all, or even take the best defended (such as Social Security) first. You just need a breakthrough somewhere.

• TURN FORTRESS STRENGTHS AGAINST ITSELF. During the 1999 budget debate, President Clinton handed foes of the entitlement state an opportunity, his new USA proposal, but they failed to recognize it. Clinton's USA would have had higher caps for deposits and greater flexibility in withdrawals than current IRAs. Congress should have counterproposed not just that deposits and earnings into USAs be tax-deductible, but that withdrawals for educational or medical expenses be deductible, too. The prospect of a family accumulating tens of thousands of dollars in USAs, with which they can escape the control of public school monopolies, onerous HMOs, and government regulators, should have been an enticing one. Clinton was lucky that Republicans did not use his proposal against him.

• RAM THE GATES WHEN POSSIBLE. The entitlement state is most vulnerable in areas where middle-class Americans don't perceive their own livelihoods to be at stake. Early reform efforts of farm subsidies and cash welfare programs identified these vulnerabilities. Use the battering ram of legislative action against other weak points such as corporate welfare, which is immensely unpopular across the political spectrum and provides liberal politicians with the one thing they can offer potential donors in the business community.

• BUILD SIEGE TOWERS. Identify and promote private-sector alternatives to welfare programs, including those operated by charities and churches. Route resources to expand these alternatives through such means as a Private Assistance Tax Credit that would allow dollar-for-dollar reductions in government welfare spending when individuals make contributions to the private institutions of civil society.

• CUT OFF SUPPLIES. The cause of "defunding the Left"—of reducing the extent to which taxpayers subsidize the garrisons of the entitlement state—has never been more important. A host of supply lines must be attacked, from the Legal Services Corporation and the National Council of Senior Citizens to public broadcasting and public employee unions. As stated earlier, an effective attack on corporate welfare will destroy much of the Left's ability to attract financial support from business for their political campaigns.

• MAINTAIN AN ARTILLERY BARRAGE. Keep the entitlement garrison reeling and guessing with catapulted missiles such as philosophical attacks on the welfare state, statistics demonstrating the poor returns and shaky fiscal health of particular entitlements, and effective quantification of the cost of big government such as Tax Freedom Day. Politicians, staffers, and activists who work in the trenches, as it were, of campaigns and legislation sometimes forget how important it is to seize the moral high ground. Taking money from the people who earn it to give to those who do not is wrong. At some fundamental level, most Americans—most human beings—know this. Virtually every religion and moral code in existence vilifies it. Judeo-Christians learn commandments against stealing and coveting a neighbor's property. The Buddha taught that one of eight behaviors from which one should abstain was "taking what is not given." Property rights are deeply imbedded in Islamic teaching and tradition. Critics of America's welfare state should not question the intentions or goals of its defenders. However, they should clearly challenge the underlying immorality of writing envy into law.

• LOOK FOR DEFECTORS. Some of the most effective recruiters to the cause of freedom have been former socialists, liberal academics "mugged by reality," open-minded liberal politicians, and community leaders in areas where government dependency is especially acute. Think of Polly Williams and Reverend Floyd Flake on school choice, former Senator Bob Kerrey on entitlements, or Charles Murray on poverty. Another way to think about this tactic is to emphasize how the current entitlement regime harms groups such as women, African Americans, or the families of workers who die prematurely. These arguments may well create new allies with powerful ammunition of their own.

A NOTE ABOUT FUNDAMENTAL TAX REFORM

To some free-market conservatives, the strategy outlined above will seem heretical. They are advocates of fundamental tax reform. In their view, the conservative movement should invest its scarce political resources in an attempt to push through a single big idea, a sort of 1986 Tax Reform Act multiplied many times over. They differ on the details of what the bill should look like but not on the importance of enacting it as a whole. If the federal welfare state and the monstrous tax code it has spawned is, indeed, a castle, these conservatives wish simply to remount their horses, couch their lances, and charge, with a banner flapping behind them that says "Flat Tax" or "National Sales Tax" in bright, bold letters.

These are smart people whose experience and analytical skill are far greater than mine. They know that their cause is noble but risky. They view a heroic defeat as an acceptable price to pay for principle. Perhaps in their minds, the role they wish to play is that of El Cid, the inspirational leader of the Spanish revolt against the Moors who even in death led his troops to battle as a corpse strapped to his steed. But I see another Spaniard on that horse. He is Don Quixote.

Too many tax reformers have lost their way in the fight against the federal income tax code, letting their rhetoric and the internal logic of their ideas blind them to reality. They focus on taxes to the exclusion of the spending side of the ledger, where the strength of the federal leviathan lies. Nobody likes to pay taxes, certainly not of the magnitude and intrusiveness of today's code. However, Americans have come to value the services the taxes fund. No fundamental tax reform is worth fighting for if it does not result in a substantial long-term reduction in the size and scope of government. Nor is it practical in the short term if it does not constitute a large, visible tax cut for the vast majority of Americans.

Perhaps the most insidious element of the flat tax/sales tax debate is its assumption about the virtue of simplicity. Certainly, the tax code is immensely complex, and the deadweight loss to the economy of complying with it sizable. But for most Americans, tax compliance doesn't seem costly at all. They take the standard deduction, rather than itemizing. If they don't fill out the 1040EZ form, they often pay someone else a relatively small amount of money to do their taxes for them. As far as the payroll tax is concerned, few realize just how much it reduces their take-home pay, or where it goes. Ditto for the local property tax, which many homeowners with mortgages pay via escrow accounts and thus never feel the sting of writing the annual check. Worst of all is the sales tax, which for consumers has become a hardly noticeable routine. They need not figure it, nor are they provided an annual bill to know how much they have paid. It seems simple, yes, and is the least hated of taxes. For that reason, advocates of freedom and limited government should think twice about relying on it more in the future.

The fact of the matter is that the American welfare state grew throughout the twentieth century largely because it promised to make life simpler. For many, the promise has been kept. Instead of having to worry about saving and investment your own money for retirement, the federal government does it for you. Worried about elder care for your parents or college for your kids or losing your job? Washington politicians promise to ease your mind. If the welfare state did not exist, if Americans were responsible for managing their own money and planning for their future needs, their lives would seem more complicated, not less. That they would feel an increased sense of control over their lives is true, too. The two go hand in hand, just as they do in the case of children, dependent but largely without responsibilities as well, who grow to be self-sufficient adults with jobs, mortgages, checking accounts, car problems, and children of their own.

Fundamental tax reform is needed. It must, however, be a goal rather than a bill. Its basic principles should be neutrality, efficiency, and the benefit principle. First, neutrality means striving as much as possible to treat all citizens in like circumstances in a like manner. No special preferences for well-connected interest groups. No "progressive" tax rates that treat people differently based on wealth or income. No distortions of market decisions by, for example, taxing deferred consumption—in the form of physical, human, or intellectual capital formation at a higher real rate than current consumption. Efficiency means making sure that the tax code itself, however admirable its goals, does not become a net drag on economic growth. Although neutrality might call for careful identification of every form of investment in the human capital of children, for example, efficiency tells us that probably the best course of action is to exclude a few large categories of clearly defined investment—such as a fixed amount of health-care and education expenditures—and then estimate the rest with a simple personal allowance. Similarly, neutrality might demand that corporations clearly delineate the share of some kinds of expenditures, such as travel or computer purchases, that represents a deductible investment in worker productivity instead of a form of non-wage, taxable compensation. Efficiency, on the other hand, recommends allowing corporations to take broad but possibly capped or depreciated deductions for these expenditures.

The benefit principle means choosing the right tax to fund the right government program. For some services, such as local water and sewer service or state incorporation, the right tax is no tax at all. These services can be priced relatively easily and their users charged a fee. For local services such as police and fire protection, streets, sanitation, and the purchase of land for "open space," your physical stake in the community is directly related to the benefits you derive from the effective performance of the services. So a tax levied on the value of real property, including land and major assets such as homes, automobiles, or machinery, is a reasonable way to fund them. What does not matter is from whose pocket the money ultimately comes. If a retail store is able to pass along its property taxes to its customers, they are in effect paying for the local services needed to keep shoppers and the store safe and to ensure the absence of force or fraud in the transactions performed there. Similarly, one can argue that the number and location of economic transactions is itself related to consumption of services such as courts or regulators, so a sales tax applied at retail is appropriate to fund them (my own view is that the sales tax will become increasingly difficult to collect in a world of Internet commerce, thus leading to its demise under the efficiency principle).

Finally, the remainder of government services—the funding of education, public health programs, and the provision of a basic social safety net, for instance—do not necessarily relate to asset ownership. It is your stake in the society-at-large, not in the physical landscape, that determines the degree to which you "benefit" from these programs. Admittedly, many of the programs in this category probably should not be government responsibilities at all. But for those that are, and those that for the time being remain deeply imbedded in the public consensus, the right way to allocate financial responsibility is by consumption. The higher the consumption, the higher the standard of living and thus the more benefit you receive from residing in the jurisdiction. Of course, the same rate should apply to all. If I consume ten times as much as you do, I should shoulder roughly ten times as much of the burden of general government.

The current income tax violates all of these principles. Because it relies on a fuzzy and misleading definition of income, it violates the first principle by not excluding from taxation the expenditures that both corporations and individuals undertake to enhance future (taxable) consumption at the expense of current consumption. For higher-income individuals and most corporations, it thoroughly ignores the second principle of efficiency entirely in favor of a mind numbing, inconsistent, and in some cases mysterious system that even the Internal Revenue Service admits it cannot understand. Finally, its multiple rates shift far more of the burden of government on entrepreneurs, the thrifty, retirees, and other high-bracket households than the benefit principle allows.

Unfortunately, most flat tax or national sales tax plans fall short of fulfilling these principles adequately. In their zeal to rid the code of all or nearly all deductions or exclusions, they unwittingly impose double taxation on human capital investment in the form of education and health care, or tax income that is not consumed by the earner at all but that is taken in state and local taxes. More importantly, they make the mistake of ignoring or minimizing the huge transition costs that sudden shifts in tax policy, even justifiable ones, can bring. In my view, the best model for fundamental tax reform is the consumed-income tax. Exclude all savings from income before taxing it with a single marginal rate, and tax withdrawals from savings later on. One of the best things about this system is that, unlike other models, you can achieve it gradually. A combination of IRA expansion and rate reduction will do it, augmented by other tax-deferred savings accounts such as ESAs, MSAs, and USAs and the substitution of individual, capped deductions for human capital investments for the current array of credits and tax subsidies for higher education, employer-provided health insurance, and the like.

The consumed-income tax would also tend to spread taxation out over a taxpayer's life. The flat tax, for example, equalizes the tax treatment of investment by taxing the principle but then exempting returns. While faultless from an economic perspective, what it means is that a young stockbroker or software engineer will pay full tax initially on deposits into his 401(k), but then earn interest or dividends on that money the rest of his life and pay no tax when he withdraws and spends them. Here is where the image of the wealthy "coupon clipper" living high on the hog and paying no tax comes from. In reality, he has already paid a stiff tax up front—but who remembers that? In my view, it makes for better politics to deduct the principal when he earns and invests it, then tax him when he withdraws his earnings—likely later in life when he is wealthier and less sympathetic. Yes, interest and dividends still accrue tax free, but he cannot spend them unless he withdraws and pays taxes on them.

Finally, any fundamental tax reform worth having cannot stand alone but must be part of a larger strategy to contain and contract the welfare state. Here is where simplicity is not necessarily helpful. Perhaps the more elegant solution would be to have one tax-deferred account, diversified and professionally managed, from which Americans could draw their retirement income or pay for health care, education, and the like. But the welfare politics of the New Deal brought forth an alphabet soup of "helpful" government programs, and we have become accustomed to them. It is a genie not easily returned to its bottle. In my view, Americans will want to move slowly, to open up an ESA and see how it performs, to see how a neighbor's USA helps him leave a thankless job and go back to school. It does not matter if the landscape of tax reform remains a bit hilly for a while, with ridges and dips and some roundabout byways, as long as reformers remember where they are going—to the flat valley beyond.

CONCLUSION

The siege against big government will not be won easily or quickly. The entitlement fortress exists because of the patient, steady work of builders who knew what they were doing and who still passionately believe that government is a better guarantor of American security and prosperity than are free enterprise, personal initiative, and personal responsibility. The good news is that, even as Americans have developed strong attachments to individual entitlement programs, they have retained their overall disdain for expansive, expensive government. They need only be presented with a realistic plan for moving gradually away from government dependency without losing their ability to handle the big-ticket items of life: losing a job, paying for health care and education, buying a home, developing a disability, or retiring.

The savings account strategy offers just such a plan. It accomplishes the main goals of both fundamental tax reform and entitlement reform without waiting for a mythical time at some point in the future when all the parties will be willing to sit down and negotiate a "grand deal" to eliminate the income tax or privatize Social Security. Reform will not come at one stroke. Like the explosion of IRAs and 401(k)s during the past two decades, it will likely appear to come out of nowhere, the result of small policy changes that lead to major transformations in the way people organize their lives and plan for the future. Advocates of smaller government and greater personal freedom will not prevail by reckless and futile charges. The congressional meltdown in 1995 and 1996 demonstrated that fact clearly. The welfare state's foes will win only by undermining support for entitlements over time, by giving Americans alternative ways of meeting their long-term needs. Only at the end of this process can they finally, triumphantly, knock down the walls and take the citadel.

CONCLUSION
THE NEW INVESTOR POLITICS

I N A MUCH-CITED 1999 PAPER FOR THE WASHINGTON-based Cato Institute, journalist Richard Nadler summarized the political case for broadening and deepening the ownership of private securities in the United States. "The most significant demographic shift of this century is the rise of history's first mass class of worker capitalists—men and women whose wealth-seeking activities include both wage earning and capital ownership," wrote Nadler, who also headed the American Shareholders Association. The implications of this development went well beyond the economic well-being of shareholding families. According to the surveys of public opinion and voter behavior summarized by Nadler, researchers had found a powerful correlation between ownership of stock and a variety of free market views. "Shareholders display favorable attitudes toward programs that reduce taxes on savings and investment for retirement, education, health care, and other major life-cycle occurrences," he reported. "At the same time, they register high levels of skepticism toward government 'investments' for these same purposes." Stockholders were more likely than other Americans—even after adjusting for income, race, and other characteristics—to favor such ideas as unlimited IRAs, lower taxes on capital gains, and expanded tax deductions for education and health care.[1]

As I observed in the introduction to this book, the fundamental insight of Investor Politics—that policies to encourage personal savings and investment offer the prospect of returning America to its limited-government roots—is hardly new. It is an old, even ancient idea. Aristotle observed that land ownership was essential for self-government to succeed. "Great is the good fortune of a state in which the citizens have a moderate and sufficient property," the philosopher wrote. His was a political, not an economic, argument. Only cranks believe that economic progress is possible without urbanization, without economies of scale, without specialization, without change. But only the hopelessly naïve can fail to see how economic change—particularly the transformation of a society from agrarian to industrial—affects political behavior. In a free enterprise system, people will naturally discover how best to employ their knowledge and talents to benefit their fellow citizens. However, their adherence to the very principles that underlie free enterprise will not come so naturally. Indeed, as we have seen, it is difficult to find examples in which urbanization and the decline of asset ownership have not led to a growth in government.

In the spirit of rediscovering Thomas Jefferson's Investor Politics, I have taken a second, and far more favorable, look at the writings of the so-called "New Agrarians." These were scholars, novelists, poets, and others—most of them from the South and Midwest—who in the 1930s began to form a cadre of intellectuals opposed not just to the New Deal but to industrial and cosmopolitan society more generally. Their prescriptions on economic policy are embarrassing and painful to read today. Indeed, my own early impressions of such writers as Richard Weaver and Liberty Hyde Bailey were formed mostly by snickering at what I considered their economic illiteracy. Yet, as I return to the writings of the New Agrarians with a different purpose in mind, I find much wisdom. Like Jefferson's argument for an agrarian republic, the New Agrarian critique is not about economics at all, but about politics and personal virtue. The New Agrarian economist Ralph Bordosi, for example, argued that families ought to be as self-sufficient as possible, even in the midst of modern industrial processes and organizations that made mass production far more efficient. The rationale was not that families would be better off in a material sense if they personally generated two-thirds of all they consumed (his proposed ratio). As author Allan Carlson has observed, Bordosi's point was that the truly "free person" was not "merely the man who has the infinitesimal fraction of the political power represented by a vote" but rather was "so independent" that he could "deal with all men and all institutions, even the state, on terms of equality."[2]

In a 1934 essay, the historian Herbert Agar made a similar point in an essay entitled "The Task for Conservatism." Agar criticized the application of the term "conservative" to those who advocated industrial capitalism. Instead, he preferred to associate the term with political and cultural virtue. Agar wrote that a true conservative who wanted to keep government from corrupting men would seek "the widest possible distribution of [productive] property." He contended that Jefferson, John Adams, and other Founders had viewed such diffusion of property as necessary for "enterprise, for family responsibility, and in general for institutions that fit man's nature and that gave a chance for a desirable life." In Agar's view, it was greed that had motivated Americans by the 1930s to abandon the farm and the small shop in favor of factories, urban density, and high finance. He and other New Agrarians were thus attracted to what even they called "radical" policies to redistribute property ownership so that Americans would recover the virtues they had lost. Such a redistribution "must be produced artificially and then guarded by favorable legislation," he admitted.[3]

In blaming "greed" for the economic transformation of American society, the New Agrarians often sounded more like left-wing radicals than the right-wing radicals they considered themselves to be. In terms of economic policy prescriptions, at least, there was a surprising amount of agreement between the two poles. But this need not be evidence of heresy. Indeed, there is an element of the Investor Politics insight in the writings of Karl Marx himself. After all, the notion of workers owning the means of production—and thus aligning the interests of capital and labor in a stateless society—has seen its successful application not in socialist countries, but in capitalist ones with modern securities markets. Through pensions, profit sharing, stock options, 401(k)s, and IRAs, American workers can realize the advantages of capital ownership without sacrificing the separation of ownership and control that characterizes the corporate form. Workers thus own much of the means of production—but not necessarily, or even frequently, the means they themselves use to produce goods and services: a synthesis of classical economics and Marxist sociology. Unfortunately, when the savings strategy of reconciling free markets and political stability was most needed—during the Great Depression—it was not feasible.

At the start of the twentieth century, the Populist and Progressive movements had radicalized America's two main political parties. The Democrats and Republicans, divided during previous decades on issues such as trade and sound money, now vied with each other to break up corporate trusts and instigate new welfare programs, first at the state level and later in Washington, that expanded the scope of government. There was a brief but brilliant resurgence of free market thinking during the 1920s, marred only by the monetary manipulation of the recently created Federal Reserve Board. After its inflationary bubble popped and Herbert Hoover's protectionism and interference with markets resulted in a deep recession, desperate Americans turned to Franklin Roosevelt for deliverance. He won election as a fiscal conservative but soon abandoned entirely the old Democratic philosophy to create modern-day welfare politics. The crowning achievement of the New Deal was the Social Security Act of 1935, which created not only a government transfer program for retirees but also cash welfare for mothers with children and a government monopoly over unemployment insurance. Subsequent administrations, Democratic and Republican, used the 1935 act as a model for their own welfare legislation, culminating in a massive expansion of government power in the Social Security amendments of 1965 that created Medicare and Medicaid.

The stock market crash and the Great Depression destroyed public confidence in the private financial markets which were, in fact, the only practical alternative to government for families seeking a way to finance their retirement, education, health care, and emergency savings. Because Social Security appeared to be such a good deal—a mirage generated by the windfall realized by early generations of retirees who had paid little into the system—Americans swallowed their traditional skepticism about big government and entrusted more and more of their lives to its management and protection.

REDEFINING THE POLITICAL DIVIDE

Because such ideas as privatizing Social Security, expanding IRAs, or creating tax deductions for education and health care have been associated with conservative Republicans in the past two decades, some might question whether Investor Politics is merely a new name for an old ideology. I do not think so. For one thing, both political parties are learning to speak in Investor Politics terms. Bill Clinton, one of the most successful Democratic politicians of the twentieth century, helped to burnish his credentials as a "New Democrat" by offering rhetorical support, and occasionally more, to pro-savings proposals. He signed legislation creating Educational Savings Accounts and proposed tax-free Universal Savings Accounts. His vice president, Al Gore, nearly became his successor by fudging the differences between his policies and those of his rival George W. Bush. In the 2000 presidential race, both candidates favored tax cuts, more tax-deferred savings accounts, some variety of school choice, and more equal tax treatment of health-care investments. Consequently, Bush won only a small majority among Americans with stock portfolios—proof not that Investor Politics has yet to arrive but that it has already affected both the rhetoric and the platforms of both major parties.

The terms "liberal" and "conservative," which lost their original meanings long ago but remained useful labels for two contrasting philosophies of American government during the twentieth century, have now truly outlived their usefulness. Particularly because they connote views on a variety of issues beyond this scope of my inquiry, in such areas as reproductive rights or foreign policy, they are insufficient to describe the emerging politics of the twenty-first century. Some thinkers in both camps are starting to comprehend this. Michael Joyce, head of a conservative-leaning philanthropy in Milwaukee called the Bradley Foundation, argues that the term "compassionate conservatism" is an attempt at describing a distinct governing philosophy that began to emerge in the late 1990s. Joyce prefers the term "new citizenship," but his observations will sound familiar. In the 1970s, Democrats failed to keep the welfare state under control, and the consequences led to Republican resurgence. However, GOP efforts at "frontal assault" on the welfare state in the early 1980s and again in the mid-1990s also failed. Now the new approach, which attempts to use conservative means to accomplish what have traditionally been thought of as liberal ends, promises to reframe the debate about government, he says. If passive recipients of welfare programs become active participants in programs that build both financial and human capital, the political calculus shifts. "How are liberals going to expiate their guilt if the people they are dealing with are not victims but are active citizens, just as important as they are?" Joyce asks.[4]

On the left, economic journalist Robert Kuttner is a reliable proponent of Keynesian economics and redistributive social programs. He nevertheless recognizes the prospect of a "shareholder nation" contributing to a political realignment. Observing that the limits of income redistribution have probably been reached, Kuttner suggests that an increasing number of liberals and Democrats might shift their emphasis to new ideas such as promoting savings. "If liberals like me are to get off the defensive and resume progress toward a more egalitarian democracy," he writes, "it won't be via further redistribution but through wealth-broadening in the spirit of [Thomas] Jefferson" and other advocates of widespread asset ownership.[5]

Many of the older political distinctions—having to do with differences in culture, values, ethnicity, even geography—will persist in the coming years. But I still think that the main issues of federal policy will divide American politicians and their constituents into new rival camps. In the absence of a better suggestion, I would like to suggest that this political divide be redefined as consisting of Welfare Politics and Investor Politics. Here are some of the differences:

• Welfare politicians encourage dependency. Investor politicians promote independence.

• Welfare politicians promise to remove risk from the lives of voters. Investor politicians promise only to help them and their families manage risk and reap its rewards.

• Welfare politicians believe voters to be fundamentally incapable of saving, investing, and planning for their future needs and thus need government to perform these tasks on their behalf. Investor politicians believe that individuals can and should manage their own financial affairs, with the public sector's role remaining secondary and circumscribed (but not nonexistent, a concession that most modern-day conservatives and libertarians appear to be willing to make).

• Welfare politicians think government action is necessary to guarantee sufficient investment to stimulate economic growth. Investor politicians know that the private sector is the better investor and that, except for cases in which it is difficult to charge accurate prices to users of an asset, government "investment" rarely lives up to the term.

• Welfare politicians believe that individuals should trust the taxing power of Washington to guarantee them the resources they will need for retirement, educating their children, buying a home, and handling medical or financial emergencies. Investor politicians believe that individuals should trust the wealth creation of Wall Street and Main Street to provide resources for these "big-ticket" items of life.

• Welfare politicians believe that government should encourage some forms of private investment, such as housing and college educations, over others. Investor politicians trust private individuals, operating within competitive markets, to determine how best to allocate their investment activities. Their focus is on making sure that proper tax policies exist to shield these activities from double taxation.

• Welfare politicians think that large-scale investment is best accomplished through government action. Investor politicians favor moving as many such investments—be they highways, water and sewer systems, education, or health care—into the private, competitive marketplace through the sale of assets, competitive contracting, load shedding, public-private partnerships, and consumer-choice mechanisms.

• Welfare politicians believe that government should provide generous, long-term welfare benefits to the able-bodied poor. Investor politicians believe that such programs ensnare the poor, rather than truly helping them, and that government's role should be limited to the provision of short-term assistance to those with emergency needs (justified by the need to maintain order).

• Welfare politicians believe that disabled individuals must be maintained indefinitely as wards of the state. Investor politicians believe that people with disabilities represent unused human capital that the public sector can help to tap through training, technology, and job placement programs designed to promote independence and self-sufficiency.

• Welfare politicians believe that a large number of American workers are incapable of earning enough money to be self-sufficient in a free market economy. Thus, they favor higher minimum wages and a generous Earned Income Tax Credit to subsidize the incomes of workers indefinitely. Investor politicians believe that competitive markets efficiently compensate workers for their productivity. In their view, insufficient income is evidence of insufficient capital formation, so public policy should address not the symptoms but the disease itself.

There are signs that this realignment between Welfare Politics and Investor Politics is already underway. Some prominent Democrats are touting market-based reforms of Social Security and Medicare.[6] Some Republicans, on the other hand, oppose these ideas as being either too radical or threatening to the family. One can see a possible political future in which investment-oriented Democrats detach themselves from a party still devoted to welfarism and gravitate towards the Republican Party of Ronald Reagan and George W. Bush. On the other hand, divisions on social issues, trade, and foreign policy might lead to a split within the GOP, generating a new party of disaffected Republicans and Democrats.

That the coming Investor Politics of the twenty-first century will help one particular party or candidate over another would be an uncertain prediction at best. But its coming seems to me to be the inevitable outcome of two parallel trends: first, growth in financial sophistication, which will make personal investing even easier to undertake and understand; and second, growth in the elderly population as Baby Boomers begin to retire. Sustaining the old income-transfer programs of the twentieth century will prove impossible. Reinventing them as new savings programs of the twenty-first century will constitute the majority of public policymaking over the next two decades.

NOTES

NOTES TO INTRODUCTION

1. Proverbs 6:6–10, New American Standard Version Bible.

2. Quoted in Saul K. Padover, ed., *Thomas Jefferson on Democracy* (New York: Pelican Books, 1946), 70.

3. Ibid.

NOTES TO CHAPTER 1

1. Ruth Barlett, *Insect Engineers: The Story of Ants* (New York: William Morrow, 1957), 66–90.

2. Jack Weatherford, *The History of Money: From Sandstone to Cyberspace* (New York: Crown, 1997), 15.

3. Douglass C. North, *Structure and Change in Economic History* (New York: W. W. Norton, 1981), 4.

4. Mark Kishlansky, Patrick Geary, and Patricia O'Brien, *Civilization in the West to 1715*, vol. 1 (New York: HarperCollins, 1991), 4–5.

5. North, 72–90.

6. Barry Cunliffe, *The Oxford Illustrated Prehistory of Europe* (Oxford: Oxford University Press, 1994), 499.

7. Ibid., 38.

8. Frank Knight, *Risk, Uncertainty and Profit* (London: London School of Economics and Political Science, 1935), 245.

9. Ibid., 61.

10. Ibid., 64–65.

11. Ibid., 67.

12. Carroll L. Riley, *The Origins of Civilization* (Carbondale: Southern Illinois University Press, 1969), 16.

13. North, 6.

14. Robert C. Allen, "Agriculture and the Origins of the State," *Explorations in Economic History* 34 (1997): 142.

15. Richard Pipes, *Property and Freedom* (New York: Alfred A. Knopf, 1999), 86.

16. Kishlansky, 7.

17. Ibid., 25–26.

18. North, 95.

19. Ibid., 21–22.

20. Allen, 144–46.

21. Some scholars have observed that, contrary to the suggestions of the early "hydraulic" theorists, irrigation of the Nile and similar waterways did not require huge scale but was more

likely a series of locally created and controlled entities. Still, local governments performed the task, rather than families or voluntary associations. See Allen, 135–36.

22. Ibid., 24–25.

23. Weatherford, 48.

24. William N. Goetzmann, *Financing Civilization* (1999), http://viking.som.yale.edu/will/finciv/chapter1.html.

25. Ibid.

26. Pipes, 98–99.

27. Ibid.

28. Ibid.

29. Larry Reed (1998), commentary at www.Mackinac.org.

30. Subhi Y. Labib, "Capitalism in Medieval Islam," *The Journal of Economic History* (March 1969): 93–95.

31. Quoted in Nathan Rosenberg and L. E. Birdzell, Jr., *How the West Grew Rich: The Economic Transaction of the Industrial World* (New York: Basic Books, 1986), 127.

32. Ibid.

33. Ibid., 118.

34. Ibid., 117.

35. North, 141.

36. Rosenberg and Birdzell, 122–23.

37. North, 133.

38. Ibid., 144.

39. Ibid., 157.

40. Rosenberg and Birdzell, 191–93.

41. Thomas Sowell, *Conquests and Cultures* (New York: Basic Books, 1998), 10–11.

42. North, 165.

43. Rosenberg and Birdzell, 145–46.

44. Ibid., 147.

45. North, 158–61.

NOTES TO CHAPTER TWO

1. Wilbur Cohen, quoted in Sylvester J. Schieber and John B. Shoven, *The Real Deal: The History and Future of Social Security* (New Haven: Yale University Press, 1999), 121.

2. Dr. Nicholas Balabkins, "The German Historical School of Economics: Welfare Capitalism Begins," *Great Economic Thinkers: The Audio Classics Series* (Knowledge Products, 1988), tape 1.

3. Alicia H. Munnell, "Social Security," and Frederick B. M. Hollyday, "Otto von Bismarck," *New American Encyclopedia* (New York: Grolier, 1991), B:298–99 and Sne:14.

4. Edward Bellamy, *Looking Backward 2000–1887*, online ed., http://xroads.virginia.edu/~HYPER/BELLAMY/ch09.html, chapter 9.

5. Clarence B. Carson, *A Basic History of the United States: The Growth of America 1878–1928*, 5 vols. (Greenville, Ala.: American Textbook Committee, 1985), vol. 4, 75–76.

6. Ibid., 78.

7. Hugh Lefler and Patricia Stanford, *North Carolina*, 2d ed. (New York: Harcourt Brace Jovanovich), 324–28.

8. Samuel Eliot Morrison, *The Oxford History of the American People* (New York: Oxford University Press, 1965), 790.

9. James West Davidson and Mark H. Lytle, *The United States: A History of the Republic* (Englewood Cliffs, N. J.: Prentice-Hall, 1986), 413–15.

10. Carson, 76.

11. See Lawrence W. Reed, *A Lesson from the Past: The Silver Panic of 1893* (Irvington-on-Hudson, N.Y.: Foundation for Economic Education, 1993).

12. Davidson and Lytle, 419.

13. Ibid., 459.

14. Historical homeownership rates obtained by author from Mike Hovland, History Staff, Bureau of the Census, Washington, D.C.

15. Carson, 124–26.

16. Davidson and Lytle, 464–65.

17. George Brown Tindall and David E. Shi, *America: A Narrative History* (New York: W. W. Norton, 1989), 616.

18. Richard W. Leopold, Arthur S. Link, and Stanley Cohen, eds., *Problems in American History* (Englewood Cliffs, N. J.: Prentice-Hall, 1996), 196.

19. Ibid., 198.

20. Davidson and Lytle, 478–80.

21. Price V. Fishback and Shawn Everett Kantor, "The Adoption of Workers' Compensation in the United States: 1900–1930," working paper no. 5840, National Bureau of Economic Research, Cambridge, Mass., 1996, 4–16.

22. Ibid., 11.

23. Ibid., 13–15.

24. Ibid., 16.

25. Ibid., 49, table 3.

26. Carson, 194–96.

27. Ibid., 249, 256.

28. Unemployment Compensation Commission, "Origin of the Unemployment Insurance and Employment Service Programs in North Carolina," by Silas F. Campbell, Bureau of Research and Statistics, Raleigh, N.C., 1995, 1–2.

29. Milton Friedman, *Free to Choose: A Personal Statement* (New York: Harcourt Brace Jovanovich, 1980), 98–99.

30. Ibid., 100.

NOTES TO CHAPTER THREE

1. Larry Schweikart, *The Entrepreneurial Adventure: A History of Business in the United States* (Orlando: Harcourt College Publishers, 2000), 144–46.

2. Ibid., 147–48.

3. George B. Tindall and David E. Shi, *America: A Narrative History,* 2d ed. (New York: W. W. Norton, 1989), 460.

4. Nathan Rosenberg and L. E. Birdzell, Jr., *How the West Grew Rich: The Economic Transformation of the Industrial World* (New York: Basic Books, 1986), 189.

5. Robert Hessen, *In Defense of the Corporation* (Stanford, Calif.: Hoover Institution Press, 1979), 37–38.

6. Ibid., 43.

7. Schweikart, 81.

8. Ibid., 97.

9. Ibid., 85.

10. "The pioneer years: A new industry is founded," Dun & Bradstreet web site, November 8, 1999.

11. Schweikart, 116.

12. Jack Weatherford, *The History of Money: From Sandstone to Cyberspace* (New York: Crown, 1997), 170.

13. Schweikart, 182.

14. Ibid., 185.

15. Rosenberg and Birdzell, 199.

16. Ibid., 221.

17. Schweikart, 256.

18. Ibid.

19. Rosenberg and Birdzell, 224.

20. Donald J. Boudreaux and Thomas J. DiLorenzo, "The Protectionist Roots of Antitrust," *Review of Austrian Economics* 6, no. 2 (1993): 81–96.

21. Clarence B. Carson, *A Basic History of the United States: The Growth of America, 1878–1928*, 5 vols. (Greenville, Ala.: American Textbook Committee, 1985), vol. 4, 97.

22. Schweikart, 257.

23. Carson, 92.

24. Rosenberg and Birdzell, 225.

25. Schweikart, 258.

26. Rosenberg and Birdzell, 220.

27. "Dow Jones Industrial Average," Dow Jones web site, 2000, 1.

28. "About Moody's," Moody's Investors Service web site, 2000.

29. Christopher Howard, *The Hidden Welfare State: Tax Expenditures and Social Policy in the United States* (Princeton, N.J.: Princeton University Press, 1997), 52.

30. Rob Norton, "Corporate Taxation," in David Henderson, ed., *The Fortune Encyclopedia of Economics* (New York: Warner Books, 1993), 325.

31. Theodore Roosevelt's views on trust busting evolved even during his presidency towards acceptance and regulation rather than litigation and breakup. See Samuel Eliot Morrison, *The Oxford History of the American People* (New York: Oxford University Press, 1965), 821.

32. Schweikart, 298.

33. Ibid., 330.

34. Richard Nadler, "The Rise of Worker Capitalism," policy analysis no. 359, The Cato Institute, Washington, D.C., November 1, 1999, 3.

35. Joseph Nocera, *A Piece of the Action: How the Middle Class Joined the Money Class* (New York: Simon & Schuster, 1994), 35–38.

36. Schweikart, 333.

37. Tindall and Shi, 608.

38. Carson, 159.

39. Ibid., 171.

40. Schweikart, 332.

41. Richard Timberlake, "Money in the 1920s and 1930s," *The Freeman: Ideas on Liberty* (April 1999): 37–39.

42. Joseph Salerno, "Money and Gold in the 1920s and 1930s: An Austrian View," *The Freeman: Ideas on Liberty* (October 1999): 34–35.

43. Benjamin M. Anderson, *Economics and the Public Welfare: A Financial and Economic History of the United States, 1914–1946*, 2d ed. (Indianapolis: Liberty Press, 1979), 145–46.

44. Lawrence Reed, "Great Myths of the Great Depression," Mackinac Center for Public Policy, Midland, Mich., 2000, 3.

45. Schweikart, 347.

46. John Downes and Jordan Elliot Goodman, *Barron's Finance and Investment Handbook*, 3d ed. (New York: Barron's, 1990), 853–54.

47. Ron Chernow, "The New Deal's Gift to Wall Street," *The Wall Street Journal*, 11 November 1999.

48. Nadler, 3.

49. Howard, 55.

50. For a full discussion of these issues, see Michael Schuyler, *Consumption Taxes: Promises and Problems* (Washington, D.C.: The Institute for Research on the Economics of Taxation [IRET], 1984), 8–11.

51. Howard.

52. Ibid.

53. Richard Nadler, "Special (k): What else Reagan wrought," *National Review* (April 19, 1999): 52.

54. Arthur Kennickell et al., "Recent Changes in U.S. Family Finances: Results from the 1998 Survey of Consumer Finances," *Federal Reserve Bulletin* (January 2000): 13.

55. Nocera, 39.

56. Ibid., 42.

57. Ibid., 49.

58. Bruce Bartlett, "Thank You, Federal Reserve," *The American Enterprise* (March 2000): 20–22.

59. Nocera, 79–82.

60. *Fact Book 1999* (New York: Investment Co. Institute), 85.

61. Nocera, 120.

62. *Fact Book 1999*, 45–69.

63. Department of Commerce, *Statistical Abstract of the United States,* Economics and Statistics Administration, 117th ed., 527–29.

64. Stephen M. Bainbridge, "In Defense of the Shareholder Wealth Maximization Norm: A Reply to Professor Green," *Washington and Lee Law Review* 50, no. 4 (fall 1993): 1429.

65. Hessen.

66. Ibid.

NOTES TO CHAPTER FOUR

1. Samuel Eliot Morrison, *The Oxford History of the American People* (New York: Oxford University Press, 1965), 935.

2. Quoted in Frederick L. Allen, *Since Yesterday* (New York: Harper & Brothers, 1940), 38.

3. Carson, *A Basic History of the United States: The Welfare State 1929–1985,* 5 vols., (Greenville, Ala.: American Textbook Committee, 1985), vol. 5, 17.

4. James West Davidson and Mark H. Lytle, *The United States: A History of the Republic* (Englewood Cliffs, N.J.: Prentice-Hall, 1986), 530.

5. Ibid.

6. Carson, vol. 5, 18.

7. Davidson and Lytle, 553.

8. Carson, vol. 5, 19.

9. Davidson and Lytle, 554.

10. Henry Hazlitt, *The Failure of the "New Economics"* (New York: D. Van Nostrand, 1959), 421.

11. Lawrence Reed review of *The Roosevelt Myth* by John T. Flynn, *The Freeman: Ideas on Liberty* (September 1999): 5.

12. Carson, vol. 5, 14.

13. Davidson and Lytle, 553.

14. Reed, 62.

15. Carson, vol. 5, 26.

16. John T. Flynn, *The Roosevelt Myth* (New York: Devin-Adair, 1948), 61.

17. Morrison, 957.

18. Flynn, 42.

19. Davidson and Lytle, 565, 570.

20. Ibid., 566.

21. Carson, vol. 5, 48.

22. Ibid., 50.

23. Davidson and Lytle, 567.

24. Carson, vol. 5, 52.

25. Ibid., 55.

26. Morrison, 969.

27. Arthur Schlesinger, Jr., *The Coming of the New Deal* (Boston: Houghton Mifflin, 1958), 290.

28. Morrison, 969.

29. Phillip Longman, *The Return of Thrift: How the Collapse of the Middle Class Welfare State Will Reawaken Values in America* (New York: The Free Press, 1996), 33.

30. Davidson and Lytle, 571.

31. Ibid., 581.

32. Seymour Martin Lipset and Gary Marks, "How FDR Saved Capitalism," *Hoover Digest* (November 2000), excerpted from Lipset and Marks, *It Didn't Happen Here: Why Socialism Failed in the United States* (New York: W. W. Norton, 2000).

33. Robert Higgs, "Regime Uncertainty: Why the Great Depression Lasted So Long and Why Prosperity Resumed After the War," *The Independent Review* 1, no. 4 (spring 1997): 575.

34. Sylvester J. Schieber and John B. Shoven, *The Real Deal: The History and Future of Social Security* (New Haven: Yale University Press, 1999), 27–28.

35. Bernard Roshco, "The Devil's Tunes and the Sirens' Song: Privatizing Social Security," *Public Perspective*, Roper Center for Public Opinion Research, University of Connecticut (October/November 1999): 26.

36. John Flynn argues that the second New Deal, when stripped of all its other "rabbits in a hat," was left as a "spending rabbit." Flynn, 61.

37. George B. Tindall and David E. Shi, *America: A Narrative History*, 2d ed. (New York: W. W. Norton, 1989), vol. 5, 723.

38. Hazlitt, 421.

39. Carson, vol. 5, 86.

40. Hazlitt, 421–22.

41. Davidson and Lytle, 581.

42. Morrison, 987.

43. Longman, 33.

44. Henry Hazlitt, *The Conquest of Poverty* (New Rochelle, N.Y.: Arlington House, 1976), 93.

45. John T. Flynn, "The Social Security 'Reserve' Swindle," *Harper's* (March 1939): 241–42.

46. Longman, 34–39.

47. Tindall and Shi, 725.

48. John Maynard Keynes, *A Treatise on Money* (New York: Harcourt Brace, 1931), vol. 1:172.

49. Hazlitt, 434.

50. Ibid., 379.

51. Paul Johnson, *Modern Times: The World from the Twenties to the Eighties* (New York: Harper & Row, 1983), 255.

52. Higgs, 566–67.

NOTES TO CHAPTER FIVE

1. Arthur H. Vandenberg, "The $47,000,000,000 Blight," *Saturday Evening Post* (April 24, 1937): 7.

2. Letter from Arthur Altmeyer to Arthur Vandenberg, August 27, 1943, published in *Congressional Record* (4 September 1943).

3. Sylvester J. Schieber and John B. Shoven, *The Real Deal: The History and Future of Social Security* (New Haven: Yale University Press, 1999), 70.

4. Ibid., 42.

5. Ibid.

6. Henry Hazlitt, *The Failure of the "New Economics"* (New York: D. Van Nostrand, 1959), 421.

7. Schieber and Shoven, 54.

8. Ibid., 57–58.

9. Ibid., 82–83.

10. Ibid., 90–91.

11. Office of Management and Budget, *Budget of the United States Government, FY 2000*, 247–53.

12. General Accounting Office, *Social Security: Disability Programs Lag in Promoting Return to Work,* GAO/HHS report 97–46 (March 17, 1997), 5.

13. John F. Cogan, "The Congressional Response to Social Security Surpluses, 1935–1994," *Essays in Public Policy* 92 (Stanford, Calif.: The Hoover Institution, 1998).

14. Office of Management and Budget, 248.

15. Schieber and Shoven, 100–1.

16. William Styring III and Donald K. Jonas, "Running on Empty," *American Outlook* (November–December 2000): 12.

17. Harry Dolan, "Unhappy Returns," *The Freeman: Ideas on Liberty* (February 1999): 22.

18. Schieber and Shoven, 170–74.

19. Ibid., 174.

20. Ibid., 182.

21. Ibid., 188–90.

22. Ibid., 192–93.

23. Daniel J. Mitchell, "Social Security's Trust Fund Report Shows Program's Finances Getting Worse," backgrounder no. 1273, The Heritage Foundation, Washington, D.C., April 20, 1999, 3.

24. David Henderson, "The Social Security Crisis: Why It Happened and What We Can Do," Contemporary Issues Series 90, Center for the Study of American Business, Washington University, June 1998, 8.

25. John Goodman, "Social Security and Race," executive summary of policy report no. 236, National Center for Policy Analysis, Dallas, Tex., 1–3.

26. Henry J. Aaron, "The Myths of Social Security Crisis: Behind the Privatization Push," *The Washington Post*, 21 July 1996.

27. Matt Moore, "Facts about Social Security," brief analysis no. 341, National Center for Policy Analysis, Dallas, Tex., September 26, 2000, 1.

28. Aaron.

29. Office of Management and Budget, 255–56.

30. Ibid., 362.

31. Howard Gleckman, "The National Debt," *Business Week* (August 9, 1999): 32.

32. Rudolph Penner, Sandeep Solanki, Eric Toder, and Michael Weisner, "Saving the Surplus to Save Social Security: What Does It Mean?" brief series no. 7, The Retirement Project at the Urban Institute, October 1999, 6.

33. "Saving the Surplus," executive summary of policy report no. 241, National Center for Policy Analysis, Dallas, Tex., 2001, 2.

34. Peter J. Ferrara, "Making the Most of the Surplus," *Policy Review* (October/November 2000): 59–61.

35. Bruce Bartlett, "It Doesn't Pay to Pay Down the Debt," *The Wall Street Journal*, 30 June 1999.

36. Quoted in Bartlett.

37. Quoted in Grace-Marie Arnett, ed., *Empowering Health Care Consumers Through Tax Reform* (Ann Arbor: University of Michigan Press, 1999), 17.

38. "Don't Blame the Market," *Investor's Business Daily*, 28 October 1999, A26.

39. Howard Gleckman and Rich Miller, "Social Security Will Play the Market," *Business Week* (October 9, 2000): 140–41.

40. Office of Management and Budget, 41.

41. Henry J. Aaron and Robert D. Reischauer, "A Look at the Future of Social Security," *The Washington Post*, 19 April 1998.

42. Peter J. Ferrara, "Social Security Is Still a Hopelessly Bad Deal for Today's Workers," Social Security privatization paper no. 18, The Cato Institute, Washington, D.C., November 29, 1999, 6.

43. Melissa Hieger and William Shipman, "Common Objections to a Market-Based Social Security System: A Response," Social Security privatization paper no. 10, The Cato Institute, Washington, D.C., July 22, 1997, 9.

44. Aaron and Reischauer.

45. Daniel J. Mitchell, "Why Government-Controlled Investment Is a Bad Idea," in David C. John, ed., *Improving Retirement Security: A Handbook for Reformers* (Washington, D.C.: The Heritage Foundation, 2000), 114–15.

46. Martin Feldstein, "How to Save Social Security," *The New York Times*, 27 July 1998.

47. Kevin A. Hassett and R. Glenn Hubbard, "Where Do We Put the Surplus?" *The Wall Street Journal*, 29 January 2001.

48. David C. John and Gareth G. Davis, "The Costs of Managing Individual Social Security Accounts," backgrounder no. 1238, The Heritage Foundation, Washington, D.C., December 3, 1998, 1–2.

49. Ferrara, "Social Security," 10.

50. David John and Gareth Davis, "Keeping Administrative Costs Low," in *Improving Retirement Security*, 144.

51. Mike McNamee, "Privatize Social Security? Nobody's Laughing Now," *Business Week* (February 5, 1996): 55.

52. See Michael Tanner and Peter Ferrara, *A New Deal for Social Security* (Washington, D.C.: The Cato Institute, 1998).

53. See James M. Taylor, "Facilitating Fraud: How SSDI Gives Benefits to the Able Bodied," policy analysis no. 377, The Cato Institute, Washington, D.C., August 15, 2000.

54. General Accounting Office.

55. Ibid.

56. Merrill Matthews, Jr., "A 12-Step Plan for Social Security Reform," brief analysis no. 267, National Center for Policy Analysis, Dallas, Tex., June 4, 1998.

57. Merrill Matthews, Jr., and Shanon Gutierrez, "Latin Lessons on Social Security," *The Washington Times*, 22 January 1998.

58. Aaron, 2.

59. Steven Pearlstein, "Myths fuel Social Security debate," *The News & Observer* (Raleigh, N.C.), 9 January 1997, A2.

60. Hieger and Shipman, 11.

61. C. Eugene Steuerle, "Mandated Saving and the Fallacy of Aggregation," Urban Institute reprint of *Tax Notes* column, 1996, 1–2.

62. Bruce Bartlett, "Personal Retirement Accounts Would Increase Savings," brief analysis, National Center for Policy Analysis, Dallas, Tex., August 12, 1998.

63. Martin Feldstein, "Privatizing Social Security: The $10 Trillion Opportunity," Social Security paper no. 7, The Cato Institute, Washington, D.C., January 31, 1997.

64. Mike McNamee, "How Should We Fix Social Security?" *Business Week* (January 20, 1997): 25.

65. Neil Howe and Richard Jackson, "Natural Thrift Plan Project," National Taxpayers Union Foundation and Center for Public Policy and Contemporary Issues, Washington, D.C., November 15, 1996.

66. James Poterba, Steven Venti, and David Wise, "Personal Retirement Saving Programs and Asset Accumulation: Reconciling the Evidence," working paper, National Bureau of Economic Research, Cambridge, Mass., May 1996.

67. Daniel J. Mitchell, "Creating a Better Social Security System for America," backgrounder no. 1109, The Heritage Foundation, Washington, D.C., April 23, 1997, 25.

NOTES TO CHAPTER SIX

1. Robert Helms, "The Origin of Medicare," *The Washington Times*, 1 March 1999.

2. Gene Koretz, "It's Not Just Social Security," *Business Week* (October 26, 1998): 26.

3. Terree Wasley, *What Has Government Done to Our Health Care?* (Washington, D.C.: The Cato Institute, 1992), 44.

4. Ibid., 45–47.

5. Ibid., 48–49.

6. Ibid., 50.

7. William Styring III and Donald K. Jonas, *Health Care 2020: The Coming Collapse of Employer-Provided Health Care* (Indianapolis: Hudson Institute, 1999), 20.

8. Wasley, 55.

9. Data found in Wasley, 56, and Robert Helms, "The Tax Treatment of Health Insurance: Early History and Evidence, 1940–1970," in Grace-Marie Arnett, ed., *Empowering Health Care Consumers Through Tax Reform* (Ann Arbor: University of Michigan Press, 1999), 2–6.

10. Helms, 4.

11. John C. Goodman and Gerald L. Musgrave, "Controlling Health Care Costs with Medical Savings Accounts," policy report no. 168, National Center for Policy Analysis, Dallas, Tex., January 1992, 3.

12. Selma J. Mushkin, "Health as an Investment," *The Journal of Political Economy* (October 1962): 137; and Goodman and Musgrave, 2.

13. Office of Management and Budget, *Budget of the United States Government, FY 2000,* 279–82; and Ellen Licking, "Health Care," *Business Week* (January 10, 2000): 114.

14. Charlotte Twight, "Medicare's Origin: The Economics and Politics of Dependency," *The Cato Journal* 16, no. 3 (1997): 3.

15. Ibid., 4.

16. Ibid.

17. Ibid., 5.

18. Martha Derthick, *Policymaking for Social Security* (Washington, D.C.: The Brookings Institution, 1979).

19. Twight, 6.

20. Sylvester Schieber and John Shoven, *The Real Deal: The History and Future of Social Security* (New Haven: Yale University Press, 1999), 121.

21. "Medicare Now 30 Years Old," *Associated Press* online, 28 July 1995, 1.

22. Helms, 3.

23. Ibid.

24. "Medicare Now 30 Years Old."

25. Stuart Butler et al., "What to Do About Medicare," backgrounder no. 1038, The Heritage Foundation, Washington, D.C., June 26, 1995, 4–5.

26. Susan Mandel, "While Congress Slept . . . ," *National Review* (July 9, 1990): 19.

27. Butler.

28. Spencer Rich, "Red Tape Isn't Encouraging Doctors to Heel Themselves," *The Washington Post Weekly Edition*, 14 October 1990, 34.

29. Spencer Rich, "A Cost-Cutting Program that Actually Works," *The Washington Post Weekly Edition*, 2 September 1990, 33.

30. R. A. Zaldivar, "Democrat: Cut Medicare," *The Charlotte Observer*, 13 December 1991, A8.

31. John C. Liu and Robert E. Moffit, "A Taxpayer's Guide to the Medicare Crisis," The Heritage Foundation, Washington, D.C., September 27, 1995, 5

32. Haley Barbour, "Memorandum for Republican Senators and Republican Representatives: Medicare Polling," Republican National Committee, Washington, D.C., 1–2.

33. Kenneth J. Cooper, "Trying to Sell a GOP Alternative to Medicare," *The Washington Post Weekly Edition*, 3 September 1995, 9.

34. Howard Fineman, "Mediscare," *Newsweek* (September 18, 1995), 38–39.

35. Robert Pear, "House Republicans Offer Medicare Plan," *The New York Times*, 4 June 1997.

36. Laurie McGinley and Joseph White, "Medicare's Big Overhaul Is Bringing More Choice—and Anxiety," *The Wall Street Journal*, 5 June 1998.

37. Kenneth Walsh and Joseph Shapiro, "The Medicare Plan Everyone's Waiting For," *U.S. News and World Report* (June 14, 1999): 22.

38. Social Security and Medicare Boards of Trustees, *Status of the Social Security and Medicare Programs: A Summary of the 2001 Annual Reports*, Social Security Administration, Washington, D.C., rev. April 2001, 1–7.

39. Andrew J. Rettenmaier and Thomas R. Saving, "Saving Medicare," policy report no. 222, National Center for Policy Analysis, Dallas, Tex., January 1999, 7.

40. J. T. Young, "Left's New Effort to Block Tax Cuts," *Investors' Business Daily*, 16 February 2001.

41. Mark V. Pauly, quoted in Robert B. Helms, ed., *Medicare in the 21st Century: Seeking Fair and Efficient Reform* (Washington, D.C.: American Enterprise Institute, 1999), 15.

42. "Unto Him That Hath . . . ," *The Economist* (August 2, 1997).

43. U.S. House Republican Conference, "Health Care Chartbook," issue brief, April 28, 1994, 7.

44. Office of Management and Budget, 280.

45. Health Care Finance Administration, "Medicaid Recipients as a Percentage of Population by Age," HCFA web site, www.hcfa.gov/medicaid/msis/2082-9.htm (2000), table 9.

46. Health Care Finance Administration, "Medicaid Eligibility," data and statistics page, HCFA web site, updated October 18, 1996.

47. Ibid.

48. Office of Management and Budget, 223.

49. Michael Tanner, Stephen Moore, and David Hartman, "The Work vs. Welfare Trade-Off," policy analysis no. 240, The Cato Institute, Washington, D.C., September 19, 1995, 8–12.

50. Jane Huntington and Frederick Connell, "For Every Dollar Spent—The Cost-Savings Argument for Prenatal Care," *The New England Journal of Medicine* 331, no. 19 (November 10, 1994): 1303–7.

51. Christopher M. Wright, "SSI: The Black Hole of the Welfare State," policy analysis no. 224, The Cato Institute, Washington, D.C., April 27, 1995, 5.

52. Office of Management and Budget, 223.

53. Health Care Finance Administration, "Medicaid Vendor Payments by Type of Service," data and statistics page, HCFA web site, updated October 18, 1996, table 5.

54. Agency for Health Care Policy Research, "Examining Long-Term Care," research in action page, Department of Health and Human Services web site, updated February 22, 1996.

55. John Merline, "Time to Plan Ahead for Long-Term Care," *Consumers' Research* (January 1996): 13.

56. Census Bureau, *Sixty-Five Plus in the United States*, statistical brief, May 1995.

57. Gene Koretz, "Medical Costs of the 'Old Old,'" *Business Week* (January 31, 2000): 34.

58. Gene Koretz, "It's Not Just Social Security," *Business Week* (October 26, 1998): 26.

59. H. E. Freeman and C. R. Corey, "Insurance Status and Access to Health Services among Poor Persons," *Health Services Research* 28, no. 5 (December 1993): 531–42.

60. Theodore W. Schultz, "Reflections on Investment in Man," *The Journal of Political Economy* (October 1962): 1–2.

61. Mushkin, 150–52.

62. Michael A. Schuyler, *Consumption Taxes: Promises and Problems* (Washington, D.C.: The Institute for Research on the Economics of Taxation, 1984), 8.

63. Eugene Steuerle and Gordon Mermin, "A Better Subsidy for Health Insurance?" in Arnett, 76.

64. John Sheils, Paul Hogan, and Randall Haught, "Health Insurance and Taxes: The Impact of Proposed Changes in Current Federal Policy," National Coalition on Health Care, Washington, D.C., October 18, 1999, 1–2.

65. See Mark Pauly and Bradley Herring, "Expanding Coverage via Tax Credits: Outcomes and Trade-Offs," *Health Affairs* (January/February 2001): 1–18.

66. "Tax Credits for Health Insurance," backgrounder history for reporters, National Center for Policy Analysis, Dallas, Tex. (1999), at ncpa.org/about/pphistory.html.

67. See Mark Pauly, A. Percy, and Bradley Herring, "Individual versus Job-Based Health Insurance: Weighing the Pros and Cons," *Health Affairs* (November/December 1999): 28–44.

68. Greg Scandlen, "Why MSAs Are So Slow to Catch On," *Consumers' Research* (September 1998): 21–24.

69. Steuerle and Mermin.

70. Rettenmaier and Saving, 20.

71. Ibid., 21.

72. Stuart Butler, "Reorganizing the Medicare System to Ensure a Better Program for Seniors," backgrounder no. 1294, The Heritage Foundation, Washington, D.C., June 14, 1999.

73. James Frogue and Robert E. Moffit, "A Closer Look at Clinton's Medicare Proposal," backgrounder no. 1346, The Heritage Foundation, Washington, D.C., February 17, 2000.

74. Daniel J. Murphy, "Medicare in Urgent Need of Reform As Population Ages, Costs Skyrocket," *Investor's Business Daily*, 23 October 2000.

75. Robert J. Blendon et al., "Risky Business: Reforming Social Security and Medicare," *Public Perspective*, Roper Center for Public Opinion Research, University of Connecticut (January/February 2000): 40.

NOTES TO CHAPTER SEVEN

1. Christopher Howard, *The Hidden Welfare State: Tax Expenditures and Social Policy in the United States* (Princeton, N.J.: Princeton University Press, 1997), 52–54.

2. Thomas Sowell, *Conquests and Cultures: An International History* (New York: Basic Books, 1998), 101–4.

3. Of course, not all streets in a city grid are used by the general population. Commercial and residential developers have long built private streets, stables, and (much later) parking lots. But their value stems in large measure from their connectivity to a public system.

4. Adrian A. Paradis, *From Trails to Superhighways: The Story of America's Roads* (New York: Simon & Schuster, 1971), 19–24.

5. Ibid., 25–33.

6. Larry Schweikart, *The Entrepreneurial Adventure: A History of Business in the United States* (Fort Worth, Tex.: Harcourt College Publishers, 2000), 97.

7. James West Davidson and Mark H. Lytle, *The United States: A History of the Republic* (Englewood Cliffs, N.J.: Prentice-Hall, 1986), 218.

8. Schweikart, 98.

9. Davidson and Lytle, 219.

10. Schweikart, 105.

11. Ibid.

12. Ibid.

13. Carter Goodrich, "The Revulsion against Internal Improvements," *The Journal of Economic History* 2, no. 2 (November 1950): 146.

14. Schweikart, 124–25.

15. Ibid., 151.

16. Ibid., 156.

17. Ibid., 153–54.

18. Michael Lowrey and Jonathan Jordan, "Sidetracked: Transit and Transportation Policy in North Carolina," policy report no. 18, John Locke Foundation, Raleigh, N.C., April 1997, 3–4.

19. Ibid.

20. Davidson and Lytle, 423.

21. Census Bureau, "Historical Census of Housing Tables: Homeownership," web site, January 6, 2000.

22. Alvin S. Goodman, "Water Supply," *New American Encyclopedia* (New York: Barnes & Noble, 1990), 56.

23. Peter C. Christensen, *Retail Wheeling: A Guide for End-Users* (Tulsa, Okla.: PennWell Books, 1995), 12.

24. Davidson and Lytle, 533.

25. Kathy Neal et al., "Restructuring America's Water Industry: Comparing Investor-Owned and Government Water Systems," Reason Public Policy Institute, Santa Monica, Calif., 1996.

26. Lowrey and Jordan, 4–5.

27. Ibid., 5.

28. "A Brief History of the Trucking Industry," Pittsburgh Diesel Institute web site, January 16, 1997.

29. "State Expenditures by Function," in Scott Moody, ed., *Facts and Figures on Government Finance*, 33d ed. (Washington, D.C.: The Tax Foundation, 1999), 164.

30. Davidson and Lytle, 535.

31. "Local Government Expenditures by Function," in Moody, 246.

32. Davidson and Lytle, 535.

33. Howard, 96–100.

34. Ibid.

35. David W. Berson and Eileen Neely, "Homeownership in the United States: Where We've Been, Where We're Going," *Business Economics* 32, no. 3 (July 1997): 7–12.

36. Phillip Longman, *The Return of Thrift: How the Collapse of the Middle Class Welfare State Will Reawaken Values in America* (New York: The Free Press, 1996), 123–24.

37. Ibid., 124.

38. "The Mortgage Industry," Advisor Capital Products web site, advisormortgage.com/history.htm (1999), 1–2.

39. "Growth of Fannie Mae and Freddie Mac Poses Threat of Expensive Taxpayer-Financed Bailout, Warns New AEI Study," news release, American Enterprise Institute for Public Policy Research, Washington, D.C., March 6, 2000.

40. Computed by author using data from Moody, various tables.

41. John Hood, "Factory-Built Housing: The Path to Ownership?" *Consumers' Research* (August 1998): 16.

42. Howard, 104.

43. Ibid., 104.

44. Tom Herman, "Tax Notes," *The Wall Street Journal,* 12 January 2000, A1.

45. Ibid., 108–11.

46. Ibid., 113.

47. Office of Management and Budget, *Budget of the United States Government, FY 2001.*

48. See, for example, Daniel J. Mitchell, "Jobs, Growth, Freedom, and Fairness: Why America Needs a Flat Tax," backgrounder no. 1035, The Heritage Foundation, Washington, D.C., May 25, 1995, 24.

49. At least a few economists and policy analysts are finally speaking up about the diminishing returns of federal housing subsidies. See Patrick Barta and Gregory Zuckerman, "Homeownership: The Perils of Success?" *The Wall Street Journal,* 22 January 2001, A1.

50. Ibid.

51. Loren Lomasky, "Autonomy and Automobility," Competitive Enterprise Institute, Washington, D.C., June 1995.

52. Gabriel Roth, "How to Improve America's Highways," *Consumers' Research* (February 1991): 12.

53. Lowrey and Jordan, 7.

54. Calculations by author based on information from Moody, various tables.

55. David T. Hartgen and Elizabeth L. Presutti, "Resources vs. Results: Comparative Performance of State Highway Systems, 1984–1996," Center for Interdisciplinary Transportation Studies, University of North Carolina-Charlotte, April 30, 1996.

56. Ibid.

57. "Transportation Statistics Annual Report 1999" (Washington, D.C.: U.S. Department of Transportation, 1999), chapter 1, 14-17.

58. Daniel Machalaba, "Slow Going: As Economy Hums, Congested Freeways Exact a Heavy Toll," *The Wall Street Journal,* 30 August 2000, A1.

59. Peter Gordon, "How to Build Our Way Out of Congestion," Reason Public Policy Institute, Santa Monica, Calif., January 1999.

60. Angela Antonelli and D. Mark Wilson, "Why Congress Should Cut the Gas Tax," executive memorandum no. 664, The Heritage Foundation, Washington, D.C., March 21, 2000, 2.

61. Edward V. Regan, "A New Approach to Tax-Exempt Bonds," public policy brief no. 58A, Jerome Levy Economics Institute of Bard College, December 1999, 1–4.

62. S. Jay Levy and Walter M. Cadette, "Overcoming America's Infrastructure Deficit," public policy brief no. 40A, Jerome Levy Economics Institute of Bard College, May 1998.

63. "Living with the Car: No Room, No Room," *The Economist* (March 20, 1997).

64. Robert Poole, "Private Toll Roads: A Transportation Alternative for North Carolina," policy report no. 4, John Locke Foundation, Raleigh, N.C., October 1991.

NOTES TO CHAPTER EIGHT

1. Theodore W. Schultz, "Reflections on Investment in Man," *The Journal of Political Economy* 2, supplement (October 1962): 1–2.

2. Moses Abramovitz, "The Search for the Sources of Growth: Areas of Ignorance, Old and New," *The Journal of Economic History* 53, no. 2 (June 1993): 224.

3. "2000 Industry Report," *Training* magazine, www.trainingmag.com, October 2000.

4. Ibid. See also Department of Education, National Center for Education Statistics, "Total expenditures of educational institutions, by level and control of institution," *Digest of Education Statistics 2000*, 35, table 32.

5. Ibid.

6. Department of Education, National Center for Education Statistics, "Student proficiency in reading, by age, amount of time spent on homework, and reading habits," *Digest of Education Statistics 1998*, 129, table 111.

7. Department of Education, National Center for Education Statistics, *The NAEP 1998 Reading Report Card for the Nation* (March 1999), by L. Donahue et al., 107.

8. Ibid., 22.

9. NAEP test score data, Department of Education, *Digest of Education Statistics 1998*, 134–45.

10. Donahue, 70–85.

11. *Digest of Education Statistics 1998*, 134.

12. Department of Education, Office of Educational Research and Improvement, "Highlights from TIMMS," 1999, 7.

13. Herbert J. Walberg, "Spending More While Learning Less," Thomas B. Fordham Foundation, Washington, D.C., July 1998.

14. Andrew Coulson, *Market Education: The Unknown History* (New Brunswick, N.J.: Transaction Publishers, 1999), 73–74.

15. Jack High and Jerome Ellig, "The Private Supply of Education," in Tyler Cowan, ed., *The Theory of Market Failure: A Critical Examination* (Fairfax, Va.: George Mason University Press, 1988), 367–73.

16. Ibid., 369.

17. Coulson, 84.

18. Quoted in Coulson, 79–80.

19. Hugh Lefler and Patricia Stenford, *North Carolina*, 2d ed. (New York: Harcourt Brace Jovanovich, 1972), 325–27.

20. James West Davidson and Mark H. Lytle, *The United States: A History of the Republic* (Englewood Cliffs, N.J.: Prentice-Hall, 1986), 436.

21. Department of Education, *Digest of Education Statistics 2000*, 12 and 50.

22. Coulson, 111 and 171.

23. Department of Education, *Digest of Education Statistics 2000*, table 38, 48. Data adjusted for inflation using Consumer Price Index-Urban Areas.

24. Ibid., 122.

25. Ibid., 48.

26. Ibid., 146.

27. Coulson, 180–84.

28. Department of Education, *Digest of Education Statistics 2000*, various pages and author computations.

29. Ibid., 331–32.

30. Edwin S. Rubenstein, "The College Payoff Illusion," *American Outlook*, The Hudson Institute (fall 1998): 18.

31. Department of Education, *Digest of Education Statistics 2000*, 334 and 397.

32. Office of Management and Budget, *Budget of the United States Government, FY 2001*, 233 and 385.

33. Rubenstein, 14–15.

34. Ibid., 16.

35. Frederic L. Pryor and David L. Schaffer, *Who's Not Working and Why* (Cambridge, U.K.: Cambridge University Press, 1999), 13:6.

36. Office of Management and Budget, *Budget of the United States Government, FY 2001*, 239.

37. For further analysis of government training programs, see Patrick F. Fagan, "Liberal Welfare Programs: What the Data Show on Programs for Teenage Mothers," backgrounder no. 1031, The Heritage Foundation, Washington, D.C., March 31, 1995; Marc Levinson, "Everyone's Magic Bullet; Why job training is no cure for the economy's ills," *Newsweek* (September 21, 1992): 44; and Jonathan Walters, "The Truth about Training," *Governing* (March 1995): 32–35.

38. Alan Eck, "Job-Related Education and Training: Their Impact on Earnings," *Monthly Labor Review* (October 1993): 21–36.

39. Thomas Jefferson, "Notes on Virginia, Query 14," in Saul Padover, ed., *Thomas Jefferson on Democracy* (New York: Penguin Books, 1939), 87.

40. Department of Education, *Digest of Education Statistics 1998*, 335.

41. "Social Security and Education," executive summary of policy report no. 240, National Center for Policy Analysis, Dallas, Tex., 2001, 1.

42. See Dr. Jay Greene, "An Evaluation of the Florida A-Plus Accountability and School Choice Program, Manhattan Institute" (February 2001), http://www.manhattan-institute.org/html/cr_aplus.htm; and Greene, "A Survey of Results from Voucher Experiments: Where We Are and What We Know," civic report no. 11, Manhattan Institute, New York, N.Y., July 2000.

43. Saul J. Blaustein, Christopher J. O'Leary, and Stephen A. Wandner, "Policy Issues: An Overview," *Unemployment Insurance in the United States* (Kalamazoo, Mich.: W. E. Upjohn Institute for Employment Research, 1997), 3–4.

44. Office of Management and Budget, *Budget of the United States Government, FY 2001*, 250.

45. Don Carrington and Jonathan C. Jordan, "Savings & Loans: Reforming Unemployment Insurance Through Competition and Compound Interest," policy report no. 21, John Locke Foundation, Raleigh, N.C., April 1998, 16–20.

46. Martin Feldstein and Daniel Altman, "Unemployment Insurance Savings Accounts," working paper no. W6860, National Bureau of Economic Research, Cambridge, Mass., December 1998, 7.

47. As laid out in Carrington and Jordan, 20–31.

48. Ibid., A1 through A4.

49. Feldstein and Altman, 29–30.

50. Michael Tanner, *The End of Welfare* (Washington: The Cato Institute, 1996), 34.

51. John Locke, "Draft of a Representation Containing a Scheme of Methods for the Employment of the Poor," October 6, 1697, in David Wooten, ed., *Political Writings of John Locke* (New York: Penguin Books, 1993), 447–49.

52. Tanner, 38–39.

53. Clarence B. Carson, "The General Welfare," in *Taxation and Confiscation* (Irvington-on-Hudson, N.Y.: The Foundation for Economic Education, 1993), 23.

54. Ibid., 39 and 49.

55. Tanner, 53.

56. Census Bureau, "Persons Below Poverty Level and Below 125 Percent of Poverty Level," table in *Statistical Abstract of the United States,* 446 in the 1981 ed., 475 in the 1997 ed.

57. Studies by Anne Hid, June O'Neill, Mary Corcoran, and Roger Gordon, summarized in Robert Rector and Sarah Youssef, *The Impact of Welfare Reform: The Trend in State Caseloads 1985–1998* (Washington, D.C.: The Heritage Foundation, 1999), xv–xvi.

58. Christopher Howard, *The Hidden Welfare State* (Princeton, N.J.: Princeton University Press, 1997), 65–72.

59. Bureau of National Affairs, *Daily Labor Report,* March 21, 1988, 2.

60. Rector and Youssef, 100–1.

61. Ibid., xiii.

62. Howard, 141.

63. Office of Management and Budget, *Budget of the United States Government, FY 2001,* various pages.

64. Howard, 154–55.

65. Rector and Youssef, xiv.

66. See Robert Friedman and Michael Sherraden, "Economic Security in the 21st Century," *Ideas in Development,* 1999 annual report, Corporation for Enterprise Development, 7–10.

67. Bruce Bartlett, "Low-Income Tax Cheaters," National Center for Policy Analysis, Dallas, Tex., December 20, 1999.

68. "Unintended Consequences," *Investor's Business Daily,* 1 July 1998.

69. National Science Foundation, "Sixth Year of Unprecedented R & D Growth Expected in 2000," by Steve Payson and John Jankowski, data brief (November 29, 2000), www.nsf.gov/sbe/srs/databrf/nsf01310/sdb01310.htm; and John Hood, "Government Science Cuts Are No Big Deal," *Consumers' Research* (October 1997): 25–27.

70. Hood.

71. Payson and Jankowski.

72. Zoltan J. Acs, "Where New Things Come From," *Inc.* (May 1994): 29.

73. See John Steele Gordon, "Technology of the Future," *American Heritage* (October 1993): 14.

74. Terence Kealey, *The Economic Laws of Scientific Research* (New York: St. Martin's Press, 1996), 2.

75. Peter Coy, "Blue-Sky Research Comes Down to Earth," *Business Week* (July 3, 1995): 78–80.

NOTES TO CHAPTER NINE

1. Office of Management and Budget, *Budget of the United States Government, FY 2001,* various pages.

2. "State Budget Actions 2000," National Conference of State Legislatures, Denver, Colo., online ed.

3. "Tax Freedom Day 1999," Tax Foundation, Washington, D.C., www.taxfoundation.org.

4. Karlyn Bowman, ed., "Opinion Pulse," *The American Enterprise* (November/December 1997): 91–94.

5. "Portrait of a Skeptical Public," *Business Week* (November 20, 1995): 138.

6. John Keegan, *A History of Warfare* (New York: Alfred A. Knopf, 1993), 151–52.

7. History shows one other way to win a siege: decapitation. The idea was to seize or kill the defending commander, devastating the morale of the city and depriving garrisons of effective leadership. A good tactic in theory, this was obviously very difficult to do in practice. A famous success was the 1568 Mogul capture of Chitor Garh, the last fort of the rebellious Rajput princes

during the consolidation of Moslem rule in India. The Rajputs (literally "sons of kings") had put up a valiant struggle against long odds. They had defeated every tactic: bombardment, undermining, siegeworks. The Mogul commander, the Emperor Akbar, was surveying a breach in the wall soon to be the location of renewed hand-to-hand struggle. He spotted a Rajput wearing a chieftain's armor. Akbar took out a matchlock and fired. An hour later, he received reports of a sudden Rajput abandonment of defenses. He had killed Jaimal, the Rajput prince. Chitor Garh fell without further serious opposition. Obviously Akbar had better aim than Ken Starr. Jeffrey Say Seck Leong, "Storming the Last Hindu Fortress," *Military History* (February 1999): 59–64.

8. Mark Wayne Biggs, "Forty Days At Jotapata," *Military History* (April 1999): 27–33.

9. Robert Payne, *The History of Islam* (New York: Dorset Press, 1959), 263–64.

10. J. Arthur McFall, "Taking Jerusalem: Climax of the First Crusade," *Military History* (June 1999): 31–37.

11. Payne, 263.

12. See, for example, "Strong Support for Major Reform Among Younger Investors," *Business Wire* (April 19, 1999); Merrill Matthews, "What Americans Want in Social Security Reform," *Investor's Business Daily* (November 30, 1998); "Most Americans Favor Some 'Privatization' of Social Security," (May 22, 1999), www.nandotimes.com; and "New Poll Finds Public Convinced That Significant Reform Is Needed Now," U.S. Newswire, May 24, 1999.

13. Richard Nadler, "The Rise of Worker Capitalism," policy analysis no. 359, The Cato Institute, Washington, D.C., November 1, 1999.

NOTES TO THE CONCLUSION

1. Richard Nadler, "The Risk of Worker Capitalism," policy analysis no. 359, The Cato Institute, Washington, D.C., November 1, 1999.

2. Allan Carlson, "Compassionate Conservatism: Ten Lessons from the New Agrarians," *The Intercollegiate Review* (fall/spring 2000–2001): 42.

3. Ibid., 41.

4. Paul Gigot, "Bush's Politics: More Ambitious Than It Sounds," *The Wall Street Journal*, 2 February 2001.

5. Robert Kuttner, "Broaden the Wealth: An Idea Even Conservatives Love," *Business Week* (September 22, 1997): 22.

6. Jeremy Hildreth, "Dems Go Cato," *National Review* online, February 14, 2001.

INDEX